TREKKING in

ECUADOR

ECUADOR

Robert & Daisy Kunstaetter

THE MOUNTAINEERS BOOKS

> *Caminante, no hay camino, se hace camino al andar.*
>
> *Wayfarer, there is no path, you make the path as you go.*
>
> Antonio Machado, *Proverbios y Cantares* (1912),
> translated by Alan S. Trueblood

Published by
The Mountaineers Books
1001 SW Klickitat Way, Suite 201
Seattle, WA 98134

First edition, 2002

Published simultaneously in Great Britain by Cordee, 3a DeMontfort Street, Leicester, England, LE1 7HD

Manufactured in the United States of America

Project Editors: Laura Slavik and Julie Van Pelt
Editor: Lois Kelly
Cover and Book Designer: Kristy L. Welch
Layout Artist: Kristy L. Welch
Mapmaker: Ben Pease
Illustrator: Kevin Burkhill
Photographers: Robert and Daisy Kunstaetter unless otherwise noted

Cover photograph: *Daisy climbing to the crater of El Altar*
Frontispiece: *Trekkers below south flank of Chimborazo (Trek 22)*
Design photo: *Mural near Latacunga* (Photo: Michael Resch)

Library of Congress Cataloging-in-Publication Data
Kunstaetter, Robert.
  Trekking in Ecuador / Robert and Daisy Isacovici Kunstaetter.— 1st ed.
    p. cm.
  ISBN 0-89886-535-2 (pbk.)
  1. Hiking—Ecuador—Guidebooks. 2. Ecuador—Guidebooks. I.
Kunstaetter, Daisy. II. Title.
  GV199.44.E2 K86 2002
  918.6604'74—dc21
                                        2002001433

 Printed on recycled paper

TABLE OF CONTENTS

MAP LEGEND

2800 / 3000 (contour lines)	Contour lines (elevations in meters)
Tungurahua ▲ (5023)	Mountain summit (elevations in meters)
Laguna Minsas (lake, glacier)	Lake, glacier
Río Ulba (stream, waterfall)	Stream, river, waterfall
(bog, underground river)	Bog, underground river
Baños	City or town
○ Ulba	Village
▬▬▬	Paved road
▬▬▬	Unpaved road
+ + + + +	Railroad track
- - - - - - -	Well-defined trail
. . . .	Faint trail or cross-country route
) (	Mountain pass or saddle
♠	Hotel or inn
◤	Trail shelter
▲	Site suitable for camping
▪	Building or buildings
•	Point of interest
♙	Ranger station
⊼	Picnic area
♨	Thermal baths or hot springs
P	Parking
S	Start of trek
N	Compass arrow

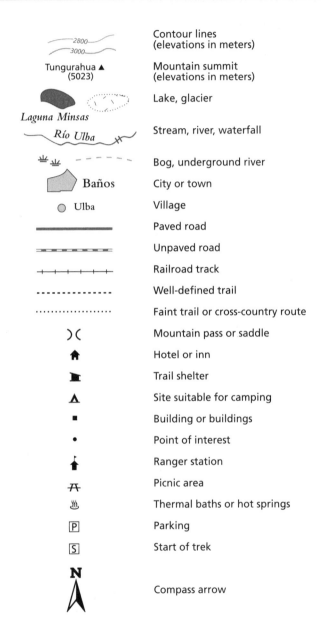

FOREWORD

By South American standards, Ecuador is a small country. You only have to look at a map to verify that. Its compactness means that the visitor can cover a lot of ground and see a wide range of geographical regions in a relatively short time. This is especially true if you are using wheels.

This book, however, is not aimed at the bus passenger, the driver, or even the cyclist. Those who use it will be on foot, and anyone who sets out to trek in Ecuador will soon realize that it is a big country. This is not to imply that distances are unmanageable or that mountain slopes cannot be climbed—rather, that the individual will feel humbled by the majesty of the volcanoes, the variety of the forest habitats, and the longevity of the indigenous peoples' impression on this beautiful landscape.

The days of the idle vacation are long gone. People want more than the beach, or the bus trip from tourist site to tourist site. Their urge is to explore, to get closer to the country they are visiting. Robert and Daisy Kunstaetter have helped countless travelers realize ambitions of going beyond the beaten track. With this book, they concentrate on just one aspect of adventure tourism. They put treks in their proper context. They give the trekker the confidence to be completely self-sufficient if he or she so desires—or to choose a group led by experienced guides.

It may be obvious to state that trekking in Ecuador is not simply a question of packing a pan, buying a few bananas and a bottle of water in the market, and heading for the hills. You need to have the highways and byways at your fingertips: the best places to settle for the night, the best value for supplies, and the best location for the best advice. You also should have environmental and cultural awareness. In other words, this book is blunder-proof.

The secret of Robert and Daisy's success lies in what, by their own admission, is their "notoriously leisurely" approach to trekking. Having traveled with Robert and Daisy in Ecuador—both on foot and by car—I can vouch for the merits of this approach firsthand. Why *not* make a detour down this track? Why *not* try this new flavor of ice cream from the shop on the corner? To quote the dictum of medieval educators, it is the spirit of "*enseñar deleitando*," imparting knowledge through enjoyment. If they did not take the time to pause, to look, to talk, to savor, they would not be able to communicate their enthusiasm for the intimate details that are to be found in this grand country.

—Ben Box, editor, *South American Handbook*

PREFACE

This book is an invitation to experience the wonders of trekking in Ecuador. Come to Ecuador for leisure and learning, sport and adventure. Come to have a great time. There is so much here to discover and enjoy!

We also invite you to open your eyes and your mind to the complex realities of Ecuador. Begin by reading "Trekking Today: A True Story" in Chapter 1. As you trek and travel, take in the awesome natural beauty of this country, but also be sensitive to the difficult challenges faced by its people. Perhaps—at a time and in a way you least expect—you might be able to help them. Perhaps some of the insights you gain while trekking in Ecuador will influence the way you think about our beleaguered planet and species.

Finally, we invite you to contribute your own experiences, and welcome any corrections to the text and maps to help improve future editions. Please write to us at *authors@trekkinginecuador.com* or P.O. Box 17-17-908, Quito, Ecuador. Although we cannot plan your treks or travels for you, we will gratefully acknowledge all correspondence.

We wish you safe and pleasant trekking.

A NOTE ABOUT SAFETY

Safety is an important concern in all outdoor activities. No guide-book can alert you to every hazard or anticipate the limitations of every reader. Therefore, the descriptions of roads, trails, routes, and natural features in this book are not representations that a particular place or excursion will be safe for your party. When you follow any of the routes described in this book, you assume responsibility for your own safety. Under normal conditions, such excursions require the usual attention to traffic, road and trail conditions, weather, terrain, the capabilities of your party, and other factors. Keeping informed on current conditions and exercising common sense are the keys to a safe, enjoyable outing.

Political conditions may add to the risks of travel in Ecuador in ways that this book cannot predict. When you travel, you assume this risk, and should keep informed of political developments that may make safe travel difficult or impossible.

—The Mountaineers Books

ACKNOWLEDGMENTS

Researching and writing this book were both a delight and a great deal of work. The very generous and capable assistance of many different people made our task easier and the experience all the more enjoyable. We offer our sincere thanks to all of the following:

The late Yossi Brain, a sorely missed friend, provided invaluable inspiration. Yossi, we are so sorry you are not here to see the result! Lou Jost helped us in more ways than we can list, foremost among them with his friendship and encouragement. He also reviewed the entire manuscript on very short notice, as well as supplied specialist contributions (flora and fauna, Mountain-Toucan), a photo, and an illustration. Popkje van der Ploeg provided her excellent editorial skills and flawlessly coordinated the efforts of other contributors. They include Kerry Alley, Miguel Cazar, and Luís and Elisabeth Reyes; all are professional guides who conscientiously researched a number of treks. Kevin Burkhill greatly enhanced this book with his charming illustrations; he donated the entire proceeds of his effort to a conservation organization working in Ecuador.

We are grateful to the following specialists who either contributed or reviewed sections in their respective areas of expertise: Craig Downer (Mountain Tapir and *páramo*), Dr. Minard (Pete) Hall and Dr. Patricia Mothes (geology and vulcanology), Dr. Stephen Bezruchka (medicine), Dr. Steve Manock and Ana María Velasco (snakes). We thank Grace and Marcelo Naranjo as well as Susana Bermeo for keeping things running while we were off trekking, and Michael Resch for finding and photographing the mural.

We are grateful to Dr. Nelson Gómez, president of the Centro Internacional de Estudios de los Espacios y Sociedades Andinas (CIESA), for his ongoing guidance and unwavering support. We likewise acknowledge the auspices of Ecuador's Ministerio de Turismo. Our thanks also go to project editors Laura Slavik and Julie Van Pelt, copy editor Lois Kelly, and the entire team at The Mountaineers Books; it is a pleasure to work with such dedicated professionals.

For their hospitality and assistance along the trail we thank: Familia Apunte, David Beatty, Oswaldo Cedeño, Familia Coronel, Graciela Jaramillo, Familia Lara, Elías Lascano, Gonzalo Llerena, Fernando Manzano, Luís Miranda, Gavin Moore, Rigoberto and José Musha, Familia Naranjo,

Charlie and Sarah Nodine, Antonella Ronco, Familia Salazar, and Daniel Villacís.

Other people who helped in many different ways include: Boris Aguirre, Jorge and Mariana Alvarez, Carlos Andi, Katherine Baccala, Patricio Ballesteros, Jean Brown, Gastón Bucheli, Chris Canaday, Ciro Cazar, Nancy Cifuentes, Rodrigo Donoso, Eva Ehrenfeld, Professor Dick Gerdes, Mark Honigsbaum, Roberto Isacovici, Carla Játiva, Ron Jones, Harry Jonits, Paul Jost, Craig Kolthoff, Irene Kunstaetter, Nelson and Zoila Lema, Ilse Luraschi, Xavier and Beatrice Malo, Jaime and Durga Mendoza, Rodrigo Ocaña, Ricardo Ordoñez, Silvia Ortega, William Reyes, Dr. John Rosenberg, Johnny Saltos, Carmen Sánchez, Kay Sibbald, Ricardo Soto, Kate Stephens, Robert Strauss, Rodrigo Tapia, Eloy Torres, Alfonso Vallejo, and Thomas Walsch.

We have shared many special moments over the years with our trekking companions, friends and relatives who (at times willingly) joined us for a walk. The experience was always memorable.

Rare glimpse of Sangay from the north (Treks 23, 24, and 25)

Section 1
INTRODUCTION

CAMINANTE NO HAY CAMINO
SE HACE CAMINO AL ANDAR

Chapter 1
WHY ECUADOR?

Ecuador's special appeal to trekkers, day-trippers, and nature lovers can be summed up in one word: accessibility. The country's unique combination of small size, exceptional geographic and biological diversity, and good transportation infrastructure places an outstanding variety of splendid natural experiences within easy reach of the adventurous visitor.

Ecuador boasts more than forty-five protected natural areas, including national parks and private reserves, almost all of which offer trekking and day-hiking possibilities. There are also innumerable opportunities for excellent day trips close to cities and towns. Many longer treks span several natural regions, from the highlands down toward the Amazon jungle or coastal plain.

Travel costs in Ecuador, although gradually rising, remain modest by international standards. Since the country is located closer to North America and Europe than the continent's other trekking destinations, airfares to Ecuador are also lower.

Ecuador receives many visitors (approximately 500,000 a year), but as yet relatively few people come specifically to trek. Unlike well-known trekking venues such as Nepal, the Inca Trail to Machu Picchu in Peru, and Chile's Torres del Paine National Park, trails in Ecuador are never crowded and offer virtually unlimited scope for exploration. Trekking in Ecuador is easily combined with a visit to the country's more traditional destinations: the Galápagos Islands, colorful indigenous markets, Amazon jungle lodges, or Pacific coast beaches.

Trekking options in Ecuador are as diverse as the country's natural areas. With altitudes ranging from sea level to more than 6000 meters (20,000 feet), there are tropical rainforests, cloud forests, high moorlands known as *páramos*, and rocky ridges right up to the snowline. The highlands offer the greatest number of trekking opportunities, and the Andes provide the perfect backdrop—with magnificent scenery and an incomparable top-of-the-world feeling. Trekkers often find themselves literally above the clouds!

Although Ecuador has wet and dry seasons, they are not the same in all parts of the country and may even vary from one valley to the next. Hence, conditions are suitable for trekking somewhere in Ecuador throughout the year.

HISTORY OF TREKKING IN ECUADOR

Well before Columbus's arrival in the new world, native cultures of Ecuador traded with one another and created an extensive network of trails that crisscrossed the Andes and connected them with lowlands to the east and west. During the reign of the Inca Empire, many of these trails were consolidated into a vast continent-wide road network (see Trek 26, Inca Trails), which later facilitated the Spanish conquest. These early roads continued to form the backbone of the nation's transport infrastructure until the construction of the Ecuadorean railway in the early 1900s. Today, old paths are still used by people in the countryside to reach their crops, move their flocks, or access the more remote villages. Although most Ecuadoreans are not aware of trekking as a sport or leisure activity, foreign trekkers here are not an invention of the twenty-first century.

As far back as the 1730s, a group of French scientists, led by Charles Marie de la Condamine, explored much of Ecuador in order to determine whether the earth bulged at the equator. (It does.) In the early nineteenth century, the German Baron Alexander von Humboldt traveled the country as part of his scientific explorations of South America. In the 1850s and 1860s, the Victorian botanist Richard Spruce covered an extensive area of Ecuador looking for quinine to help build the British Empire (see "The Cascarilla Story" in Trek 17). Another Englishman, Edward Whymper, traveled throughout the Andean hinterlands of Ecuador between 1879 and 1880. Whymper is best known for his climbing achievements, but the experiences he recorded continue to inspire contemporary trekkers.

TREKKING TODAY: A TRUE STORY

The wood in Señora Juana's hearth fire had crackled loudly all morning, a sure sign that unexpected visitors would soon arrive. And so we did, sopping wet in our high-tech hiking gear, cautiously eyeing the narrow, slippery log cast over the flooded river. This tenuous bridge was the only access to Don Teodoro and Juana's house—the last house on the trail.

Teodoro suddenly appeared on the other shore, dressed in rags in the drenching rain but wearing a broad smile. *"Bienvenidos,"* he shouted. Welcome! "Need a hand crossing with those great big backpacks?" We gratefully accepted his offer, and he scooped up a handful of sand at the river's edge and carefully sprinkled it on the log as he crossed toward us. He then nimbly carried our packs over and led us to his home.

Teodoro and Juana lived alone in a typical Ecuadorean *casita de campo,* which rural dwellers build in their fields so they can take shelter if caught overnight or in bad weather. For this couple in their sixties, however, the windowless, rough-hewn planks of timber, topped with a rusty tin roof, constituted their permanent two-room home. Nine of their ten children had grown up and left. Their youngest daughter, twelve-year-old Maritza, lived with relatives so she could attend school in the nearest village (a two-day walk from her parents' home).

When we arrived, however, Teodoro and Juana were not alone. The crackling hearth fire had foretold the arrival of seven unexpected visitors in all: Maritza, a nephew, a grandson, two distant neighbors, and us. No sooner were we all safely over the log bridge than a sudden gush of muddy brown water swept it away like a toothpick.

"May we pitch our tent in your pasture?" we asked.

Teodoro replied, "You're welcome to do as you please, but there's quite a storm out there and you'll find it more comfortable in the house. You can have the kitchen floor all to yourselves; the seven of us will be fine in the bedroom. We have two beds, you know." The tone of Teodoro's voice made it clear that there was no point in arguing.

When night fell we were indeed grateful for our spot by the hearth, but we could hardly have imagined that this would become our home for the foreseeable future. As the storm raged ever more fiercely, with the river swollen to levels Teodoro swore he had never seen before, the bridges washed away, and landslides thundering down the surrounding hills, we began to wonder if we would ever leave at all. The predicament gave the nine of us a special opportunity to get to know one another.

Teodoro and Juana had not always lived at the end of the trail. They once owned another small house, near their hometown on the far side of the *cordillera* (mountain range), but were dispossessed of communal lands and could no longer feed their rapidly growing family. Their story was not unique, although most homesteaders had crossed the *cordillera* fleeing drought rather than land disputes. Generations of deforestation had rendered parts of their naturally dry former home a sterile desert.

Teodoro had been one of the early explorers of what was to become his new home, crossing the mountains barefoot during his first visit in the 1950s. During the 1960s he guided a team of foreign scientists and still vividly recalled how awestruck they had been by the beauty of the area's cloud forests. In the 1970s he guided the first cartographic expedition of the Instituto Geográfico Militar, and he smiled with deep satisfaction when we showed him our topographic map. The place names were all there, just as he had given them. In the 1980s he came to live, clearing a parcel of land above the river, planting his subsistence crops, and introducing domestic animals including cattle.

The self-sufficiency Teodoro and Juana had achieved on their isolated farmstead was remarkable—even by the standards of backcountry Ecuador. Had it rained for forty days and forty nights, the nine of us would not have gone hungry. Their orchard grew an abundance of corn, peas, beans, squash, carrots, two kinds of sweet potato, manioc, onions, garlic, herbs, sugar cane, bananas, strawberries, and passion fruit. Chickens, ducks, pigs, and cattle provided generous amounts of meat. Cheese was made twice a week and, since two calves were born during our visit, we savoured the delicacy of colostrum: the first milk. Teodoro and Juana even produced their own coffee and tobacco, and boasted that they needed to purchase little more than matches and salt on their infrequent visits to town.

The price of this remarkable self-sufficiency had been incredibly high, however— in terms of both the ongoing effort it required from the aging couple and the destruction of the surrounding environment. Teodoro noticed our politely veiled chagrin at the cloud forest that lay in ruins around us. "Look," he protested, "I came to live here because I had to, because they took away my land and my kids were going hungry. Even then I purposely left all the big trees in the pasture but they just dried up and died." These gaunt skeletons of the forest still surrounded us, succumbing one by one to Teodoro's ax, to feed the hearth fire.

When we stooped to examine a tiny orchid on a recently felled trunk, Teodoro became contentious. "What's that thing good for anyway," he snapped. "Food, clothing, medicine?" But there was also a hint of sadness in his voice. Later, as the bare and burnt hillsides collapsed around us, the poor sandy undersoil saturated with water, he grew outright despondent. "This won't last beyond my generation. Everything we have eked out here will perish. Sure, I can still grow a few crops and run some cattle, but this land will soon be useless, and then it will never recover."

Would it rain for forty days and forty nights? At times, as we watched the endless sheets of water propelled by the wind or lay in the darkness listening to the flapping tin roofing, we felt as though we were aboard a small vessel in a gale at sea. Indeed we *were* in a Noah's ark of sorts—Teodoro and Juana's ark at the end of the trail. In the bedroom someone lit a candle and the sound of prayer began to waft gently across the wall—a welcome, soothing sound.

After 6 long days the rain finally stopped, the clouds parted, and the sun shone. Instead of a dove bearing an olive branch, a young falcon appeared and perched atop one of the skeletal tree trunks near the house. "That bastard's come to steal chickens. Get me the rifle!" was Teodoro's reflex reaction. His eyes were no longer as good as they used to be, but they were still good enough: the rifle cracked and the falcon fell dead in the orchard. Again our silence must have been eloquent, for Teodoro replied, "I would never harm a creature that is not a threat to me or my livelihood. This place is still full of birds." Right on cue, a large flock of parrots swirled overhead, squawking loudly as they too celebrated the reappearance of the sun.

When it came time to part, Teodoro and Juana would not hear of accepting money. "If you want to help us though, maybe you can convince the authorities to build a concrete footbridge up here, something that won't wash away the next time it rains." Then they handed us a wrinkled old dollar bill and asked us to put it in the alms box when we arrived at our destination. They had our interests in mind, for on a righteous mission we would come to no harm.

Were our hosts heroes or villains? We feel we have no right to judge such courageous people. Rather, we have an obligation to help them. How? A concrete footbridge would benefit Teodoro and Juana, to be sure—but it also would help those who might extract the last remnants of timber from one of the most savagely deforested regions of Ecuador. Their actions would provide a recipe for certain disaster during the next heavy rains.

To best help Teodoro and Juana, their children and grandchildren, we must broaden our perspective. Community development through sustainable agriculture, reforestation, improved education, family planning, and perhaps ecotourism all come to mind. At the same time, our good intentions are tempered by the experiences of Latin American history. The past five hundred years warn us loud and clear about the pitfalls of solutions devised and imposed from outside. Before we can do any good, we must learn not to do any more harm.

Tough as ever: Don Teodoro rebuilding the washed-out bridge

Chapter 2
ECUADOR AND ITS PEOPLE

Imagine! A country where the land is higher than the clouds.
—Yoel Nimelman, an astonished immigrant to Ecuador

GEOGRAPHY

Ecuador is located in the northwest of South America; it lies along the Pacific coast and the equator. It is one of the smallest nations of the continent, with a surface area of approximately 270,000 square kilometers (104,000 square miles). Its neighbors are Colombia to the north and Peru to the south. The principal topographic feature of the country is the Andes, a massive mountainous spine that runs from north to south. The Andes Mountains divide the Ecuadorean mainland into three regions, from west to east: the Pacific coast, the highlands, and the Amazon basin. A fourth geographic region is made up of the Galápagos Islands, situated 1000 kilometers (620 miles) offshore (directly along the equator). Ecuador is divided into twenty-two provinces, which in turn are subdivided into cantons and parishes for local administration.

Andean Highlands

Two roughly parallel ranges of the Andes, connected by transverse ridges, form the Ecuadorean highlands known as La Sierra. In the northern Sierra, ten snowcapped volcanic summits tower more than 5000 meters (16,500 feet) above sea level. These volcanoes are set some distance apart from one another, each majestically dominating its own territory. In the southern Sierra the mountains are older, lower, more eroded, and nonvolcanic, resulting in a confused topography of bare sculpted peaks and deeply incised valleys.

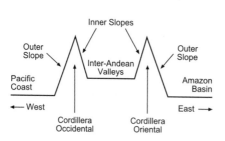

The Ecuadorean geographer Dr. Nelson Gómez describes the high Andes as a world of striking contrasts: "massive glaciers on the equator, snow and volcanic steam, dense fog and brilliant sunshine, severe cold and intense heat." The two main ranges of the Andes are the Cordillera Occidental (the western range) and the Cordillera Oriental (the eastern range). Between them lies a series of gentle green valleys between 2000 and 3000 meters (6500 and 10,000 feet) above sea level. These inter-Andean valleys are densely populated and intensively cultivated right up the mountain slopes, producing fruits, vegetables, grains, and dairy products.

A wilder landscape is to be found on the outer slopes of the Andes, which are covered with cloud forests known as *ceja andina* (eyebrows of the Andes). They are perpetually shrouded in the mists that rise from the tropical lowlands toward the icy mountaintops.

Pacific Coast

The coastal region, known as La Costa, is a broad alluvial plain drained by several rivers, including the Guayas (the largest river on the west coast of South America). Much of La Costa is densely populated and given over to large-scale agriculture, with corporate enterprises producing bananas and shrimp for the export market as well as other crops for local consumption.

Amazon Basin

The eastern lowlands, known as El Oriente, are part of the enormous Amazon River basin, which covers much of tropical South America. Low mountain ranges at the foot of the Andes, tropical rainforest, and large navigable rivers to the east are the principal geographic features of continental Ecuador's least densely populated region.

Galápagos Islands

These islands of volcanic origin, independent from the mainland, sit near the junction of the Nazca and Cocos tectonic plates. There are eight main islands, six smaller islands, and many islets spread over a large expanse of ocean. Since trekking is not permitted in Galápagos, we will not describe them further in this book.

GEOLOGY

Geology surrounds the trekker in Ecuador. The magnificent landscape we see today has been forged by geologic events over many millions of years, most significant among them the uplifting of the Andes. The growth of these colossal mountains results from the collision of the Nazca tectonic plate with the South American plate. The upper Amazon River, which some twenty-five million years ago flowed to the Pacific as a much smaller

waterway (through what is today southern Ecuador), found its route blocked by the rising Andes and eventually made its way to the Atlantic. The Amazon and coastal plains were both formed by alluvial sediments derived from the Andes.

Over the millennia, volcanic activity (the result of plate subduction) also repeatedly changed the topography. Volcanic eruptions, tectonic movements, as well as wind, water, and glacial erosion, are all forces that have molded the Andes and continue to do so today. The northern highlands in particular remain a land of earth tremors, active volcanoes, and glaciated summits. Fifty-five volcanic craters dot the landscape, and three of them are currently visibly active: Guagua Pichincha near Quito, Tungurahua by Baños, and Sangay southeast of Riobamba. Although less evident to the layman, many other volcanoes are considered active by geologists and often have hot mineral springs nearby.

CLIMATE

A journey through Ecuador is comparable to a trip from the Equator to the South Pole.
            —Alexander von Humboldt, nineteenth-century explorer

The Andes, trade winds, and ocean currents all shape Ecuador's extremely variable climate. You will find every imaginable type of weather here, from oppressively hot and humid on the coast and in the jungle, to ice and snow above 4500 meters (15,000 feet).

In the most general terms, there are two seasons: *verano* (summer, meaning dry rather than warm) and *invierno* (winter, meaning wet rather than cold). The seasons are not well defined and vary considerably from one region to another. There can be long dry periods during the wet season and heavy rain in the dry season. Neither is the concept of clearly marked seasons part of the local way of thinking; if there is a shower, you will be told it is the wet season. If the sun is shining half an hour later, then it must be the dry season. *As a trekker, you should be prepared for all kinds of weather throughout the year.*

The temperature in a given area will fluctuate more in the course of a day, and in relation to altitude, than from one season to another. As a general rule of thumb, you can expect that for every 200 meters you climb, the temperature will drop one degree Celsius (approximately one degree Fahrenheit for every 350 feet). In the inter-Andean valleys around 2500 meters (8000 feet), the climate year-round comes close to eternal spring, with temperatures seldom dropping below 10 degrees Celsius (50 degrees Fahrenheit) at night nor rising above 22 degrees Celsius (72 degrees Fahrenheit) during the daytime. In the *páramos* between 3500 and 5000 meters (11,500 to 16,500 feet), temperatures can drop below freezing at night, fog is common, and it may rain, snow, sleet, or hail. On the outer slopes of the Andes there is even more humidity than in the inter-Andean valleys.

Highlands

Every valley seems to have its own microclimate. One important factor is whether a particular place receives a greater influence from the west or the east. As a general rule, the dry season for the western slopes is between June and September; July and August are driest. The wet season is between October and May, March and April have the highest rainfall, and there is sometimes a brief dry period in December and January. On the eastern slopes the dry season is between October and February; November and December are driest. The wet season is between March and September, with the highest precipitation in June and July, sometimes reaching extreme proportions. There is also variation from north to south, with the southern highlands generally receiving less annual rainfall.

Coast

Due to the interplay of warm and cold Pacific Ocean currents, the climate in coastal Ecuador is also most varied, with very high precipitation (up to 5000 millimeters or 200 inches annual rainfall) in parts of the north and semidesert conditions (300 millimeters, 12 inches) in the south. The driest and coolest months are June through September. January through May is the hottest and rainiest time of the year.

Amazon Basin

It is said that during the dry season (peak November to February) it rains every day, while during the wet season (peak March to June) it rains *all* day. The average yearly rainfall for the region is 2000 to 3000 millimeters (80 to 120 inches), but some areas receive up to 4000 millimeters (160 inches), and a few isolated spots are even wetter.

The El Niño Phenomenon

This global climatic phenomenon occurs in an irregular five- to ten-year cycle and brings unusually heavy rains, high tides, and flooding to coastal Ecuador. It is associated with a warming of the western Pacific Ocean. The precise areas affected and the strength of the disturbance vary from one El Niño to another. Flooding can be so severe that roads are destroyed and bridges washed out, while exceptionally high tides sometimes swallow beachfront property. Drier than usual conditions in parts of Oriente are sometimes associated with the El Niño phenomenon, while flooding has also taken place in some highland regions.

FLORA AND FAUNA

Ecuador's complex topography and climate patterns have endowed it with an exceptionally wide variety of life zones. Nowhere else on earth will you find so much biological diversity in such a small area. The different zones blend into one another, and the altitude at which they occur varies depending on the latitude, type of soil, humidity, topography, and degree of human intervention.

Outer-Slope Cloud Forest

The external slopes of the Andes rise abruptly from the coastal and Amazon plains. The humidity that constantly ascends from these lowlands nurtures lush cloud forests with tall trees, exceptionally rich in epiphytes and mosses. Some of the native trees found in these forests include the alder, *erythrina* species with bright red or orange flowers and a large seedpod, and several species of *pumamaqui*, with leaves shaped like a puma's paw. A number of palms also thrive at lower elevations. Of particular interest among these is the tagua or ivory nut (described in the sidebar "Vegetable Ivory"), which can be seen along the trail in Treks 16 and 17.

The greatest diversity of orchids in the world occurs in the cloud forests of Ecuador, where many breathtaking varieties of all sizes and colors can be found. In these forests you are also likely to encounter mixed flocks of foraging birds, among which many colorful tanagers often stand out. Spectacular birds such as the Plate-billed Mountain-Toucan (see Trek 7,

Toucan Trail) in the west, and its eastern counterpart, the Black-billed Mountain-Toucan, also make their homes here. As you reach higher elevations, the number of insects diminishes and many species of beautiful hummingbirds take over their role as pollinators.

Mammals are harder to find in the cloud forest, but there are capuchin, spider, and howler monkeys at lower elevations of the western slopes and Amazon species, such as the woolly monkey, in the east. Among the large mammals are the Spectacled Bear (see sidebar later in this chapter) and the Mountain Tapir (see Trek 13, Tapir Trail).

VEGETABLE IVORY

The tagua or ivory nut is a palm that grows below about 1200 meters (4000 feet) in the outer-slope cloud forest and surrounding plains. This palm reaches a height of up to 6 meters (20 feet) and produces a very long compound flower made up of sweet-smelling, slightly sticky fuzz-balls. These develop into clusters of oval seeds, about the size and shape of a hen's egg, which become extremely hard. This unusual hardness and their creamy white color have earned them the name "vegetable ivory." The palms are commercially exploited on the northern Pacific coast, and the seeds can be harvested without damaging the tree.

During the late 1800s, tagua was produced extensively in Ecuador and used to make buttons and crafts, but it was later displaced from the market by plastics. Toward the end of the twentieth century, the tagua tradition was revived and Ecuador is once again exporting button blanks for use in ecologically friendly garments. At the same time, local artisans have begun to produce a wonderful variety of tagua crafts, which make excellent souvenirs since they promote conservation rather than destruction of the forest areas where the palm grows.

Páramo

Above about 3000 meters (10,000 feet) is a transition zone between the cloud forest and *páramo*. Trees get gradually smaller, and small bushes of the daisy and blueberry families are scattered amidst grasses. Some of the more common species of trees in this area are the polylepis, with a characteristic peeling red bark, the *piquil* or *fical*, with daisy-like yellow flowers and a velvety underside on the leaves, and the *quishuar*, with similar but longer leaves.

The *páramo* proper, starting at about 4000 meters (13,000 feet) in the northern highlands or as low as 3300 meters (11,000 feet) in the south, has continuous vegetation cover. There is a predominance of grasses, clumps of the *Calamagrotis, Stipa,* and *Festuca* genera, giant and dwarf rosettes, cushion plants, and dwarf bushes. Plants here have developed special characteristics (such as small waxy leaves), which allow them to survive in very harsh conditions. There are many colorful flowers such as the gentians and *chuquiraguas*. Other characteristic flora are club mosses and terrestrial bromeliads known as *achupallas*.

The *páramo* is home to the White-tailed Deer, its predator the Mountain Lion, and a miniature deer (the *pudú*) which is quite hard to see. Rabbits are very common in the high grasslands, supporting their predators the Andean Fox and Great Horned Owl. The *páramo* is also home to the majestic Andean Condor, the Chimborazo Hillstar hummingbird, and such aquatic birds as the Andean Coot, Andean Teal, and Andean Gull. Many high lakes were seeded with trout in the 1970s and still offer good fishing. The *páramos* of Ecuador are vital to the well-being of other ecosystems located downslope (see "A Living Sponge" in Trek 15).

As you approach the snowline, the soil becomes sandy and vegetation more scarce. Although the ground appears bare, careful observation will reveal that, in addition to mosses and lichens, there are a number of small plants with tiny bright flowers growing in the most inhospitable conditions.

Paepalanthus ensifolius *is a rosette often found in boggy páramo.*

A SPECTACLED BEAR

This species earned its imaginative name because of the white patches usually found around the eyes, while the rest of its coat of thick fur is jet black. The only bear native to South America, it is also the smallest member of family *Ursidae*. Adult males reach 2 meters (6.5 feet) in length and weigh up to 175 kilograms (385 pounds), while females are usually only two-thirds this size. Widely distributed throughout the Andean countries, Spectacled Bears in Ecuador are found on both the eastern and western slopes of the Andes right up to 4700 meters (15,500 feet), wherever their cloud forest and *páramo* habitats have not been destroyed by man.

Perhaps because of its relatively small size and mostly vegetarian diet, the Spectacled Bear has traditionally been considered innocuous. It does, however, like to supplement

its usual menu of bromeliads (especially *achupallas*), fruits, and bamboo shoots, with small rodents, rabbits, and even the occasional deer or Mountain Tapir. Although the bears are shy and seldom seen by trekkers, evidence of their activity is easy to spot in the form of chewed or shredded *achupallas*. In such areas you should not keep food in your tent: this little Latino bear deserves just as much respect as its more intimidating northern cousins.

Inter-Andean Valleys

Sheltered by both ranges, this area is drier than the outer slopes of the Andes. The region has been taken over by agriculture and ranching, even up in the *páramos*. Introduced species such as eucalyptus and pine are most common, but a few remnants of native vegetation can be found in the many *quebradas* (ravines, valleys, or canyons). Likewise, there are many domestic animals and at higher elevations you are likely to see domesticated Andean camelids: the llama and alpaca. Vicuñas are their wild relatives, found only on the slopes of Chimborazo following a successful reintroduction program (see Trek 21, Vicuña Trail).

Domestic Andean camelids: llama with young (Photo: Kerry Alley)

Northern Pacific Rainforest

The northern coastal plain has some of the wettest rainforest in the world, but it is also an area threatened by logging. This is the southern end of the Chocó Bioregion of neighboring Colombia (see Trek 2, Ecuador's Chocó). Much of the flora and fauna here is shared not only with Colombia, but also with Central America. The shore in this area has beautiful mangroves; alas, many are being cut to make way for shrimp farms.

Dry Southern Coast

In contrast with the north, the southern Pacific coast of Ecuador is very dry (almost a desert in the far south). There are deciduous forests here, and the flora and fauna are that of the Tumbesian Bioregion shared with northwestern Peru. The large pot-bellied kapok tree is characteristic of this area.

Amazon Jungle

Biological diversity reaches its peak in Ecuador's Oriente. One hectare of rainforest can have more than 300 species of trees, although the epiphytes are not as abundant as in the cloud forest. In a single site, 14 species of primates and 550 species of birds have been recorded. In addition to the primates, mammals include 5 species of cats, 3 anteaters, sloths, lowland tapir, 2 species of dolphins, rodents, and many varieties of bats. Among the reptiles are several caimans and snakes of all descriptions, including the anaconda (the largest in the world). Many of the birds are striking; there are macaws and parakeets, many water birds, and the impressive Harpy Eagle, which preys on monkeys. There are as many as 700 species of butterflies at a single site, including several large fluorescent blue morphos. Life in the lakes and rivers is no less diverse, with giant catfish, piranhas, stingrays, and eels.

CONSERVATION

The immense value of Ecuador's unique biological diversity is something regrettably few Ecuadoreans are able to take to heart. In a country where most people are beset by chronic poverty, and most economic and political leaders are beset by concepts of progress rooted in unsustainable forms of development, there has been little scope for conserving the natural environment.

Many rural Ecuadoreans continue to clear patch after patch of primary forest, in the hope of feeding their steadily growing families. As a result, the annual rate of deforestation is estimated to exceed two percent. For their part, the authorities continue to permit (even encourage) extensive petroleum and mining operations in the very heart of national parks, in the hope of keeping up with interest payments on the country's steadily growing foreign debt.

Despite this sometimes grim picture, however, there is real hope. In addition to Ecuador's extensive national park system, many private reserves have been created during the past two decades. There are also a growing number of community-based environmental protection and ecotourism projects sponsored by local and international nongovernmental organizations (NGOs; see "Conservation Organizations" in Appendix A). Trek 16, The Great Cascade Trail, provides a close-up look at one particularly successful community development project.

There is also some positive news at the government level. Environmental issues no longer depend on the Ministry of Agriculture. The Ministerio del Ambiente (Ministry of the Environment), created in 1998, is responsible for the administration of Ecuador's national parks and reserves. As in other developing countries, there has been talk of swapping foreign debt for environmental conservation, but there are no major achievements on this front to date.

As a trekker you can do your part to encourage conservation and sustainable development in Ecuador. If local people perceive tangible economic benefit from your presence in their area, then they will have an incentive to conserve the forest or *páramo* so that other visitors may follow. When appropriate, hire a local person to guide you or pack animals to help with your load. Buy some fruit from their orchards or provisions at the local shop. Show you care and are willing to share your wealth as well as your ideas. You might also consider contributing some of your time or money to one of the NGOs working for conservation in Ecuador.

Sadly, many campesinos continue to clear patch after patch of primary forest.

HISTORY

Archaeological studies date the presence of man in current-day Ecuador to approximately 10,000 B.C. Many early cultures flourished in different regions and later amalgamated into larger, more powerful nations—the ancestors of contemporary native groups. In the fifteenth century, the northward-expanding Inca Empire encountered much resistance from these pre-Ecuadorean nations, but eventually subjugated them. Quichua became the common language (still spoken today) and Quito the northern capital of the Inca Empire. A civil war between two heirs to the Incas' throne, Atahualpa in Quito and Huascar in Cusco, weakened the empire and facilitated the Spanish conquest. Spanish *conquistadores*, led by Francisco Pizarro, landed on the Pacific coast of South America in 1531. In 1534 Spanish colonial Quito was founded over the remains of Inca and pre-Inca cities.

Spanish Colonial Rule

Almost three centuries of colonial rule followed the conquest. The Spaniards were given large tracts of land, and all the Indians who lived there became their property. The indigenous population was decimated by disease and forced labor. The last vestiges of this feudal system were still in place in 1964, when agrarian reform was finally introduced. Ironically, perhaps, the same reforms marked the beginning of deforestation for many natural areas of Ecuador, because they deliberately encouraged colonization of unpopulated parts of the country.

Over the years the population of *mestizos*, of mixed Indian and Spanish blood, grew and became the majority. This group spearheaded the drive for independence from Spain. The first attempts at secession took place in 1809, but the Spanish were finally expelled from Quito in 1822. At that time Ecuador became a part of Simón Bolívar's Gran Colombia, which also included modern-day Colombia and Venezuela. In 1830, this federation dissolved and its members became independent states.

The Republic

The history of Ecuador as an independent nation is marked by many long periods of political instability (corresponding to times of economic hardship), with brief interludes of calm during less frequent episodes of prosperity. In 170 years the country has had sixty-one presidential terms of office and eighteen constitutions. Power has traditionally alternated between conservative groups from the highlands and liberal groups from the coast. Although many of the changes of government were the result of uprisings, these generally took place without widespread violence and had little or no effect on the day-to-day lives of the people.

In 1979, following seven years of military rule, Ecuador entered its most recent period of constitutional democracy. The 1980s and 1990s were marked by repeated government attempts to introduce neoliberal economic reforms. These reforms were always opposed by the country's labor unions and (in more recent years) by the indigenous movement, which has become an important political player. It was and is a time of increasing economic hardship and corresponding social unrest. Governments were overthrown without bloodshed in 1997 and 2000, and a nominally democratic solution was found to both crises.

POPULATION

Ecuador is among the most densely populated countries in Latin America. The 1990 census recorded 10.2 million inhabitants (37.8 inhabitants per square kilometer, 97.8 per square mile). By the turn of the millennium, population was estimated at 12 to 13 million. Urban dwellers account for over half of the population. The main cities are Quito, the capital; Guayaquil, the main port and largest metropolis; and Cuenca, a cultural center in the southern highlands.

You can expect to meet a few folks on the majority of treks. Most Ecuadoreans are friendly people who warmly welcome foreigners. Many have a genuine curiosity and want to learn from and about their visitors. In the lowlands, people are often outspoken and easygoing, while highlanders (especially those in the countryside) are usually more reserved. Be prepared to receive stares and giggles, particularly from children, when you trek by remote villages; and don't be surprised if along the way you are called *míster* or *gringo*. People in isolated rural areas are occasionally suspicious of outsiders. Since trekking is not a common activity, locals may have a hard time understanding why you have come so far just to see the forest or waterfall they take for granted. Surely you must be searching for gold or some other hidden treasure!

CULTURES

Contemporary Ecuador is home to many cultures. Although the majority of the population is *mestizo*, of mixed Spanish and Indian blood, many native people retain their cultural identity and belong to a number of different nations. There are also Afro-Ecuadoreans (descendants of slaves brought from Africa in the eighteenth century), a few direct descendants of Spaniards, and other smaller minorities.

The coastal plain is the most densely populated region, with just over half of the country's people. Here you find the *montubios*, a generic term for coastal country dwellers. The northern coastal province of Esmeraldas has the highest concentration of Afro-Ecuadoreans. There are also a small number of coastal native people, such as the Awas, Chachis, and Tzachilas or Colorados.

The inter-Andean region was historically the most heavily populated in the country, dating back to pre-Inca times. Today it is home to the highest proportion of native people, with a common language (Quichua) inherited from the Incas. These natives live mainly in rural areas throughout the Sierra, and their typical dress and hats vary from one region to another. Highland native groups with a distinct cultural identity include the Otavaleños, Salasacas, Cañaris, and Saraguros. You are sure to meet many highland native people along your treks.

Although the Amazon lowlands (El Oriente) account for less than four percent of the country's population, this has been the area of fastest growth and greatest natural destruction since 1972, when petroleum extraction began in the region. Most colonists migrated to the Oriente from the highlands and settled in towns along the foothills west of the jungle, while many natives maintain a seminomadic lifestyle in the rainforest.

As a result of increased contact with colonists and oil workers, cultural assimilation among rainforest native people is running high. The most numerous of Amazon native groups are the Quichuas del Oriente, a group distinct from highland Quichua speakers. Smaller groups include the Shuar, Achuar, Huaorani, Cofán, Siona, Secoya, and Záparo. As a rule, if you plan to trek in Oriente you will need a permit (often several permits) from native communities along the way. It is best for you and the native people you might encounter if you go with a qualified guide.

RELIGION AND FIESTAS

The majority of Ecuador's population is Roman Catholic, although other Christian and non-Christian religions are also present. Ecuadorean traditions reflect a degree of syncretism (mixture or fusion) between Catholicism and aboriginal customs. One example, which you are likely to encounter while trekking, is the presence of crosses. Their Catholic significance is obvious, but before the Spanish conquest native people also made cairns (pyramids of rough stones) and put crossed sticks over them to mark important intersections.

Religion in Ecuador is closely related to the festival calendar. *Día de fiesta* is not an easy concept to translate. It is at once a festival, a feast, a party, a holiday, and a holy day. It is a day to be looked forward to and prepared for; a day in which to be very happy, or very solemn, or very patriotic. It is a day when the restraints of social hierarchy may be temporarily relaxed, when rich and poor can celebrate together.

Most authentic are the *fiestas de pueblo* (village festivals), held to honor a community's patron saint, to commemorate the founding of a canton or parish, or to celebrate the season's harvest. There is not a hamlet too small to have its own special *fiesta*. This is usually celebrated with a solemn mass, a parade with floats and folk dancing, exhibits, bull fights,

Pase del Niño parades, such as this one in Chordeleg, are an important Christmas tradition.

live music, dancing, fireworks, traditional foods, and much drinking.

If your trek happens to take you through a village during its *fiesta*, take advantage of this special opportunity. You may be invited to dance, have something to eat, and even more likely, you will be offered *chicha* (a fermented corn beverage) or *aguardiente* (literally "fire-water"—home-brewed cane liquor). People will be offended if you do not accept, and you must find a polite way to say no if you wish to abstain or when you have had enough.

Note that if you are planning to get transport, a local guide, or pack animals, you might have to wait until the *fiesta* ends and town residents sober up before these are available. Transport to a village is likely to be crowded during festivities, hotels may be full, and shops and services closed.

ECONOMY AND DEVELOPMENT

> *Ecuador is a beggar sitting on a chest of gold.*
> —Alexander von Humboldt, nineteenth-century explorer

The mainstay of the Ecuadorean economy has traditionally been agriculture. Industrial banana plantations occupy most of the arable land on the coast. (Ecuador is the world's number-one banana producer and exporter.) Shrimp is also grown on the Pacific coast, in artificial ponds built by destroying most of the country's mangroves. Other agricultural exports include fish (mainly tuna), coffee, cocoa, and cut flowers.

Although agriculture remains very important, since 1972 petroleum has been the main source of foreign revenue. The extraction of oil from the Amazon basin has brought devastation to parts of the rainforest and some of its native people. At the same time, tourism has been growing steadily, and in 2000 it became the country's third major source of foreign income. Dubbed "the industry without a chimney," tourism has the potential to promote sustainable development—but only if it is responsibly managed.

Despite the country's great natural wealth, most people in Ecuador are poor. Since independence, the country has been saddled with the burden of its debts to richer nations—a vicious cycle of ongoing borrowing and endless interest payments. Resources badly needed for education, health care, and housing go instead to service the foreign debt and to line the pockets of a notoriously corrupt bureaucracy. Not much is left for social programs. Many Ecuadoreans have migrated (legally or illegally) to North America and Europe in search of better opportunities. Since the late 1990s, the number of migrants has increased dramatically.

In 1999 the Ecuadorean economy collapsed altogether, following a series of fraudulent bank failures, and the Sucre (the country's currency since 1883) devalued into oblivion. In a desperate bid for stability, the United States dollar was adopted as the national currency. Monetary stability was indeed achieved, but at the cost of further diminishing the purchasing power of most of the population.

Keep these issues in mind when you meet people during your treks. Especially in rural areas, many people are poor (although they are less likely to be hungry than those who live in urban slums). No matter how low your income, you are almost certainly far better off than the people you encounter or hire to help you, so you can afford to be generous (within reason). By visiting Ecuador you are contributing to its economy and helping its people—but only if you adhere to the principles of responsible travel and trekking.

Chapter 3
WHAT TO EXPECT

This is the country where nothing is easy but everything is possible.
—Arduino Cercená, ice-cream maker and prophet

INDEPENDENT VERSUS ORGANIZED TREKKING

Several key factors will determine how you choose to trek in Ecuador: time, money, language skills, trekking experience, and personal preference.

Trekking with an International Company

Several companies from Australia, Europe, and North America offer trekking trips in Ecuador (see Appendix A). This is the easiest and most expensive option. Everything will be arranged for you, and your guide and companions will speak your language—you just have to show up. The drawbacks are lack of flexibility regarding routes, reduced exposure to local culture, and (of course) the price.

Trekking with an Ecuadorean Company

Trekking with a local company has the advantages of lower cost than international companies, greater flexibility regarding routes and schedules, and usually the opportunity for more local interaction. Prices vary considerably; the range at present is about $30 to $100 per person per day, everything included. Arrangements can be made on-site at the last minute, or in advance from abroad. Many Ecuadorean trekking operators speak English and sometimes other European languages; they are easy to contact by e-mail.

Although the quality of these treks varies, a number of very reputable Ecuadorean agencies run good trekking tours. Quito agencies arrange tours throughout the country, and agencies in regional centers are also a worthwhile option. The latter may know their areas better and offer a greater variety of routes (but they will not necessarily know all the treks described in this book). If you do not speak Spanish, make sure you are assigned a guide who speaks your language. Appendix A has an alphabetical list of agencies for each trekking center in Section II.

Organized versus independent trekking: a matter of personal preference (Group photo: William Reyes)

Independent Trekking

This is the most economical choice and offers the greatest flexibility and challenge. You plan your walk, choose the route and pace that best suit you, make your own preparations, and rely exclusively on your own abilities to get in and out safely. To trek independently you should have enough time, a flexible travel itinerary, adequate experience, clothing and equipment, and a more-than-basic knowledge of Spanish. If you meet these requirements and are so inclined, then independent trekking is by far the most satisfying option. It will give you an opportunity to explore the many wonders of backcountry Ecuador. This book is written with independent trekkers in mind.

Note, however, that it is not safe to trek alone. If you were to get into any trouble—even something as minor as a sprained ankle—nobody would be there to assist you or to seek help. Lone trekkers are sometimes a target for thieves. A trekking party of two people is fine, and four is ideal; more than six is too many. If you are traveling alone, it is easy to find trekking partners; post a notice in hotels and restaurants frequented by travelers, or just work the *gringo* grapevine.

Hiring a Local Guide

Even if you meet all the criteria for trekking independently, there are still some circumstances in which hiring a local guide is advisable. Such is the case with jungle routes, for example, where navigation is difficult and native communities are particularly sensitive to the presence of outsiders. You will need additional time to find an appropriate guide and make the necessary arrangements. Choose carefully, as the quality of the guide will in large measure determine the quality of your experience. Prices vary greatly, but count on paying $10 to $25 per day for a local guide. You must also provide food, usually a tent, and sometimes a backpack or waterproof clothing for your guide.

Pack Animals and Porters

There is nothing quite as simple and satisfying as carrying everything you need on your own back. If you wish to lighten your load, however, some routes are suitable for pack animals, which may be hired near the trailhead. This too requires additional time to organize. You must also provide the same food and equipment for a muleteer as you would for a local guide. While your main pack rides on the horse, donkey, mule, or llama, take a day pack in which you carry everything you may need during the day: your valuables, maps, navigation instruments, camera, extra film, warm jacket, raingear, water, snacks, etc. The cost will run approximately $5 to $15 per animal per day—plus the same amount for the muleteer, who can usually handle up to three animals.

Crossing the Río Limón del Carmen (Trek 17)

In a few places in Ecuador you may be able to hire porters to carry some of your gear. Unlike pack animals, porters can travel on any trail you can. Hiring porters is not a common practice, however, and it opens a Pandora's box of social issues. Do you provide porters with clothing and equipment equivalent to your own, or do they manage as best they can with a well-worn poncho for a blanket and a sheet of plastic for a tent? Of course this question also applies to the muleteers and local guides mentioned above. Indeed, these rather artificial categories (local guide, muleteer, and porter) often overlap in practice, and all are occasional sidelines for a few rural Ecuadoreans rather than anyone's profession. Porters charge between $5 and $15 per day, plus food and equipment as above.

RESPONSIBLE TREKKING
As a trekker, take care to minimize the harmful effects of your trip on both the natural and cultural environments. Many treks go through vulnerable remote areas; you might be among the first tourists to visit these sites and should be especially careful not to spoil them.

Protecting the Natural Environment
In Ecuador, as elsewhere, elemental standards of conduct apply: "Pack it in, pack it out"; "take nothing but photos, leave nothing but footprints." In order to minimize your impact on the areas you trek through, stay on available trails. If walking cross-country, be careful to do as little damage as possible. Many treks go through *páramo* where the vegetation, in particular the cushion plants, are very delicate and grow extremely slowly. In these areas, try to step on the straw instead.

When camping, always keep your impact to a minimum: disturb as few plants as possible, do not dig gutters, do not build a fire unless it is indispensable, and avoid staying at the same site for several days (so as not to damage the area). Your goal should be to leave the spot where you camped as you found it.

Culcitium nivale, *a delicate relative of the sunflower, growing on a cushion plant*

Ecuadoreans sometimes show a lack of awareness about the importance of discarding trash properly. You can help with your good example and by *insisting* that guides and companions pack out all refuse. Toilet paper and sanitary napkins represent a particular eyesore in this regard, as anyone who has come across the last trekker's latrine in the middle of the trail can testify. Do your business well away from water sources, trails, and campsites. Consider using leaves or grass as a substitute for toilet paper, and pack out sanitary napkins or tampons.

Water sources must also be protected. Although oats are organic, the scraps of your porridge don't belong on the shore of that pristine stream. Wash your dishes, your clothes, and yourself well away from water sources.

Although some locals hunt and fish to supplement their diet, make sure you are not creating a demand for wild game to feed trekkers. Never permit your guide to kill such endangered species as Mountain Tapir or Spectacled Bear. You can also help protect endangered plants and animals by being selective when you buy souvenirs.

Protecting the Cultural Environment

The impact of our interaction with local people is not easily measured, but clearly negative consequences of tourism have been experienced in areas that receive a large number of visitors.

Communication is the first step toward a positive cultural exchange; the more Spanish you speak, the more meaningful your experience will be. Ecuadoreans are very polite people. Greeting when you step into a shop and even as you pass someone on the trail is important. The formal *buenos días* (good morning), *buenas tardes* (good afternoon), and *buenas noches* (good evening) are most commonly used. Handshakes and farewells (*hasta luego*) are also expected, and a smile is always welcome.

The Lara family of San Juan de Llullundongo

If you are invited to stay in someone's home or given assistance along the trail, always offer to pay. Ask, *"Cuánto le debo?"* How much do I owe you? In untouristed areas, money will be refused or the amount left to your discretion. Be generous but reasonable. Giving too much will create an unfair expectation of the next trekker. Whether or not you pay, remember to share in other ways: some of your food, a token gift from your home (a postcard or flag lapel-pin), and of course your ideas and insights.

In the mountains, folks dress more conservatively than on the coast or in the jungle. It is not appropriate to wear shorts in a church, religious shrine, or cemetery. Shorts are acceptable on the trail, but nude bathing is not. Try not to offend people by ignoring their customs and beliefs.

"Soul thievery" is the most common indiscretion committed by tourists. Some native people believe that a photograph steals their soul. Folks dressed in colorful indigenous outfits or cute local children may be seriously offended if the first thing you do is point a camera at them. *Always ask for permission before you take someone's picture.* Offering to send a copy of the picture is a small courtesy that is always appreciated. (Be sure to keep your word.) Never offer, or give, money for photographs; that is asking someone to sell his or her soul.

Begging is a particularly difficult issue. Ecuador has some genuinely destitute people for whom a contribution may make the difference between having a piece of bread and not eating that day. Others, however, have acquired the bad habit of asking any foreigner for money. Try to distinguish between the two, and if you decide to give something, consider food rather than money. Do not give anything to children. On the trail, well-meaning trekkers' gratuitous gifts of money, candies, or pens to children lead to future begging. Instead, contribute to the local school or a community development project.

TREKKING INFRASTRUCTURE

> *Trails, like rivers, flow down out of the mountains.*
> —Alfonso Barrera Valverde, *El País de Manuelito*

Trekking in Ecuador is, for the most part, an independent adventurous activity. That is precisely what makes it so rewarding. The country does not have an extensive infrastructure set up specifically for hikers. In that sense it is unlike Nepal, for example, where the foreigner arrives and automatically fits into a well-organized trekking world. In Ecuador the trekker must be self-sufficient in all respects.

Protected Natural Areas

Some of the treks described in this book go through national or private protected areas, while others follow public paths through the countryside. Many go through both protected and unprotected areas.

Ecuador's *Sistema Nacional de Areas Protegidas* includes nine national parks and seventeen reserves spread throughout the country's natural regions. In mainland Ecuador, approximately 15 percent of the land area (almost 4 million hectares, or 10 million acres) is protected. A number of parks were created in 1979 and the remainder in the 1980s and 1990s. Although these protected areas exist on paper, infrastructure is limited in the older parks and nonexistent in some of the more recently created ones. Park boundaries are seldom marked (or even clearly defined), the number of rangers is insufficient for the size of the reserves, and—with few exceptions—trails are not marked or maintained.

In addition to the national system of reserves, there are many private protected areas. Their infrastructure varies: some are wilderness areas without any services, some have research stations that allow trekkers to spend the night, and others have elaborate and expensive lodges for visitors. Some of these reserves have systems of trails that offer good trekking and day-hiking opportunities.

Vicuña reserve at Mechahuasca

Permits and Fees

Fees, payable on entry to most public and private reserves, vary from park to park and also with the time of the year (high versus low season). They currently range from $5 to $20 per person for foreigners, while Ecuadoreans pay considerably less. The facilities for collecting these fees are concentrated at a very few popular access points and, along many of the treks described in this book, there is no opportunity to pay. Instead, consider making a donation to one of the NGOs listed under "Conservation Organizations" in Appendix A.

Native communities may charge fees for passing through their land (especially in Oriente). Likewise, *hacienda* owners may charge for the right of trespass, although more frequently they simply want you to ask permission. The fees applicable to each trek are described in Section II. The Ministerio del Ambiente issues permits to those who wish to collect specimens of wild plants or animals.

Trails

Most trails you will walk along are there because locals use them to go to the next village, to reach one of their fields or pastures, or to go logging, hunting, or fishing. Very few trails in Ecuador were built for trekkers *per se*. At times, a well-defined path you are following will end frustratingly before you reach your goal. Perhaps the people who walk there only go that far and their objective falls short of yours, or perhaps you took the wrong trail.

The quality of a trail will depend on its frequency of use, its terrain, and the weather. Close to towns you will find dirt roads or wide mule tracks. In a rainy area, this is also where you will find the worst mud: the daily stomping of animals makes a real mess. Where pack animals are used regularly, their sliding creates transverse ridges, known as *camellones* because of the resemblance to humps on a camel's back (see "The Cascarilla Story" in Trek 17). Walking along a trail with *camellones*, especially when it is wet, can be a real challenge. In some places where the ground is soft, trails have been worn so deep that they become gullies, well over your head.

Always pay attention to gates along the trail, and make sure to leave them just as you found them.

Those trails that are maintained are usually looked after by the people who use them. You may run across a *minga*, a group of people working together on a community project, clearing or repairing the trail. As a fellow user of the trail, your efforts to help will be greatly appreciated.

Camellones *on the trail to La Victoria (Trek 17)*

In wilderness areas you will likely have to go cross-country or follow animal paths. Do not assume that a path necessarily goes where you want to; always keep an eye on your navigation instruments. In some places, especially grassy *páramos*, many parallel paths later diverge. In forested areas, there may be many animal paths—and it is a challenge to find the one going just where you want to.

Campsites and Shelters

One of the greatest pleasures of trekking in Ecuador is camping along the way. A great many spots to camp are not merely suitable but splendid, though few of these are marked as "campground." A very few parks have designated camping areas or shelters, where trash may be a serious problem. Whenever you can, help pack some of the accumulated trash out.

The sites suitable for camping that are described in this book generally have some flat ground on which to pitch a tent; reasonable shelter from the wind; and a water source nearby. They may have nothing else. In soggy *páramo*, lay down a generous mattress of straw before pitching your tent. (In addition to keeping you drier, this will help protect the fragile underlying soil and plants.) When camping in populated rural areas, always ask permission and offer to pay before pitching your tent in someone's backyard or potato field.

Few shelters exist specifically for trekkers in Ecuador, and even those few are generally not maintained. In remote villages, you may be offered floor space in the local school. Consider reciprocating with some pencils, pens, or notebooks.

MAPS AND NAVIGATION

The ability to read a topographic map and to navigate with a compass and altimeter are essential for independent trekking in Ecuador. For all but the easiest walks, the maps in this book must be supplemented with topos. A Global Positioning System (GPS) is recommended for more difficult treks, but remember that a GPS will not work in dense forest or deep valleys.

Maps

Topographic maps for Ecuador are produced by the Instituto Geográfico Militar (IGM) in the following scales: 1:250,000, 1:100,000, 1:50,000, and 1:25,000. The 1:50,000-scale maps, with a contour interval of 40 meters (130 feet), are the most useful for trekking. Occasionally the more detailed 1:25,000-scale maps may be helpful. GPS users should note that not all IGM topos use the same map datum. Most of the older sheets use the Provisional South American 1956 datum for Ecuador ($dX=-278$ meters, $dY=+171$, $dZ=-367$, $dA=-251$, $dF=-0.000014192702$), while a few of the newer maps use the World Geodetic System 1984 (WGS 84).

The best place to purchase all these maps, as well as aerial photos, is directly at IGM headquarters in Quito. (See "Topographic Maps" in Appendix A.) If original color maps are not available for a particular quadrant, then black and white copies are sold. Originals and copies cost $2. There are no IGM offices outside Quito. If you wish to purchase Ecuador topo maps abroad, you will have to pay considerably more and your selection will be limited (see Appendix A).

IGM maps are generally very good, although they occasionally contain errors. Keep in mind that most of these maps are quite old, and certain things may have changed over time. Glaciers, for example, have receded on many mountains; once-forested areas may now be pastures; and trails shown may have become vehicle roads or be totally overgrown.

Many names that appear in maps have indigenous roots. In the transliteration to Spanish they have sometimes been changed, so that different versions appear on maps of different scales, or what is shown on the map is different from local usage. Examples include *pungu/punku, bamba/pamba/*

pampa, pagcha/paccha, Pulinguí/Pulingue, and Guacamayos/Huacamayos. Very common place names are used repeatedly, and in the same map you may have two totally different streams that are both called Quebrada Santa Ana.

In this book, trek descriptions use the names and spellings found on IGM 1:50,000-scale topographic maps, and the text indicates when these are different from those used by local people. Note that some names on IGM maps refer to a general area, and are not associated with a specific topographic feature such as a hill or a village. Be aware that some rivers change names along their course. The changes might be shown on the maps, but it might also be a change in usage by local people along the way.

Most maps of border areas are classified as *reservado,* which means you must obtain a military permit in order to purchase them. This can be done right at the IGM and is not necessarily difficult, but may require some extra time. Among the treks in this book, only the two maps for Trek 29, Pass of the Winds, are *reservado.*

Finally, note that the Spanish alphabet has the extra letter Ñ, between N and O; this letter is used in the IGM's map grid, so when you order maps, make sure to specify whether it is N or Ñ that you need. To avoid confusion, always specify a map by both its name and its grid coordinates.

Navigation

Navigation is one of the great challenges of trekking in Ecuador, and getting it right is one of the great satisfactions. Convoluted topography, frequent fog, and the absence of signs make finding your way something of a puzzle. Your maps, instruments, and intuition, as well as the trek descriptions in this book, are all pieces of that puzzle. None should be relied on in isolation; rather, they must be brought together. You should also consult local people whenever possible, but bear in mind the following *caveats.*

Understanding Spanish does not guarantee you will understand the route directions of a *campesino* (rural dweller), nor should you assume that locals are familiar with a map and compass. Since *campesinos* nearly always move much faster than trekkers, the walking times given by locals must be multiplied several-fold. Always request details and landmarks that are as specific as possible. General inquiries usually receive the following reply: *"Hay un sólo camino, no puede perderse."* "There is only one trail, no way to get lost." This is hardly ever the case.

Trails in Ecuador are full of minor forks, far more than can be mentioned in the trek descriptions or shown on the maps in this book. When you reach one of these, explore ahead a bit. One branch will soon lead to a house or pasture, while the other continues along your route.

By definition, real explorers must spend a good deal of their time being lost (*se hace camino al andar*). If you get lost, consider it an opportunity to discover new routes. Take a break, consult your map and instruments, and think over the situation calmly. With a little patience and perseverance, you will make it safely somewhere interesting.

Chapter 4
PREPARATIONS

There is not enough space in this book to provide all the information you need to travel in Ecuador. Many excellent guidebooks have been published about the country (see Appendix B) and are a recommended companion to this volume. Internet sites and other resources are listed in Appendix A.

GETTING YOURSELF READY

To prepare yourself for trekking in Ecuador, you will need to get into the very best physical shape possible and learn Spanish. The better prepared you are in both these respects, the more you will enjoy your trip.

Since the finest trekking opportunities in Ecuador are in the highlands, where walking up and down steep mountain slopes is the rule, being in good physical condition is especially important. Even if you are in great shape, however, you will need a period of acclimatization when you arrive at high altitude. Acclimatization to altitude, immunizations, and other health preparations are discussed in Chapter 5.

Your stay in Ecuador will also be easier and more meaningful if you can communicate with its people. Although some Ecuadoreans speak English, the vast majority speak only Spanish. In remote highland areas people speak mostly Quichua, with Spanish as a second language. Appendix C lists a rudimentary trekker's vocabulary, but this is not sufficient. Learn some Spanish ahead of your trip, or begin your trip by learning Spanish. Quito alone has more than 100 Spanish language schools, and there are others in Cuenca, Baños, and Otavalo.

PASSPORT AND VISAS

Only citizens of a few African, Asian, and Central American countries require a consular visa to visit Ecuador as tourists. Others just need a passport valid for at least six months, and preferably a return or onward ticket. Once in the country you are required to carry your passport at all times, and you may be asked to present it to police on the street or at roadside checkpoints. Although you will rarely be asked for identification in the countryside, you should nonetheless always carry your passport when trekking. (Make sure you have a good plastic bag to keep it dry.)

Upon arrival, most tourists are authorized to stay in Ecuador 30 to 60 days. This may be extended to a maximum of 180 days per year at the discretion of the immigration police.

INSURANCE

Travel insurance (including medical and baggage coverage) should be considered compulsory for all visitors to Ecuador. Be sure to read the fine print, so you know what is and is not covered. Familiarize yourself with claims procedures and remember to bring the necessary contact information with you. If you should incur a loss or medical expense, notify your insurer at once. Be sure to keep all receipts and, in the event of theft, always obtain a police report. Foreign insurance companies will generally not pay directly for medical expenses in Ecuador. You will have to pay out-of-pocket and then request reimbursement. You should, therefore, always have some extra funds on hand.

CLOTHING AND EQUIPMENT

Some trekking gear can be purchased or rented in Quito. See Appendix A for a list of Quito camping stores as well as trekking agencies in other cities that may have rentals available. Consider bringing as much of your own clothing and equipment as possible, however, so you know what you have and can rely on it. Furthermore, because of customs regulations, it is expensive and time-consuming to have anything sent to you once you are in Ecuador. If you buy or rent equipment here, check it thoroughly before you head out on the trail. Our suggested gear checklist (see sidebar on the next page) is just that—a suggestion—and experienced trekkers will have their own variations. A few items, however, merit additional comment.

Adequate clothing for rain, wind, and cold is critically important to prevent hypothermia. A set of separate light sleeping clothes, which can be kept dry in a waterproof stuff-sack during the day, is likewise required.

Boots are obviously fundamental for trekking. While options abound, in our experience the simplest is the best. Calf- to knee-length rubber boots are sold economically throughout Ecuador, although very large sizes may be hard to find. They are universally worn by all *campesinos* and, when combined with a pair of warm wool socks, make for surprisingly versatile and comfortable footwear. They are a blessing on frequently muddy trails and also offer some protection against snakes. Synthetic or leather hiking boots are recommended for those treks involving ice and snow, dry rocky trails, and extensive road walking. New footwear of any kind should always be tried first on day walks; your boots and feet need time to get used to each other.

A reliable camping stove is very important; many treks are above tree line, and the existing forests should not be turned into firewood. Sealed *Camping Gaz* canisters are the most commonly available form of camping fuel in Ecuador, but such stoves do not perform well in the cold or at high altitude. White gas can be hard to find; try the *Kywi* chain of hardware stores in Quito, and ask for *combustible para lámparas Coleman*. Kerosene is available but not common. Although somewhat dirty, all gasoline (petrol) in Ecuador is unleaded and can be burnt in a pinch by some stoves. The authors have used a simple *Optimus 123* stove for many years, while others prefer more sophisticated multi-fuel models.

A machete (easily purchased throughout Ecuador) is also used by all *campesinos* but is not necessarily recommended for trekkers. If you have experience using a machete, then it can be useful in dense brush. Otherwise, the risk of serious injury and the inconvenience of additional weight may far exceed the benefits of this implement. A small pair of garden pruning shears make a safe, light, and innovative alternative to a machete.

GEAR CHECKLIST

The following is a comprehensive list. Select what you need for conditions on a given trek, and remember to think *light* and *compact*. Special gear for each trek is described in Section II.

Backpack
Day pack
Rain cover for pack
Stuff-sacks (waterproof or lined with plastic bags)
Sturdy plastic bags (various sizes)
Tent with good mosquito netting and separate fly
Plastic sheet cut to footprint of tent
Three-season sleeping bag
Insulating mat or pad
Camping stove
Fuel bottle
Pot, bowl, and spoon
Pocket knife with can opener
Water bottle
Container to fetch water (e.g., an empty one-gallon plastic mineral water bottle)

Continued on p. 52 . . .

Water purification supplies (see Chapter 5)
First-aid kit (see Chapter 5)
Sewing kit and gear repair kit
Parachute cord
Sunscreen (for both skin and lips)
Insect repellent
Washcloth and soap
Flashlight or headlamp
Matches and lighters
Maps and navigation instruments
Reliable water-resistant watch
Notebook, pen, and pencil
Breathable waterproof jacket and pants
Warmest fleece jacket
Wool or fleece pants
Wool hat
Wool gloves or mitts
Neck warmer (gaiter)
Light fleece or light wool sweater
Moisture-wicking short-sleeve T-shirt
Moisture-wicking long-sleeve T-shirt
Moisture-wicking long underpants
Light cotton or poly-cotton pants
Shorts
Underwear
Wool socks
Boots
Sunglasses
Sun hat

Optional Items

Camera
Binoculars
Down vest
Walking stick(s)
Rope
Fishing rod
Machete or pruning shears

GETTING TO ECUADOR

Ecuador is easy to reach. The air travel gateways from North America are Miami, Houston, and New York City; from Europe they are Madrid, Amsterdam, Paris, and Frankfurt. There are also flights to Ecuador from most other South American capitals, as well as Panama and Costa Rica in Central America. In Ecuador, international airports are located in Quito and Guayaquil, with Quito being the preferred point of arrival for most tourists. You are not allowed to carry flammables aboard commercial aircraft, so remember to empty your stove and fuel bottle before you fly.

For those traveling from neighboring countries, Ecuador has several land border crossings to Colombia and Peru. A new and exciting option is also becoming available: river travel along the upper Amazon from Brazil and Peru to Ecuador.

CURRENCY AND PRICES

The United States dollar is the only official currency of Ecuador. In addition to the usual bills, U.S. and equivalent-value Ecuadorean coins circulate. Other currencies are very difficult to exchange. U.S. dollar traveler's cheques, credit cards, and bank cards for internationally linked ATMs (banking machines) are all useful, but you must bring some of your funds as U.S. cash in small denominations—$20 bills and smaller. In the countryside even a $5 bill may seem big, so always carry some singles. Coins, on the other hand, are unnecessary weight while you are trekking.

Quito: the preferred point of arrival for most tourists

Ecuador remains a bargain for the international traveler. On a rock-bottom travel budget, expenses are currently about $10 per person per day. For around $25 a day you can find much more comfort, and more than $75 a day is getting into the first-class range. Prices are gradually rising, however, as the economy continues to seek equilibrium following dollarization. The above prices, and those given elsewhere in this book, are correct at the close of this edition and can be expected to slowly increase thereafter.

ACCOMMODATIONS AND MEALS

As a popular travel destination, Ecuador offers a vast array of places to stay and to eat, ranging from opulent and expensive ($220 per person per night in a luxury hotel, $40 for an elegant buffet) to basic and very cheap ($2 per person per night, $1 a meal). The widest variety is found in Quito, Guayaquil, and Cuenca, as well as in popular resort areas. All the trekking centers listed in Section II have a good assortment of such establishments. In small towns and villages, however, you are likely to find only very simple hotels and restaurants. Some places along the treks described in this book are so small that they have no such facilities, but you may be able to arrange for room and board in a private home.

COMMUNICATION

The Internet is very well developed in Ecuador and has become the mainstay of communication for travelers. There are cyber-cafés in all major cities and even in some surprisingly small towns. Rates start around $1 per hour but are usually higher in more remote locations. The telephone system is also reasonably good. Local, national, and international calls may be made from public telephone offices located in most towns (but not in very small villages). There is also a cellular phone system, including debit-card-operated public cell phones. The post office offers the least reliable form of communication; postcards, letters, and packages (even registered ones) are sometimes lost or delayed for months.

PROVISIONS

Shopping in Ecuador is fun. With many colorful markets and old-fashioned general stores *(tiendas)* to choose from, you can take in the local atmosphere while you stock up on provisions. Major cities have modern supermarkets that offer the largest variety of products, including imported items you may use at home. Be sure to check the expiration

Shopping in the Otavalo market is colorful and fun.

date on perishable goods, and keep in mind that polite bargaining is acceptable in markets but not in shops.

Dehydrated meals and name-brand energy bars are not available in Ecuador, but many nutritious, lightweight, and nonperishable foods (ideal for trekking) can be obtained locally. Don't miss the opportunity to enjoy specialties produced in areas you trek through, such as the excellent cheese in Salinas (Trek 16) or delicious trout in Atillo (Trek 20). A sample shopping list, based on local foods, is shown below. Your own list will vary according to the length of your trek, the altitude and climate, your tastes, and of course your appetite. The supper staples listed are noodles and instant mashed potatoes; since water boils at a lower temperature at higher altitude, foods like rice, dry peas, or beans take forever to cook.

GETTING TO THE TRAILHEAD

Public transport goes almost everywhere in Ecuador, and buses are by far the most common way to get around. City buses are best avoided when you are carrying your backpack, but taxis are plentiful and cheap (a recommended alternative). There are frequent departures from Quito's central bus terminal (*terminal terrestre*) to all the trekking centers described in Section II. Do not ride intercity buses at night, though, and always keep a

SAMPLE SHOPPING LIST

The following is an example of trekking provisions for two persons for 6 days. Those items marked with an asterisk (*) may be easier to find in a supermarket in Quito or another large city; everything else should be available at shops anywhere in Ecuador. The total packing weight is approximately 10 kg (22 lb).

Breakfast

*500 g (18 oz) *granola, muesli or other cold cereal* (granola, cereal)
400 g (14 oz) rolled oats (avena)
*400 g (14 oz) *cream of wheat* (semola)
500 g (18 oz) sugar (azúcar)
400 g (14 oz) milk powder (leche en polvo)
200 g (7 oz) butter or margarine (mantequilla, margarina)
200 g (7 oz) malted barley (pinol, máchica)
200 g (7 oz) raisins (pasas)
*200 g (7 oz) *dried fruit* (fruta seca)
coffee, tea, herbal teas, or cocoa (café, té, aguas aromáticas, cocoa)

Lunch

1 kg (2.2 lb) bread (pan)

careful watch on your gear at bus stations (see "Public Safety" in Chapter 5).

Getting from a regional trekking center to the trailhead usually involves a more adventurous ride in a small local bus, taxi, truck, or pick-up. Hitchhiking (always offer to pay) is generally safe and well-accepted along small country roads that lack bus service. It is unnecessary and not recommended on those routes with regular public transport.

Among the trekking centers described in Section II, only Cuenca and Loja (for Vilcabamba) receive commercial flights from Quito and Guayaquil. Cars, including sturdy four-wheel-drive vehicles, may be rented in Quito, Guayaquil, and Cuenca, but they are very expensive and seldom convenient. City driving is chaotic; vehicles cannot be left unattended at the trailhead, and most treks do not make a loop (so you would need to take public transport back to your car).

300 g (11 oz) salt crackers or biscuits (galletas de sal)
750 g (1.7 lb) *hard yellow cheese (queso maduro)
300 g (11 oz) *hard salami (salami)
2 cans (170 g, 6 oz each) of tuna fish (atún)
3 bags (150 g, 5 oz each) of salty banana chips (chifles)
2 packets (100 g, 3.5 oz each) of mayonnaise (mayonesa en sobre)
300 g (11 oz) *gorp or trail mix (prepare your own)
300 g (11 oz) assorted dry sweets from a local bakery (dulces)
200 g (7 oz) chocolate (chocolate)
150 g (5 oz) assorted candies (caramelos)

Supper

400 g (14 oz) noodles (fideos)
2 packets *instant mashed potatoes (puré de papas Maggi)
4 packets instant soup (sopas Maggi)
2 packets instant lentil stew (menestra Yastá)
200 g (7 oz) *dry soy protein (carne, vegetal, carne de soya, Carve; available in health food shops)
50 g (2 oz) *dry mushrooms (hongos secos)
4 stock cubes (cubitos Maggi)
300 g (11 oz) assorted cookies (galletas dulces)
salt and seasonings (sal, especies)

Adventurous ride: buses attempting to cross the Río Mira

Chapter 5
AN OUNCE OF PREVENTION

In Ecuador (as in other parts of Latin America) an ounce of prevention is worth *ten* pounds of cure. Safe and healthy trekking or travels are the rule here, but must not be taken for granted. Simple routine precautions will suffice to assure a wonderful experience for most visitors, yet the consequences of carelessness can be very severe. You are responsible for your own welfare in Ecuador; nobody else will keep you out of trouble.

PUBLIC SAFETY

The trekking routes of Ecuador are arguably the safest places in the country, except for a very few trails long popular with foreigners. People in the countryside are generally helpful and honest but also poor, so you should not leave your campsite unattended or valuables strewn about.

The big cities call for greater caution and a street-smart attitude. Quito, Guayaquil, and Cuenca all have their share of bag-snatching and slashing, as well as violent crime. Do not display your valuables, use a money belt for cash and passport, and choose your hotel carefully. Avoid crowds, deserted streets, and dangerous areas of town. Be wary of con tricks—and generally stay alert to your surroundings, especially at bus stations.

Highway robbery is another hazard. Since this occurs mostly at night, the obvious precaution is to travel only by daylight (which also allows you to enjoy the splendid views). Since 2000, increasing violence related to the drug trade and insurgency in neighboring Colombia has spilled over to the northernmost provinces of Ecuador: Esmeraldas, Carchi, and especially Sucumbíos. Throughout Ecuador, involvement in the drug scene could lead to sixteen years' imprisonment—or worse.

The treks in this book have been selected with public safety in mind, and potentially hazardous areas have been omitted. Where minor public safety concerns exist, these are mentioned in Section II. The overall public safety situation in Ecuador is changing with time, so it is always prudent to inquire locally before heading into an unfamiliar area.

TREKKING SAFETY

The backcountry is like a person. In order to earn its respect, you must first respect it.
—José Miguel Girón, lifelong explorer

The first step to safe trekking is to know your own abilities and limits, and to choose treks compatible with them. Never trek alone, and keep in mind the limitations of your companions as well as your own. Clear thinking and good communication among fellow trekkers is the best way to avoid most hazards and prevent accidents. Some general hazards are mentioned below; those for specific treks are described in Section II.

Hypothermia

Hypothermia, also called exposure, is a serious hazard for trekkers. The most common cause in Ecuador is a combination of wet and windy conditions, rather than extreme cold. Thin people are at higher risk. Adequate clothing is the best form of prevention (see "Clothing and Equipment" in Chapter 4). You will lose a significant amount of heat through your head, so remember to wear a wool hat in bad weather. Also important are sufficient high-calorie foods, including fat (e.g., cheese, salami, butter, margarine, mayonnaise). Severe shivering and pale skin, the first symptoms of hypothermia, should be dealt with right away. Make camp in a spot that is as sheltered as possible, remove the affected person's wet clothes, and put him or her in a sleeping bag together with a warm, naked trekker.

Dehydration

Dehydration is also a hazard—not only on very hot treks, but especially on cold ones. While trekking in the cold, you will lose moisture through sweat and breathing, but you will not necessarily feel thirsty. It can be difficult to drink very cold water. Prevent this problem by preparing generous amounts of warm drinks with breakfast, which will see you through the first part of the day. The caffeine in coffee, tea, and hot chocolate is a mild diuretic, however; too much of these can make you lose water. You can very roughly gauge your state of hydration by paying attention to your urine. If you are not urinating or it is dark yellow, then you need to drink more. Always carry at least a liter (quart) of water when heading for ridges or other areas where you know it will be scarce. (These are indicated in the trek descriptions in Section II.)

Altitude Sickness

Altitude sickness, locally known as *soroche*, occasionally affects some people. It is unpredictable, and being in good physical condition does not make you immune. The key is to give your body sufficient time to gradually adapt to the change in elevation. If you travel from sea level to Quito (2800 meters, 9200 feet), take it easy for the first day or two. Avoid too much exertion, alcohol, tobacco, and heavy food. Then you can continue your process of acclimatization by enjoying some of the lower and easier treks first.

The symptoms of *soroche* include fatigue, shortness of breath and a pounding heartbeat on mild exertion, headache, decreased appetite, difficulty sleeping, and nausea. The only reliable remedy is to descend. *Mate de coca*, an infusion of coca leaves available in Ecuador (but less common than in neighboring Peru or Bolivia), can sometimes diminish mild symptoms. The drug acetazolamide (Diamox) has been used to prevent *soroche* but should only be taken on the directions of a physician. The very best form of prevention is a sufficiently relaxed schedule, so that you do not rush into higher treks before you are ready for them.

Acute mountain sickness (AMS) is a severe and potentially fatal form of *soroche*, which can include pulmonary edema (fluid in the lungs) and cerebral edema (swelling of the brain). It is not considered a major hazard for trekkers in Ecuador but, in theory, it could affect a few people on some higher routes. Even at more modest elevations, special precautions may be required if you have had AMS in the past. This complex subject is discussed in the books mentioned in "Staying Healthy," later in this chapter. Remember that the key to prevention is gradual acclimatization, and the most effective treatment is descent.

Sun Protection

The equatorial sun is fierce (especially at higher altitudes), and sunburn can be very serious. Always wear a sun hat and good-quality sunglasses. Always apply sunscreen to both skin and lips. Remember that overcast conditions can also produce severe sunburn.

Hazardous Animals and Plants

You might encounter a few hazardous animals and plants while trekking in Ecuador. Snakes come to most people's minds, but these creatures are often shy and many are harmless. Venomous snakes in Ecuador are usually found below about 1800 meters (6000 feet), but up to 2800 meters (9200 feet) in the dry southern province of Loja. A common venomous snake is the fer-de-lance, locally called *equis*; there are also other *Bothrops* species and coral snakes. Never walk barefoot or in sandals in areas where there may be snakes; always wear rubber boots with long socks. Never grope under rocks or vegetation; always keep your hands within sight. If you see a snake, do not panic or disturb it; retreat quietly until it slithers away. In the unlikely event that a trekker is bitten, stay calm, make the injured person as comfortable as possible, and send someone for help immediately. Snakebite treatment centers are located on the coast and in the Oriente jungle (where the snakes are); they are listed under "Emergency Contacts" in Appendix A.

Insects also worry some people, although most (like butterflies and beetles) are a real delight. Mosquitoes are hazardous below about 1500 meters (5000 feet) because of the diseases they can transmit: malaria, yellow fever, and dengue fever (see "Staying Healthy" later in this chapter). When there are many mosquitoes about, wear long sleeves and long pants and use repellent and the mosquito net on your tent. Higher-altitude mosquitoes, black flies, and sand flies are annoying but not dangerous. Ticks are common in forest, brush, and pastureland, but Lyme disease (which ticks can transmit in North America) has not been reported in Ecuador. Check for ticks after trekking. You can remove them by dabbing repellent and pulling gently with a rocking motion. Minute ticks called chiggers, which are found at lower elevations and are too small to see (let alone remove), can make you very itchy but are otherwise harmless. Sulfur powder (*polvo de azufre*), available in some pharmacies, can be applied to legs and groin to repel them.

Take care to avoid the hives of bees and wasps and, if you are known to be allergic to their stings, always carry adrenaline (epinephrine). Stinging ants are found in lowland areas; watch where you sit and where you put your hands. Also in lowland areas, certain flies (locally called *tupes*) lay their eggs under the skin of cattle, horses, and (rarely) people. The larva eventually leaves to continue its life-cycle and, although unpleasant, it is not dangerous.

Dogs are ubiquitous; every house in the countryside has several of them. They are usually raucous but inoffensive. A good way to discourage them is to bend over and pick up a stone (or just to pretend if there are no stones nearby). In the unlikely event that you are bitten by a dog or any other mammal, clean the wound at once by rinsing with large amounts of water (liters and liters), and seek medical help without delay. Rabies is present in Ecuador; if you have had rabies vaccine, treatment will be simpler—but you still must see a doctor.

Cattle are frequently left to graze in large unfenced areas, and you will regularly meet them on the trail. Most are curious creatures who may take an interest in you, thinking you are bringing them salt (which they have learned to associate with backpacks and plastic bags). Wave your walking stick to keep them at a safe distance. Fighting bulls are generally raised in high *páramos* (so they will be stronger when brought down to the bull rings) and call for greater precautions. Local lore has it that a group of such bulls is usually not aggressive, but a lone *toro* must be avoided. Keep a wary eye on him from afar, and he will most likely do the same with you.

Noxious plants are not common in the areas covered by our treks. A few palms and ferns have sharp spines, so take care not to lean on them. Spines are also found on some bambusoid grasses (see Trek 15, The Llanganates Experience). Contact with the *aluvillo* tree (sumac) produces a severe skin reaction similar to poison ivy. There are occasional nettles (whose sting goes away in a few minutes if you do not scratch) and a few other stinging plants in the tomato family.

Flooded Rivers

Flash floods can occur on many rivers in Ecuador, especially those with large watersheds upstream. Never camp right at the water's edge, and keep an eye on weather conditions up-river. Take no chances fording a flooded river; wait it out instead. Once the rain stops, the water level will fall as quickly as it rose.

Losing Your Way

Getting seriously lost can be hazardous, because it causes some people to panic and do dangerous things. Keep your cool and see "Maps and Navigation" in Chapter 3. Stay calm on narrow ledges, unstable slopes, and flimsy bridges. Proceed slowly and steadily if you judge them safe; otherwise, retrace your steps to a secure location, take a break, and consider your options. If necessary, do not hesitate to discontinue the planned trek and return along the route that brought you—even if this means a big detour or reduced rations.

STAYING HEALTHY

Staying healthy while trekking and traveling merits a book all its own. Such books include *The Pocket Doctor* by Stephen Bezruchka, and *Medicine for Mountaineering and Other Wilderness Activities* by James A. Wilkerson. Internet sites also offer up-to-date health information for international travelers (see Appendix A). Some health hazards are mentioned above. The following section is limited to the most common and important general health issues before, during, and after your visit to Ecuador.

Before You Travel

A pre-travel medical checkup is advised if you have an ongoing health problem or are unsure whether or not you are fit for your journey. Be sure to obtain adequate amounts of any medications you take on a regular basis, as these may not be available in Ecuador. If you wear eyeglasses, get a clearly written prescription to bring with you in case yours are lost or broken. Contact lenses are controversial; some trekkers prefer them on the trail, while others find the cleaning solutions, etc., a serious inconvenience. At least be sure to bring a pair of glasses to Ecuador, in addition to your contacts.

Arrange for immunizations well in advance, with either your personal physician or a travel clinic. In consultation with a physician, consider receiving or updating the following immunizations before trekking in Ecuador: polio, diphtheria-tetanus, typhoid fever, hepatitis A and B, yellow fever (if you plan to visit the Oriente), and rabies.

Prevention of malaria is a complex subject. The malaria-prone regions of Ecuador are changing with time, but generally include rural areas of the Pacific coast and all of the Oriente jungle. Malaria is usually not a hazard above 1500 meters (5000 feet). A number of different medications are available to prevent malaria; discuss the pros and cons with your physician. Just as important as malaria pills are precautions against the mosquitoes that carry the disease (see "Hazardous Plants and Animals," above).

Prepare a first-aid kit. The one suggested here is very simple, but you may wish to add items. Well-stocked pharmacies are the rule throughout Ecuador, and prescriptions are required only for drugs that could cause addiction. Generic drugs are available, and you can easily obtain most items at lower cost in Ecuador than in North America or Europe. Be sure to pack your first-aid kit in several layers of plastic bags, to keep it dry.

FIRST-AID KIT CHECKLIST

Those items difficult to obtain in Ecuador are marked with an asterisk (*).

General

> first-aid guide* (e.g., First Aid, A Pocket Guide by Christopher Van Tilburg)
> space blanket*
> suture strips (Steri-Strips)*
> alcohol swabs*
> water purification tablets (tabletas para purificar agua), e.g., Micropur, as a backup even if you have another chemical purification system or a filter
> elastic bandage (venda elástica)
> gauze (gaza)
> adhesive tape (esparadrapo)
> Band-Aids or plasters (curitas)
> scissors (tijeras)
> tweezers or forceps (pinzas)
> safety pins (imperdibles)

Medications

> all your usual medications*

While You Are in Ecuador

Trekking in Ecuador usually makes you feel good—strong and healthy. Although most travelers and trekkers experience no serious illness, minor digestive and skin disorders do occur. Some can be prevented as outlined below. Treat minor ailments as suggested, and with patience and a positive attitude. Such ailments are, after all, part and parcel of the experience you have come so far to enjoy.

Drinking Water

Untreated water must not be consumed anywhere in Ecuador. Do not drink from taps, lakes, streams, springs, or wells. All water must be purified. You can boil it vigorously for one minute at sea level, or longer at higher altitudes. This requires carrying a lot of extra weight in fuel, however. Iodine, chlorine, potassium permanganate, and other chemicals can be used to purify water, and a variety of chemical water purification systems are commercially avail-

anti-malarials*; only chloroquine (Aralen) and pyrimethamine-
sulfadoxin (Fansidar) are routinely available in Ecuador
acetaminophen-codeine*, for severe pain
ciprofloxacin (cipofloxacina, Ciproxina), a broad-spectrum
antibiotic
doxycycline (doxiciclina, Vibramicina), a broad-spectrum
antibiotic
metronidazole (metronidazol, Flagyl) for amoebas and giardia
ASA (Aspirin) (aspirina) for fever, aches, and pain
kaopectate (kaopectate) for diarrhea
oral rehydration salts (sales para rehidratación oral) for young
children with diarrhea

Creams

bacitracin-neomycin (bacitracina-neomicina crema, Nebacetina)
for infected cuts and scrapes
isoconazole (isoconazol crema, Icaden) for minor fungus
infections: athlete's foot and jock itch

Antibiotic Eye Drops

gentamycin (gentamicina solución oftálmica, Garamicina) for
conjunctivitis (pink-eye) and eye injuries

able (although these are hard to find in Ecuador). Always follow instructions carefully to ensure that the water is adequately treated and to avoid poisoning yourself. Chemical purification is a good option for a couple of weeks (and can be a lifesaver in an emergency), but it is not suitable for ongoing use because the chemicals themselves are potentially harmful.

A number of portable water filters on the market can reliably remove parasites and bacteria— but not viruses such as hepatitis A. The cheaper models have a limited life span, and their filter elements (unavailable in Ecuador) may have to be replaced frequently. The higher-quality models, which contain long-lasting ceramic filters, are heavier and more expensive but are highly recommended to long-term trekkers.

A wide variety of bottled beverages are sold in Ecuador, including mineral water, soft drinks, and beer. All of these are safe, but they are obviously not practical to carry on anything longer than a day hike. When you are in cities or towns, try to purchase beverages in returnable glass bottles rather than disposable plastic ones (to avoid creating trash). Hot beverages such as coffee or tea and the very popular *agüitas* (herbal teas), which are prepared using boiled water, are safe. Long-life UHT-treated milk, sold unrefrigerated in box-like containers, can be trusted. Standards for ordinary pasteurization vary however, and regular milk sold in plastic pouches should be boiled for added safety. Raw milk, fresh from the cow, is delicious but must be boiled thoroughly.

When trekking independently, you will prepare your own food, which makes precautions that much easier. The dry trekking staples listed under "Provisions" in Chapter 4 are all safe, and just about any other food is also safe if you cook it long enough. Raw fruits and vegetables in Ecuador are particularly varied and tasty, however, and it would be a shame to miss them. Clean them thoroughly using ordinary water, then peel them or give them a final rinse with purified water. Avoid raw foods that grow in close contact with the ground and cannot be peeled (e.g., lettuce and strawberries), or rinse them with a disinfectant solution sold in most Ecuadorean supermarkets.

In cities and towns, choosing a trustworthy restaurant requires something of a sixth sense. Look around a bit, to observe general cleanliness. See if you can catch a glimpse of the kitchen and the kitchen staff. Don't be shy about leaving if the surroundings are unappealing. Be cautious about prepared food sold in markets, and avoid all food sold by street vendors.

Personal Hygiene

Personal hygiene is important when you are traveling and trekking. Don't forget to wash your hands regularly just because you are on the trail.

Market food in Saquisilí: tasty but . . .

(Politely encourage guides and muleteers to do likewise.) Washing up regularly with a washcloth is also quick and easy while trekking. Keep the use of soap to a bare minimum, however, to avoid getting it into water sources. In hot areas, loose-fitting, light cotton clothing and talc, body powder, or foot powder will help prevent superficial fungal infections such as athlete's foot and jock itch.

Gastrointestinal Illness
Even if you take all the necessary precautions, you may yet experience a minor gastrointestinal upset during your visit to Ecuador. A belly-ache, gas, or a little diarrhea are best treated with rest, dietary restraint, a lot of fluids, Kaopectate for diarrhea, and especially patience. Take care that young children with diarrhea do not become dehydrated.

Antibiotics for traveler's diarrhea, previously discouraged for uncomplicated cases, are now recommended by some specialists. Questions remain, however, about potential side effects, about becoming a carrier, and about breeding resistant organisms. The authors are inclined to avoid unnecessary medication. Moderate quantities of yogurt can help repopulate your intestine with beneficial bacteria after your symptoms have subsided.

Seek medical help if diarrhea persists for a week or more, if you develop a high fever or rash, have severe cramps, or pass mucus or blood in your stool. If you have these severe symptoms while trekking and cannot reach a medical facility, you may want to take metronidazole and either ciprofloxacin or doxycycline while you make your way to a doctor. In the case of massive watery diarrhea and vomiting, the first priority is oral rehydration. If you develop jaundice (yellowing of your skin or eyes), get a blood test for hepatitis and see a physician. Recurrent episodes of bloating, with vast amounts of foul-smelling gas from above and below, usually mean giardia or a related protozoal infection. Either can be treated with metronidazole.

Unexpectedly, perhaps, constipation can also be a problem on the trail. Most trekking foods have little fiber. Bran (*afrecho*) makes a good addition to many starchy staples, and whole wheat bread (*pan integral*) and crackers (*galletas de trigo integral*) are available in larger centers in Ecuador.

Skin Problems
Rashes, insect bites, and minor fungus infections of the skin are common. Keep them clean to prevent additional bacterial infection. Bug bites are

best left to heal on their own; the more you scratch, the longer they itch. Fleas (*pulgas*) are common and generally harmless. Scabies, locally known as *rasca bonito*, are tiny mites that burrow just below the surface of the skin and can make you incredibly itchy. Lice (*piojos*) are harder to contract but cause intense itching of the scalp or other hair-covered areas. Scabies and lice are common among some highland natives of Ecuador; treat these conditions with medicated soaps and shampoos containing gama-benzene hexachloride (Davesol or Lindano) and wash all your clothes thoroughly in hot water. More serious skin problems are, fortunately, rare. Seek medical help whenever your symptoms persist, or if you develop a sore or ulcer on your skin that does not heal.

Injuries

Injuries can occur on the trail, and should not be a cause for alarm. Clean all minor wounds with soap and a lot of water, disinfect the skin around them with alcohol (ouch!), and dress them with gauze and adhesive tape. Support sprained joints with an elastic bandage, and splint injured limbs. Patch an injured eye, keeping the eyelid firmly closed with gauze pads and adhesive tape, and apply antibiotic eye drops twice a day. An injured trekker may benefit from a day's rest, after which he or she can either continue or (if necessary) make their way out. In all cases, the trekking party should stay together and move at the pace of the slowest trekker. In the event of a serious injury, make camp in the nearest secure location and keep the injured person warm, dry, and hydrated. If there are enough trekkers, two should go together to seek help as soon as possible, while one stays behind with the injured person.

Infectious Disease

Sexually transmitted diseases, including AIDS, are a hazard for visitors to Ecuador. Prevention is simple in principle: abstain or use a condom.

Other infectious diseases in Ecuador are either uncommon or seldom affect visitors. These include tuberculosis, leishmaniasis, leptospirosis, Chagas' disease, bubonic plague, and meningococcal meningitis.

After You Return Home

If you are taking pills to prevent malaria, remember to complete the course as prescribed. If you were ill during your travels, think you have been at particular risk, or have been away for six months or more, arrange for a general medical examination.

IN CASE OF EMERGENCY

Although most trekkers find their own way out of most predicaments, it is important to have backup in case something goes seriously wrong. Facilities in Ecuador are very limited, however—so you will need to be as self-sufficient as possible.

Search and Rescue

Advise a reliable friend or relative of your planned trekking route and estimated date of return. Tell them how long to wait before beginning to look for you, and remember that delays and unexpected changes of route are common. In the absence of a friend or relative, you can try to notify your embassy of your route and schedule. Should a serious accident occur, the Ecuadorean authorities will most likely contact your embassy to coordinate and finance any rescue efforts. You should contact your embassy as soon as possible if you find yourself in serious trouble.

Cellular phone rentals are available in Quito and Guayaquil. The cellular network can be reached from a number of high elevations, even in remote locations. Such rentals are expensive, however, batteries may not perform well in the cold, and many trekking areas do not have cellular coverage.

The Asociación Ecuatoriana de Guías de Montaña (ASEGUIM), the Ecuadorean Mountain Guides' Association, provides rescue service for mountaineers and may be able to assist trekkers as well. This is a private professional service and generally very expensive. Furthermore, ASEGUIM is a loosely knit organization and can be quite difficult to reach in a hurry. (See "Emergency Contacts" in Appendix A.)

Air ambulance transport of a sick or injured trekker may be required in a very few situations. Air ambulance service within Ecuador, as well as to other countries, is available from Quito (see "Emergency Contacts" in Appendix A). Air ambulances to and from Ecuador are also operated by international specialists in conjunction with insurance companies. Such service is extremely expensive; if you want to have this option in an emergency, arrange for the necessary insurance coverage before you travel.

Medical Facilities

There are public and private hospitals as well as private clinics (*clínicas*) of varying standards in all provincial capitals of Ecuador. Smaller towns and villages may have only basic medical facilities, if that. The best facilities, and physicians who speak languages other than Spanish, are in Quito, Guayaquil, and Cuenca (see "Emergency Contacts" in Appendix A). Ask your embassy or consulate for a list of doctors and dentists who speak your language. Quality medical care is expensive in Ecuador, so make sure you have adequate insurance.

Section II
THE TREKS

CAMINANTE NO HAY CAMINO
SE HACE CAMINO AL ANDAR

Chapter 6
SELECTING A TREK

The twenty-nine treks described in this section cover diverse geographic and biological areas. They include a range of climates and altitudes, and present varying levels of difficulty. See the "Trek Summaries" table on the following pages. Treks run from 2 hours to 2 weeks in length, but can easily be combined if you are seeking a longer trekking experience. Please choose your treks carefully; the better they suit your interests and abilities, the more you will enjoy them.

There are many other trekking opportunities in Ecuador and you are heartily encouraged, once you feel comfortable here, to strike out and discover your own. The descriptions of a very few well-known treks have been intentionally omitted from this book, although they are briefly mentioned in the introduction to each trekking center. These sometimes overused routes may have public safety problems, they may need to recover from excessive use, or they are already described elsewhere. This book offers more innovative alternatives.

The treks described here are organized around eight different cities or towns, which are reflected in the chapter titles. Most are popular tourist destinations in their own right, which additionally offer access to interesting trekking areas. These trekking centers (one per chapter) are presented from north to south. Within each chapter, the treks appear in order of challenge, from the easiest to the most difficult. Some trailheads can be conveniently accessed from more than one center.

UNDERSTANDING THE TREK DESCRIPTIONS

Each trek begins with a summary of basic data. Treks are **rated** as very easy, easy, moderately difficult, difficult, or very difficult. This subjective classification is based on a combination of the trek's length, altitude, gradient, navigational challenge, climate, trail conditions, vegetation, and other factors. **Elevations** listed are the lowest and highest points of a trek, not the beginning and end. The **maps** listed are important supplements to those included in this book. Do not undertake a trek without them, unless they are indicated as optional.

The best time to visit is discussed; this is usually a matter of climate. Ecuador's highly variable weather, however, means you must be prepared for all conditions at any time of the year. Any **special gear** required for a particular trek is mentioned; rubber boots are the default for footwear. The availability of **water** along the route is described; remember that all water must be purified. **Hazards, annoyances, and permits and fees** required are also listed. Those **services** of particular interest to trekkers are described, such as accommodations on the route or whether pack animals are available. Finally, the best place to obtain **provisions** for the trek is discussed.

Every trek description begins with an overview of its special features and attractions. It then describes **access** from the trekking center to the trailhead, followed by the trekking **route** and directions for **getting back** to the trekking center. Trekking times (given in boldface) are unavoidably subjective, since everybody moves at a different pace and conditions on the same trail vary from one time to another. Times listed do not include any stops for breaks or meals—only uninterrupted walking. Your own walking times will almost certainly be different, but with experience you should be able to establish an approximate relationship between your pace and ours, so that these figures can act as a useful guide. Treks are best done in the direction indicated, for a variety of reasons; certainly walking times will be more difficult to use if you are traveling in the opposite direction.

The conversion of metric to English units (miles, feet, etc.) in the text is context-sensitive: an exact altitude such as a summit or pass is rounded to the nearest foot, while more approximate elevations and distances are rounded to the nearest 50, 100, or 500 feet. Times of day are given using the 24-hour clock. The words trek, hike, and walk are all used interchangeably, as are trail and path. Simple descriptive terminology is used whenever possible, but readers will have their own nuances for terms such as steep, gentle, or undulating. The nose of a ridge refers to the generally steep portion where the ridge begins, climbing up from a flat area or the intersection of two rivers. Plant and animal names are given in English, when English names exist. Otherwise Spanish, Quichua, or scientific (Latin) names are used. A list of common plants and animals in all these languages is found on the website *www.trekking inecuador.com.*

TREK SUMMARIES

Trek Number	Trek (Center)	Distance (km)	Elevation (m)	Days
Very Easy				
3	Parque Metropolitano (Quito)	5	2900–3050	2 hours
Easy				
1	Guinea-Pig Lake (Otavalo)	12	3050–3450	1
4	Pasochoa Reserve (Quito)	13	2800–3950	1
5	Pasochoa Summit (Quito)	9	3300–4200	1
6	Papallacta (Quito)	8	3300–3500	1
7	Toucan Trail (Quito)	16	1200–3000	1–2
11	Valley of the Waterfalls (Baños)	8	1550–1800	1
16	Great Cascade Trail (Guaranda)	20	900–3750	2–3
18	Volcano Watching (Riobamba)	15	2800–3900	2–3
26	Inca Trails (Cuenca)	15	2700–3100	1
Moderately Difficult				
8	Guacamayos Trail (Quito)	10	1350–2200	1–2
9	Hostel Hopping to Quilotoa (Latacunga)	25	2650–3900	2–3
10	Across Rumiñahui (Latacunga)	20	3000–4200	2

No.	Trek		Elevation	Days
12	Cave of the Oilbirds (Baños)	17	650–800	2–3
17	Forgotten Footsteps (Guaranda)	15	1200–3300	2–3
19	Crater of El Altar (Riobamba)	20	3100–4300	3–4
20	Atillo and Osogoche Lakes (Riobamba)	22	3500–4200	2–3
21	Vicuña Trail (Riobamba)	22	3550–4400	2–3
22	Royal Road (Riobamba)	33	2600–4250	3–4
28	Natural High (Vilcabamba)	30	1600–3600	4–5
Difficult				
2	Ecuador's Chocó (Otavalo)	45–65	600–2100	4–6
13	Tapir Trail (Baños)	14	2200–3700	3–4
14	Around Tungurahua (Baños)	25	1700–3700	4–5
23	Hot Springs in the Cloud Forest (Riobamba)	54	2850–4000	5–7
24	Black Rock of Cubillines (Riobamba)	23	3150–4450	4–5
25	High Lakes and Ridges (Riobamba)	45	3100–4600	5–6
27	Gold-Rush Trail (Cuenca)	65	1100–3700	5–7
29	Pass of the Winds (Vilcabamba)	52	1200–3600	4–6
Very Difficult				
15	The Llanganates Experience (Baños)	35	3350–4200	7–14

USING THE MAPS

The maps in this book show all elevations in meters above sea level. Contour intervals are either 100, 200, or 400 meters, as indicated. A common abbreviation used on the maps is Q *(Quebrada*—ravine, gully, or valley*)*. Vehicle roads are designated as either paved or unpaved. Unpaved roads may be earth, gravel, or cobbled.

Trekking routes fall into two categories: well-defined trails, and faint trails or cross-country routes. The distinction between them (or between a wide trail and a narrow, unpaved road) is subjective.

The maps are as detailed as possible, but they cannot show all minor forks along a route, nor every gate and little stream you will cross. Many smaller streams may be seasonal.

To avoid carrying this entire book on the trail, you may wish to make photocopies of a particular trek description, the map legend (earlier in the book), and "Emergency Contacts" in Appendix A.

Chapter 7
TREKS FROM OTAVALO

Altitude, 2500 meters (8200 feet)
Population, 30,000

After Quito and the Galápagos Islands, Otavalo is probably the most visited spot in Ecuador—and for good reason. The town's fabulous Saturday market is among the largest in Latin America, unsurpassed for color and variety. An entire plaza has been set aside for crafts (especially textiles), and you can browse or purchase an extraordinary array of beautiful wares. Otavaleños, the area's native inhabitants, also attract the attention of visitors for their traditional dress and proud bearing.

Otavalo provides ample opportunities for trekking. Among the most frequently visited spots are the Peguche waterfall near town, the summit of Mount Imbabura (not an easy climb), and the Lagunas de Mojanda to the southwest. All these areas, especially Mojanda, have experienced occasional public safety problems, so inquire locally as to the current situation before heading out. There are a number of homespun tour agencies in Otavalo; most concentrate on the region's cultural attractions and day trips, but a few may be able to organize longer treks.

Trek 1 is an easy and popular day hike, with simple access west of Otavalo and pretty views in good weather. Farther afield in the same direction, and far off the tourist trail, lies Ecuador's Chocó, Trek 2. This long, difficult, and rewarding route offers a wonderful diversity of endemic flora and fauna as well as a glimpse of the homesteaders' way of life.

| GUINEA-PIG LAKE

Research and editorial assistance by Kerry Alley
Rating: Easy, 12-kilometer (7.5-mile), full-day hike.
Elevation: 3050 to 3450 meters (10,000 to 11,300 feet).
Map: IGM 1:50,000: CT-ÑII-F1 Otavalo (optional).
Best time to visit: June through September are the driest months, but December through March have the clearest skies with only occasional rain. The wettest months are April, May, October, and November.

Special gear: None.

Water: A number of streams shown on the IGM map are often dry, but water is available at the trailhead.

Hazards: Holdups have taken place on this route. Do not take valuables. Inquire locally before doing the trek. Many species of blueberries grow around the lake. Some, which look similar to the edible ones, are poisonous. Do not pick or eat any berries.

Annoyances: None.

Permits and fees: A $1 fee is payable at the ranger station for a day visit to Laguna Cuicocha. There is a $5 fee if also visiting other areas in the reserve.

Services: Many tour operators from Quito and Otavalo visit Cuicocha. The El Mirador cabins, above the lake, offer simple accommodations for $6 per person. Phone: (06) 648-039.

Provisions: There is a restaurant at the cabins mentioned above and another by the dock. If you wish to bring your own lunch, Otavalo has well-stocked shops with a wide variety of provisions.

Laguna Cuicocha, in Cotacachi–Cayapas Ecological Reserve, is one of the most scenic lakes in Ecuador. Situated on the southern slopes of an extinct volcano called Cotacachi (4939 meters, 16,205 feet), the lake fills a volcanic caldera. About 3000 years ago, a rapid eruption emptied the underlying magma chambers, so the bulk of the original mountain fell in on itself. There are two lava-dome islands in the lake, the result of later volcanic activity. Cuicocha means "guinea-pig lake" in Quichua; it is so named

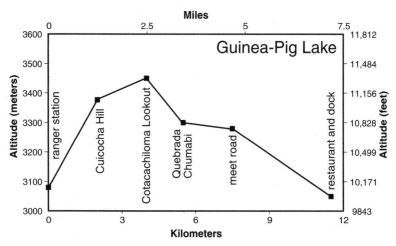

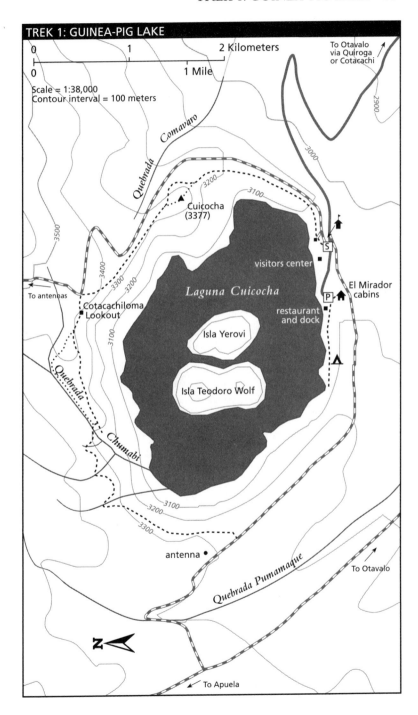

TREK 1: GUINEA-PIG LAKE

0   1   2 Kilometers

0   1 Mile

Scale = 1:38,000
Contour interval = 100 meters

To Otavalo
via Quiroga
or Cotacachi

2900

3000

Quebrada Comavaro

3200

3100

Cuicocha
(3377)

3500

3400

3300

3200

To antennas

Cotacachiloma
Lookout

Laguna Cuicocha

visitors center

El Mirador
cabins

restaurant
and dock

3100

Quebrada

Isla Yerovi

Isla Teodoro Wolf

Chumabi

3200

3100

3300

antenna

Quebrada Pumamaque

To Otavalo

N

To Apuela

because the islands resemble two guinea-pigs sleeping curled up together.

This trek follows a path along the rim of the caldera, which affords wonderful views of the lake, Cotacachi, and even peaks as distant as Cotopaxi. The area boasts a surprising variety of plants, especially orchids—the most notable being the bright purple *flor de Cristo*. Coots (chunky black duck-like birds) enjoy the reedy shorelines, at least twelve species of hummingbirds have been identified, and condors may be sighted. The visitors center has well-designed displays explaining the natural and human history of the park (entry $1). Interesting boat rides are offered for $1 per person (minimum five per trip) and last about 25 minutes.

Access: You can take a taxi to Cuicocha from Otavalo for $8, or from the central park in Quiroga for $3. Transportes Cotacachi buses leave Otavalo's bus terminal for the towns of Cotacachi and Quiroga every 10 minutes (the 30-minute ride costs $.20).

Route: The trek begins at the ranger station at the entrance to the park, a **10-minute** walk east from the dock along the paved road. At the ranger station, a cobbled road goes north; the trailhead is on the left, about 3 meters (10 feet) along the cobbled road. In **5 minutes** you will climb to a small house; cross the driveway and follow the trail above the eastern rim of the lake. After **45 minutes** you will approach Cuicocha Hill (3377 meters, 11,080 feet); on the way you will find many *flor de Cristo* orchids. A faint path goes over the top of the hill, where you have outstanding views; but the main trail contours around the hill to the east (right), as an orchid-filled trench. You will regain the rim in **10 minutes**. Another **25 minutes** ahead, the path again briefly meets the unpaved road before heading off to the west. Here you stand on Cotacachiloma (3450 meters, 11,320 feet), the highest point on the caldera rim, with good views of Cotacachi to the north. **Five minutes** farther is the covered Cotacachiloma Lookout, with wonderful views of the lake and islands.

If you opt to take the normal loop around the lake, continue west along the main trail for **25 minutes** to the first major fork, then turn north (right) to descend from the ridge. Otherwise, to take the alternate route, seek a faint path 100 meters (300 feet) beyond the lookout. Follow this path northwest down along a gentle ridge approaching an unnamed streambed. Pass through a small gulch and enter the main dry streambed filled with sand, grass, and remnants of native forest—a welcome change from the open country. Turn west to follow the streambed down to the dry, bouldery Quebrada Chumabi. Take the path along the

Laguna Cuicocha (Photo: Kerry Alley)

near (southeast) side of Quebrada Chumabi left (southwest) and downhill until it climbs slightly back toward the rim and meets a more obvious gravel trail. **Forty minutes** from Cotacachiloma Lookout, you will regain the main trail around the lake.

Head west across the dry riverbed of Quebrada Chumabi. **Five minutes** ahead is a muddy trickle of water, followed by a clearing. This is the only reliable source of water along the route. **Fifteen minutes** from the clearing you will cross an unnamed tributary of Quebrada Chumabi, and **15 minutes** later you will reach another *quebrada* that leads to Cuicocha. The path exits the *quebrada* some 25 meters (80 feet) downhill from where you entered. It will take about **20 minutes** to reach the first signs of agriculture along the western rim of the lake. Follow the path for an additional **15 minutes** along the edge of the caldera, past some planted pines and a red and white antenna, to reach a sign marking the end of the trail. Turn west (right) to go out to the road, in order to avoid passing through private property. The ranger station is about **1 hour** (4 kilometers, 2.5 miles) south and east along the road, or continue directly to the lake via the El Mirador cabins (where you can enjoy the best views of the lake, with Cotacachi in the background).

For a close-up view of the lakeshore and its water birds, follow a pleasant path (25 minutes each way) heading west from behind the El Muelle restaurant by the dock. A flat area along this trail is suitable for camping.

Getting back: The owners of El Mirador offer transport to Quiroga, Cotacachi, or Otavalo. You can also arrange to have a taxi wait for you or call for a taxi in Quiroga. Phone: (06)915-933. It is a 10-kilometer (6-mile) walk down to Quiroga.

7 ECUADOR'S CHOCÓ

Research and editorial assistance by Kerry Alley
Rating: Difficult, 45- to 65-kilometer (28- to 40-mile), 4- to 6-day trek.
The length depends on whether you walk or ride from Nangulví to
Barcelona.
Elevation: 600 to 2100 meters (2000 to 6900 feet).
Maps: IGM 1:50,000: CT-ÑII-C4 Apuela, CT-ÑII-E2 Vacas Galindo.
There is no topographic map for the western end of this trek.
Best time to visit: July through October are the driest months.
November through January are only moderately rainy and muddy;
February through June are the wettest.
Special gear: None.
Water: Available from the many streams and rivers.
Hazards: Poisonous snakes.
Annoyances: High humidity and deep mud in the rainy season.
Permits and fees: None.
Services: There are places to stay in Apuela, Nangulví, Junín, Reserva
Los Cedros, Magdalena Bajo, and Saguangal; details are given in the
route description. Mules can be hired in the Barcelona and Junín areas;
they are particularly useful during the wet season.
Provisions: Major shopping should be done in Otavalo or Quito.
Basic supplies are found in Apuela, Junín, Magdalena Bajo, and Saguangal.

Northwestern Ecuador shares the Chocó Bioregion with neighboring
Colombia. The Chocó is a land of forest-covered ridges dropping down
to the Pacific. There is great biological diversity, with more endemic species (plants and animals found only here) than even the Amazon basin.
Curiously, many of the animals of this region are most closely related to
those of Central America.

This trek goes through a subtropical area along the western Andean
slopes, just south of the Cotacachi–Cayapas Ecological Reserve. It proceeds from one village to another, through agricultural lands as well as
patches of magnificent cloud forest rich in mosses, bromeliads, ferns, and
orchids. The sounds of birds, bubbling brooks, and roaring rivers will
escort you along the way. As you descend, the surroundings—both natural and developed—become more and more lush. There are great views
of luxuriant ridges and valleys.

Several reserves have been created to protect the remaining forests in this region. The route goes by the community-run Junín Cloud Forest Reserve and the private Los Cedros Reserve; both are good places to spend a couple of days if you would like more time to experience the primary forest.

There is not much tourism here; people are incredibly friendly and someone might invite you to stay in their home. This is a good opportunity to learn about the life folks have made for themselves in this hilly, humid terrain. Much of the land has been given over to growing sugar cane, manioc, corn, beans, rice, and tropical fruits, as well as raising Brahmin cattle for meat.

Access: Buses to García Moreno pass through Apuela, 40 kilometers (25 miles) northwest of Otavalo, then Nangulví, 6 kilometers (4 miles) southwest of Apuela. The buses leave from Otavalo's *terminal terrestre* at 0800, 1000, 1200, and 1400 (2.5 hours to Nangulví, $1.60).

Route: The starting point of the trek is Nangulví, chosen because of its pleasant hot springs. The pools (entry $.50), restaurant, and Cabañas Nangulví (simple cabins, $1.50 per person) are run by the local community. More elaborate cabins, with hot water and restaurant, are nearby at Cabañas Río Grande; $10-12 per cabin for four, phone (06)920-171 in Otavalo. Enjoy an evening soaking in the hot springs. Next day, try to get a ride as far as possible along the road to Barcelona (labeled La Libertad on the IGM map). A ride to Barcelona saves you **5 to 6 hours** of walking. The road to Barcelona starts **40 minutes** (3 kilometers, 1.9 miles) southwest of Nangulví, on the right. During the rainy season there is at

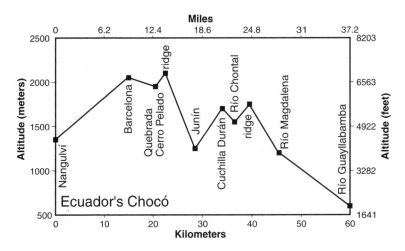

Ecuador's Chocó

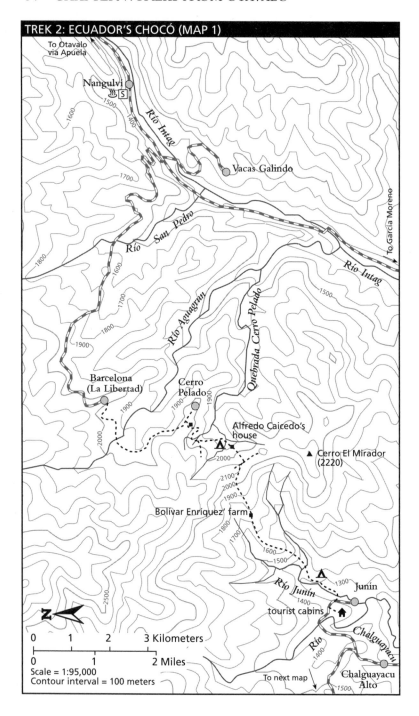

TREK 2: ECUADOR'S CHOCÓ (MAP 1)

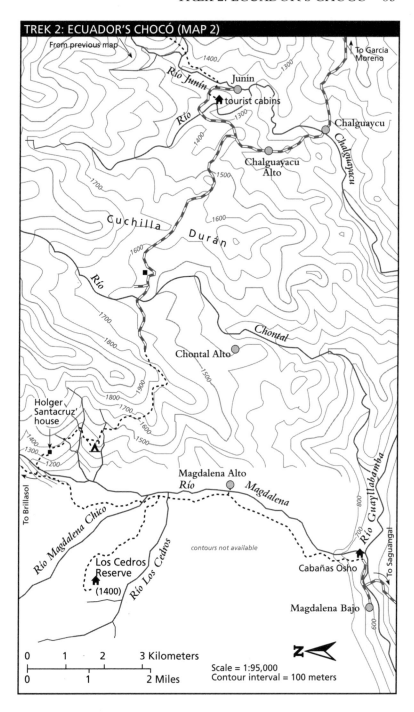

TREK 2: ECUADOR'S CHOCÓ (MAP 2)

most one truck a week, on Sundays. In the dry season, the noon bus from Otavalo continues from Nangulví to Barcelona.

Past Barcelona the road deteriorates and becomes a track that winds its way down to the Río Aguagrun and then south to the hamlet of Cerro Pelado, reached in **2 hours**. From Cerro Pelado, the route continues along a trail heading southwest. It starts on a ridge **10 minutes** before the town; ask for the path leading to Junín, or to the house of Alfredo Caicedo. As you descend, pass to the right of the first house and cross the upper Quebrada Cerro Pelado, filled with lush secondary forest. In **15 minutes** you will reach a stream filled with plants with gigantic leaves, known as elephant's ears. After crossing a second smaller stream, **10 minutes** ahead, take the left fork (the main trail continuing south and gradually climbing out of the valley). It will take **30 minutes** to reach the house of Alfredo Caicedo; there is more running water here and flat ground for camping. Do take time to converse with Alfredo and his wife, who love visitors. They also have a great view of Pichincha Volcano, which shows a very different profile than that visible from Quito.

The path continues southwest up the ridge immediately behind the Caicedo house. Just before you reach the top of the prominent ridge dividing Cerro Pelado from Junín, you will enter rich primary subtropical cloud forest. Reach the ridge line in **35 minutes**, and take a break to explore it. There is a great variety of plants here: ferns, mosses, epiphytes, and pretty flowering gesneriads, including *Columnea* with red-tipped leaves. To continue to Junín, turn right (northwest) at the fork at the top of the ridge. Continue for **3 minutes** before taking another fork left, descending the ridge on the western side. For **20 minutes**, continue walking through primary forest, with a few glimpses of surrounding hills. Another **20 minutes** ahead, reach a fence and the farmhouse of Bolívar Enríquez. The trail continues to the right of the house; look for a gate in the fence, 20 meters (65 feet) to the right of the gate leading to the farmhouse.

The path then descends along the ridge. In **1 hour** you will reach a branch of the Río Junín; wade across it (it is normally ankle deep). **Thirty minutes** ahead, you will reach another crossing—this time on a precarious bamboo bridge. Along the Río Junín, between the two crossings, are flat spaces suitable for camping. After crossing the river the second time, the trail goes west and soon meets a dirt road. To visit the village of Junín, take a left down the road and walk **10 minutes** to town, where there are

"Exciting" bridge over the Río Magdalena (Photo: Kerry Alley)

shops. This community is trying to attract tourism, to help support environmental and development projects and to keep mining companies out of the area. Residents run the Junín Cloud Forest Reserve and have built tourist cabins ($25 including meals); inquire in town. To continue the trek, take the road uphill to the right after crossing the Río Junín. In **10 minutes** you will reach the entrance to the cabins (to your left).

The trek continues along the dirt road (which sees a couple of vehicles a week when it is dry and no traffic at all in the rainy season). **Fifteen minutes** from the turnoff for the cabins, cross the Río Chalguayacu; **35 minutes** beyond, reach a fork in the road. The left branch goes to Chalguayacu Alto and on to García Moreno; take the right branch toward Chontal Alto. Follow the road for **1.25 hours** to the top of a large ridge called Cuchilla Durán, where you will enter forest again. Descend **1 hour** to reach the "suburbs" of Chontal Alto (consisting of three farms surrounded by pastures). The center of town is more than an hour southwest. Hunting is prohibited here, so some fauna (such as guans) are more common than usual for a populated area. The road continues west; **15 minutes** beyond the first house, take the left fork, which leads to an unpopulated area. **Five minutes** along this road is a wobbly wire suspension bridge crossing the Río Chontal. For the next **1 hour**, the road narrows and passes through forest until it is no longer a road but a well-traveled path. Eventually, you will notice that the forest has thickened and darkened around you, as you circumnavigate the unnamed ridge separating Chontal Alto from Brillasol. This is another beautiful stretch of primary forest; look for the unusual bromeliads with flat spatula-like pink flower stalks and purple flowers.

In **1.75 hours**, you will cross a stream. Take water here if you want to camp ahead. In **15 minutes**, you will reach a small path going left in mature forest; there is a place to camp following this trail for 5 minutes, but no water right there. **Ten minutes** beyond, in young secondary forest, is an obvious, well-traveled path approaching from the left. Continue straight rather than doubling back to the left. You will cross several small streams along the way. **Forty-five minutes** later, you will reach the home of Holger Santacruz and his family.

The path continues behind the Santacruz house. It starts as a faint track leading to the *quebrada* to the north, and continues left (down) on the far side of that small stream. Pass through fields and a wooden gate, taking the downward forks. You will reach the Río Magdalena in **15 minutes**. The roaring river and poorly maintained bridge are exciting. Cross and continue uphill for **20 minutes** to reach a larger trail. Turn left here (southwest, away from Brillasol). In **1.5 hours** you will come to the Río Magdalena Chico. Cross it on a wooden bridge that is about 20 meters (65 feet) right of the main path. **Fifteen minutes** beyond is the righthand turnoff for Los Cedros Reserve, marked with a wooden sign.

The walk up to Los Cedros takes 2 to 3 hours. The reserve protects 6400 hectares (15,814 acres) of primary cloud forest. Many new species of orchids were discovered here, and it is an excellent place for bird-watching. There is a research station, lodge, reference library, and trails. To stay overnight, reserve from Quito. Phone: (02)223-1768. Cost is $25 per night including food and transport by mule.

From the Los Cedros turnoff, our trail descends more or less parallel to the Río Magdalena, on its western bank. After **3 hours** you will come within sight of the Río Guayllabamba. Along the way, cross numerous small streams and homesteads, and see the small village of Magdalena Alto across the river. Near the junction of the Magdalena and the Guayllabamba, take the main path right; it follows the Guayllabamba downstream to the west. Here are Cabañas Osho, bamboo cabins with bath; $5 per person, they can provide meals on request. A dirt road continues west from here. In **10 minutes** it will lead to a large suspension bridge over the Río Guayllabamba. If you continue straight instead of crossing the bridge, you will reach Magdalena Bajo, also known as San José de Magdalena, in **5 minutes**. Here is Hostal Hormiga Verde, with simple dorm-style accommodations for $3 per person (mosquito nets provided). There are also simple shops and places to eat. To continue, cross the bridge over the Río Guayllabamba and follow the road west **1.5 hours** to Saguangal on the south shore of the Guayllabamba. This road ends at a T intersection. Turn right to go into Saguangal, **10 minutes** ahead. Simple accommodations are offered by Jacinto Yunga in the first house on the right ($2 per person, meals on request). In town are shops and a telephone office.

Getting back: From Saguangal there are direct buses to Quito at 0400 and 0800 daily, via Pacto and Nanegalito (5 hours, $3).

Chapter 8
TREKS FROM QUITO

Altitude, 2800 meters (9200 feet)
Population, 2,000,000

The nation's capital is the point of arrival and departure for the majority of international visitors to Ecuador. Its heart is a treasure-trove of colonial architecture and religious art. Quito also offers the widest selection of tourist services of every imaginable price and description. Many hotels and restaurants are concentrated along Avenida Amazonas and nearby streets in the neighborhood called La Mariscal. This is where you will find the majority of tour agencies. If you are looking for an organized trek, step into a couple of places for a chat, and see what is being offered. The "Trek of the Condor," was one of Ecuador's few commercially exploited routes, but it is no longer feasible. Older guidebooks may also suggest hikes from Quito to Rucu Pichincha or Cruz Loma, right above the city; sadly, both treks are now too dangerous because of armed robberies.

Despite the big city's problems of crime as well as air and noise pollution, Quito is surrounded by surprisingly pretty and tranquil countryside. The capital's strategic location and pleasant surroundings make it a logical place to begin acclimatizing with some easier treks. None is easier than Trek 3, Parque Metropolitano, literally a walk in the park. A little more challenging and 30 kilometers (19 miles) south of the city is the Pasochoa Reserve, Trek 4, ideal for a family picnic. On the other side of the same mountain, Trek 5 offers access to Pasochoa Summit—a good, easy acclimatization hike.

Trek 6, Papallacta, situated 55 kilometers (34 miles) east of Quito, makes a great 1- or 2-day outing for easy acclimatization and the country's best-developed thermal baths. Trek 7, the Toucan Trail, lies to the northwest, on the opposite side of Quito. It also offers easy hiking in a very beautiful cloud forest reserve, within city-bus reach of the capital. Back on the eastern slopes of the Andes, past Papallacta on the road to Tena, is the Guacamayos Trail, Trek 8. This moderately difficult 1- to 2-day hike goes through outstanding primary forest.

3 PARQUE METROPOLITANO

Rating: Very easy, 5-kilometer (3.1-mile), 2-hour walk.
Elevation: The park is situated between 2900 and 3050 meters (9500 and 10,000 feet).
Map: Not required, but a trail map is displayed in the park administration building.
Best time to visit: July through September are the driest months, offering the best views, but the climate is generally pleasant year-round.
Special gear: Running or tennis shoes are sufficient.
Water: City tap water is available by the administration building and picnic areas.
Hazards: The park is patrolled and generally safe, but occasional muggings have taken place. Women alone should avoid deserted areas. The park is officially open from 0600 to 1800 daily, and is not recommended after dark.
Annoyances: None.
Permits and fees: Park entry is free. There is a $1 cost to reserve a picnic area and grill.
Services: None.
Provisions: Soft drinks and snacks are sometimes sold near the administration building, or bring your own picnic.

Parque Metropolitano is a 580-hectare (1450-acre) park located on a scenic ridge top to the northeast of Quito's city center. A number of trails and a cobbled road meander through stands of eucalyptus and pine. Seventy species of birds have been identified in the deep ravine called Quebrada Ashintaco, which is clad in native vegetation. Some open areas and lookouts *(miradores)* offer great views of Quito, the suburban valleys to the east of the city, and a number of mountains including the snowcapped summits of Cayambe, Antisana, Cotopaxi, and—on a very clear day—even Chimborazo. Modern sculptures decorate some of the clearings, alongside llamas grazed for the benefit of visitors. There are sports fields, playgrounds, and picnic areas with grills and toilets. At the north end of the park is a small village called Comuna Ashintaco; many of the people in this community work in the park's maintenance.

TREK 3: PARQUE METROPOLITANO

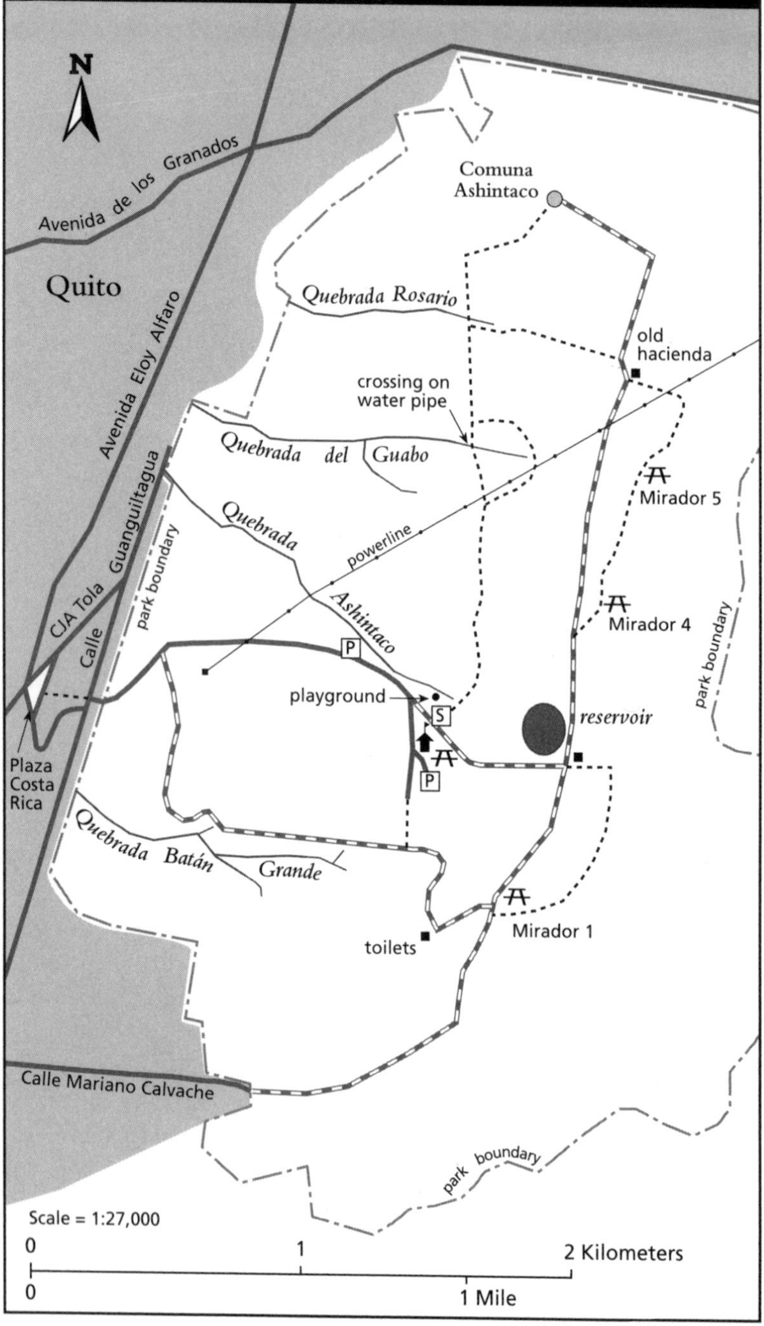

N

Avenida de los Granados

Quito

Avenida Eloy Alfaro

Calle Guanguiltagua

CJA Tola

park boundary

Comuna
Ashintaco

Quebrada Rosario

old
hacienda

crossing on
water pipe

Quebrada del Guabo

Quebrada

powerline

Mirador 5

Ashintaco

Mirador 4

park boundary

P

playground

S

reservoir

P

Plaza
Costa
Rica

Quebrada Batán Grande

Mirador 1

toilets

Calle Mariano Calvache

park boundary

Scale = 1:27,000

0   1   2 Kilometers

0   1 Mile

Parque Metropolitano is very popular with joggers and mountain-bikers, especially on weekends. On Sundays a conservation group runs bird-watching tours and invites volunteers to help with reforestation; inquire in advance with the Corporación Ornitológica del Ecuador (see "Conservation Organizations" in Appendix A).

Parque Metropolitano is the ideal place for visitors to Quito to walk in pleasant surroundings without actually leaving the city. It provides an opportunity to gently acclimatize to altitude and to orient yourself to the local geography, as well as to get a feeling for the style of trek descriptions used in this book. One possible loop is described below; there are many other options for those who want to spend more time and explore the park in greater detail.

Access: The main entrance to the park is off Avenida Eloy Alfaro, above the soccer stadium. Buses run along this avenue, or take a more frequent service along Avenida 6 de Diciembre to Estadio Atahualpa, walk east up Manuel M. Sánchez (the street just south of the stadium) to Carlos Arroyo del Río, turn right for a few meters, and continue uphill on the steps that take you to Eloy Alfaro. On the east side of Eloy Alfaro is a small park, Plaza Costa Rica; climb the steps to the east of this plaza for two blocks to Calle Guanguiltagua, where you will find the access to the park. From Guanguiltagua it is 1 kilometer (0.6 mile) to the park administration building. From the stadium it is a 15-minute walk uphill to the park access road and another 15 minutes to the administration. A taxi can also take you as far as the administration. The south end of the park can be accessed from the Bellavista neighborhood, Calle Mariano Calvache past the Guayasamín Museum.

Route: Take the trail that starts behind the small children's playground, north of the main parking area and administration buildings. Follow it uphill toward a stand of eucalyptus, past the head of Quebrada Ashintaco, and continue to the north along a wide trail through the forest. In **10 minutes** you will reach a clearing with a high-tension powerline cutting through it. The trail then descends and crosses a ravine, Quebrada del Guabo, on a large water pipe; if you are uncomfortable crossing on the pipe, then this can be detoured to the east, on a small trail through the woods. The trail then climbs out of Quebrada del Guabo and gradually descends to the next ravine, Quebrada Rosario, **10 minutes** from the powerline (**20 minutes** if you take the detour to avoid the water pipe).

At Quebrada Rosario, one trail crosses the ravine on a small wooden bridge and continues to the north. Take the loop that goes right just before the bridge, along a smaller trail that runs east, first following the edge of the ravine and later through the fragrant eucalyptus forest. In **10 minutes** you

Bird-watching in Quebrada Ashintaco

will reach a cobblestone road. This is the main road in the park; you can follow it if you do not want to use the small trails. Otherwise, follow the road right (south) for only a few meters, then take a small path to the east, by an old *hacienda* (farm house), until you reach the powerline again. Continue south along a trail through the woods and leading to a large sculpture and Mirador 5, a picnic area and lookout. This area is **15 minutes** from the road. There are views of a small reservoir and surrounding suburbs against a backdrop of high mountains (the Cordillera Oriental) to the east. Continue south along the trail that starts by the sculpture and goes through the woods to Mirador 4, **10 minutes** ahead. There are steep eroding cliffs south of here, so it is best to continue along the cobbled road. In **15 minutes** you will reach a reservoir on your right and then an intersection. The road to the right leads back to the administration buildings and park entrance.

The cobbled road climbs to the south and then descends through large meadows dotted with more sculptures and some of the best views to the south and southeast. If you wish to continue off the road, take the small trail to the left, alongside a large walled property, to a clearing overlooking the Cumbayá Valley. A trail south from the clearing contours along the hillside through a pleasant pine forest—a nice change from the eucalyptus. In **20 minutes** you will reach the Mirador 1 picnic area and lookout. Here a dirt road goes south to the Bellavista access on Calle Mariano Calvache, and the cobbled road makes a loop west (past a cabin housing toilets) and then north behind the administration buildings, **15 minutes** from Mirador 1. The cobbled road then descends to the west and in **15 minutes** reaches the main access road by the entrance gate.

Getting back: See "Access" above.

4 PASOCHOA RESERVE

Rating: Easy, 13-kilometer (8-mile), 7-hour full-day walk. There are several very easy shorter walks along the lower loops.
Elevation: 2800 to 3950 meters (9200 to 13,000 feet).
Maps: IGM 1:50,000: CT-ÑIII-C2 Amaguaña, CT-ÑIII-D1 Píntag (all optional). A simple but useful trail map is generally available at the visitor information center.
Best time to visit: July to September are the driest months; April is the wettest.
Special gear: None.
Water: Available at the park entrance and from Quebrada Santa Ana at the beginning of the walk. There is no water higher up, so carry some with you.
Hazards: None.
Annoyances: None.
Permits and fees: Park entrance costs $7 for foreigners.
Services: Use of shelters (see below) costs $3 per person, camping $1 per person. Spanish-speaking guides may be arranged in advance for $4–$6; call Fundación Natura (see "Conservation Organizations" in Appendix A).
Provisions: Bring your lunch from Quito.

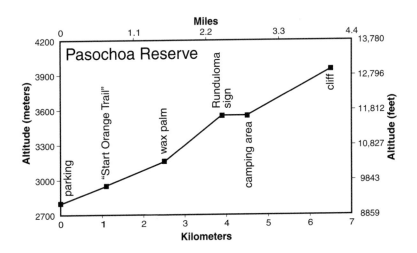

The Refugio de Vida Silvestre Pasochoa (formerly known as Bosque Protector Pasochoa) is a nature reserve on the northwest flank of the extinct Pasochoa Volcano (see Trek 5, Pasochoa Summit). It preserves a small remnant of native Andean forest, home to some 50 species of trees, 120 species of birds, and various mammals including the puma. Birds are easy to spot along the trails. At the base of the reserve, at 2800 meters (9200 feet), are an information center, environmental education center (Centro de Educación Ambiental Pasochoa, CEAP), picnic and camping sites, and two shelters accommodating twenty people.

The reserve has a system of well-signed and maintained color-coded loop trails that take from 30 minutes to 4 hours, plus one longer trail. A detailed map is displayed at the entrance, and an information pamphlet describing the reserve and its trails may also be available. The route described here follows the longer trail, which continues toward the summit of Pasochoa, crossing several Andean vegetation zones. Once the trail emerges from the forest to the *páramo*, there are excellent views of the rocky summits above, the valleys and towns below, surrounding snow-capped peaks, and the forested volcanic cauldron. Those interested in shorter walks, appropriate for young children or the elderly, should do one of the lower loops.

Access: Take a bus to Amaguaña (see Trek 5). Pick-ups and taxis from the center of Amaguaña can take you to the Refugio de Vida Silvestre for $6 one way. On weekends or public holidays there also might be enough traffic to hitchhike from the highway turnoff, southwest of Amaguaña.

Route: The entrance to the reserve's color-coded trail system is by the environmental education center, CEAP. The lower trails all head to the south side of Quebrada Santa Ana and then loop back along the north side. (Note that this is not the same Quebrada Santa Ana as in Trek 5.) Higher up, the orange trail leads to the black trail, which goes toward the summit. The most direct route to the orange trail is always to take the right-hand fork.

All routes start on a common trail, which goes through a bamboo thicket; it first drops and crosses Quebrada Santa Ana on a small wooden bridge; then it climbs gradually along a well-maintained trail with steps, to a more open area amid pastures.

Ten minutes from the start are signs for the red and blue trails, which go off to the left. Follow the yellow trail to the right; it continues to climb at first alongside a barbed-wire fence and later through forest rich in bamboo. **Ten minutes** beyond, the yellow loop goes left and the green trail starts to the right. Continue on the green trail, which climbs more steeply. In another **10 minutes** you will reach a small grassy clearing at 2950 meters (9700 feet). Enjoy views of the valley of the Río San Pedro here and the western *cordillera* (chain of mountains) beyond.

The green trail goes left and the orange trail starts to the right, by a sign reading "A la palma 45', a la cumbre 6 h, sendero naranja" (to the palm 45 minutes, to the summit 6 hours, orange trail). Follow the orange trail, which climbs steeply through more bamboo along the ridge between Quebrada Santa Ana to the north and Quebrada Sambache to the south. A couple of clearings allow for views down to the valleys and to a pasture-covered parallel ridge to the right. The trail continues along or near the ridge line, with steep sections occasionally giving way to welcome flat stretches. The vegetation gradually changes, and scrubby secondary growth yields to attractive cloud forest. You will see the first bromeliads and native trees such as the *pumamaqui*, the *cedro*, and the alder.

Thirty minutes beyond the start of the orange trail is a sign and a small clearing to the left through which you can see an Andean Wax Palm. Another **30 minutes** ahead, at 3350 meters (11,000 feet), the trail emerges from the forest onto the tussock-clad *páramo*.

The trail now climbs steeply east onto a ridge, which you will reach **30 minutes** after entering the *páramo*. At the crest is a sign, "Runduloma, 3,450 m," which is unfortunately misleading. Runduloma appears on the IGM map more than 1 kilometer (0.6 mile) north of this point. A second sign, "AL CEAP," points to the trail you just arrived on, the cor-

Lone polylepis tree on the rim of Pasochoa's crater

rect direction on the way down. You will see another trail here, which once made a long loop for the orange trail; it has not been used in many years and is not safe.

Along the right-hand fork is the black trail bearing south. Follow it first along the level ridge top and enjoy the scent of the planted pine forest to the left. In **10 minutes**, you will reach another fork; go left, following a sign: "A la cumbre" (to the summit). Just beyond is an area suitable for camping, but no water. Be sure to let the ranger at the information center know if you intend to camp here. **Five minutes** beyond, the trail crosses a fence; it then climbs toward the rim of Pasochoa's crater with nice views of Antisana to the northeast, Corazón, Ilinizas, and several towns including Machachi and Aloag to the west. As you climb the narrow ridge between the volcanic cauldron to your right and the gully of Quebrada Cañari on your left, stands of polylepis trees appear. In **20 minutes**, the trail crosses a stand of polylepis that spills over from the cauldron to the gully. It then continues to climb steeply through tussock, with more views to the northwest: of Pichincha, Ilaló, the Valle de los Chillos suburbs, and parts of Quito.

In **30 minutes** you will reach a welcome resting spot where the ground is a little flatter. From here the trail continues climbing gradually at first and then very steeply to the base of a sheer cliff, about 1 kilometer (0.6 mile) north of Pasochoa's main summit. This final grunt takes **30 to 45 minutes**, depending on your degree of acclimatization. The total time from the information center to the cliff is **3.5 to 4 hours**.

At the base of the cliff is a small ledge (a good place for a rest), and the views make the climb worthwhile. At 3950 meters (13,000 feet), it can be quite cold; fog and hail are not uncommon. The trail continues to the right of the cliff, but it is very steep and surrounded by abysses. The surface is unstable, so continuing is dangerous and not recommended. Lower down, below the base of the cliffs, and to the left of them as you are looking up, is a polylepis forest. A safer route through here is planned by the reserve administration; it will lead to a saddle and the summit trail.

The walk down takes **2 to 3 hours** along the same route—longer if you take one of the loops lower down. Remember to take the left fork by the Runduloma sign. Descending, the trail can be slippery when wet.

Getting back: You can arrange a pick-up in advance, or call Cooperativa Pacheco Jr. in Amaguaña (02)287-7047 to send a vehicle. There is a public cell phone at the information center but it does not accept coins, so be sure to take a Bell South debit card (easily available in Quito).

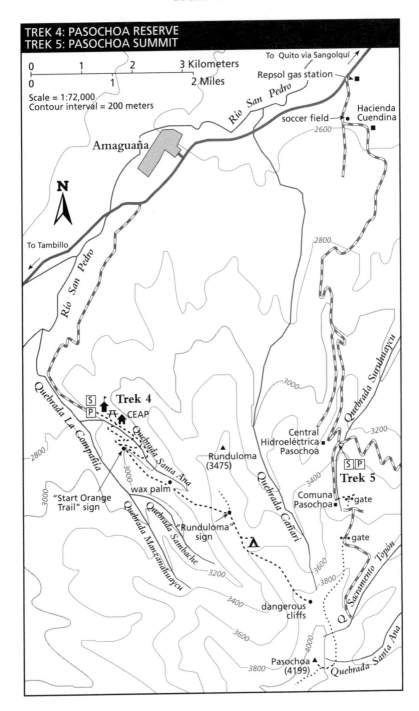

5 PASOCHOA SUMMIT

Rating: Easy, 9-kilometer (5.6-mile), full-day hike.
Elevation: 3300 to 4200 meters (10,800 to 13,800 feet).
Maps: IGM 1:50,000: CT-ÑIII-C2 Amaguaña, CT-ÑIII-D1 Píntag (both optional).
Best time to visit: July to September are the driest months, April the wettest. The temperature can drop suddenly, and dense fog rolls in at any time of the year—most commonly in the afternoon. It may be windy at the summit, and hail storms sometimes occur.
Special gear: None.
Water: Small streams along the route may dry up in summer. Take water from town.
Hazards: Bulls.
Annoyances: None.
Permits and fees: None.
Services: None.
Provisions: Take lunch from Quito.

Pasochoa is an extinct volcano located 30 kilometers (19 miles) south of Quito. It is believed to have last erupted about 100,000 years ago, when the west side of its crater collapsed, resulting in its current horseshoe shape. Pasochoa can be climbed from various directions—except the west,

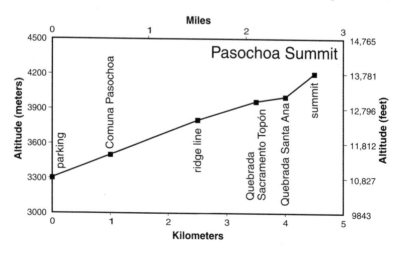

where the crater wall is nearly vertical. On the northwest flank of the mountain is the Refugio de Vida Silvestre Pasochoa, a pleasant forest reserve (see Trek 4, Pasochoa Reserve).

In clear weather the slopes of Pasochoa offer fine views of many majestic summits: Cayambe, Antisana, Sincholagua, Rumiñahui, Cotopaxi, the Ilinizas, Corazón, and their surrounding valleys. This trek also provides an opportunity to experience the tranquility of the *páramo*, within sight of Quito. Condors may occasionally be seen here. Pasochoa is a particularly good acclimatization hike in preparation for more strenuous, high-altitude trekking.

Access: To reach the trailhead, take a bus from Plaza La Marín, in Quito, to Amaguaña (frequent service 0600-1800, 1.5 hours, $.75). Beware of thieves at La Marín. You can hire a pick-up truck in the center of Amaguaña and ask to be taken to the Central Hidroeléctrica Pasochoa ($10 one way). Remember to make arrangements to be picked up in the afternoon, or be prepared to walk 10 kilometers (6 miles) down to the highway (a long slog on a cobbled road). There is not enough traffic to hitchhike here. If you are driving, the turnoff from the main paved road is at the Repsol gas station, northeast of Amaguaña.

Route: From the Central Hidroeléctrica, continue up the road for **10 minutes**, to reach a rutted dirt road that branches off to the south (right). Follow this south through the woods for **30 minutes**; it ends by a small brick building marked "Comuna Pasochoa." Turn left here, cross a stream (the beginning of the Quebrada Suruhuaycu), and follow the trail east through a small alder and pine grove to a barbed-wire fence. Turn right through a gate into a pasture (beware of bulls from here on) and head south to cross this pasture (and a second abutting one) to a dirt road on the far side. Turn left and follow the road east for 100 meters (300 feet) until it meets a larger road. It will take **20 minutes** from Comuna Pasochoa to this point. Turn right on this road, cobbled at first, and follow it south for **30 minutes**. After crossing another gate, leave the road at the base of a tussock-covered ridge (duck under the barbed-wire fence to your right) and proceed south cross-country, climbing **15 minutes** to the crest of the ridge. Then follow the ridge line for **30 minutes**, as it climbs gently to the southwest toward the east flank of Pasochoa.

From here on you will have a view of the craggy rim of the crater, including the summit. There are several indistinct cattle trails throughout the *páramo*, but the topography should be your guide in preference to

Collapsed crater of Pasochoa from the west

these. Take note of the ridge you are on as you approach the flank of the mountain to make sure you follow the same one on your descent. From the ridge top there are fine views of the surrounding mountains, the Río Pita Valley to the east and the Río San Pedro Valley to the northwest. Contour south along the east flank of Pasochoa for **1 hour**, through the waist-deep tussock grass, below several rocky outcrops to your right. Cross a small boggy area formed by Quebrada Sacramento Topón and reach the steep gully of Quebrada Santa Ana, which you can cross without difficulty.

On the far side of the *quebrada* a trail (indistinct at first but clearer as you go higher) leads west toward the summit. This is the steepest part of the walk and should be taken slowly (**30 minutes to 1 hour**) if you are not acclimatized. The final 100 meters (300 feet) are over bare rock—a little slippery when wet, but otherwise quite safe.

Just beyond the summit is a small, rocky platform ideal for lunch amid spectacular views of the collapsed crater and surrounding mountains. Continuing south beyond the base of the summit, there is access to other rocky outcrops along the crater rim (which can also be climbed). In all, it takes **3 to 4 hours** up from the Central Hidroeléctrica Pasochoa to the summit, **2 hours** back down.

Getting back: See "Access" above.

6 PAPALLACTA

Rating: Easy, 8-kilometer (5-mile), full-day hike; very easy, 2-kilometer (1.2-mile), 1-hour walk along the lower loop called Sendero de la Isla (The Island Trail).
Elevation: 3300 to 3500 meters (10,800 to 11,500 feet).
Maps: IGM 1:50,000: CT-ÑIII-B4 Oyacachi, CT-ÑIII-D2 Papallacta (both optional). A sketch map may be available at the visitors information center.
Best time to visit: The driest months are October through February. The rainy season is April through September.
Special gear: None.
Water: Available along the route but may be difficult to access, so take some with you.
Hazards: There have been occasional holdups along the road from Quito to Papallacta; this trip is safest during the daytime.
Annoyances: None.
Permits and fees: $2 for use of trails, $5 entry to thermal baths.
Services: Guiding (Spanish only) may be available from the visitors information center (El Exploratorio) at a cost of $2–$4 per person for a guided walk. Comfortable accommodations at Termas de Papallacta cost $69 a night for two persons. Reservations are recommended on weekends and holidays. Quito office phone: (02)250-4787. More economical options are available along the access road, and the cheapest basic hotels and municipal thermal baths are in the village of Papallacta.

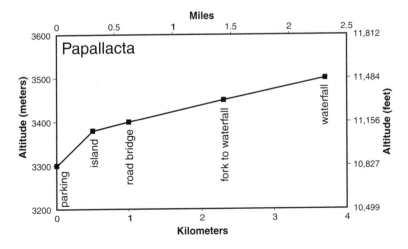

Provisions: Termas de Papallacta has a very good, expensive restaurant. There are a few more modest establishments just outside the baths and in the village of Papallacta, which also has a few basic shops.

The Papallacta region has long been a favorite for outdoor recreation. Situated in a valley on the eastern slopes of the Cordillera Oriental, and less than a 2-hour drive from Quito along a good paved road (except for the last 3 kilometers, 2 miles), it offers nice trekking opportunities through *páramo* and remnants of cloud forest. Rocky outcrops and many lakes speak of a heavily glaciated past, while forest fragments are found mainly in deep ravines. The area receives abundant rainfall year-round, and the *páramo* is often spongy. An added bonus for walking here is the opportunity to soak in one of Ecuador's most appealing thermal baths at the end of the day.

This walk lies within the boundaries of the Termas de Papallacta, a private resort with excellent accommodations, restaurants, thermal baths, a nature interpretation center, and a series of well-maintained trails in the valley of the Río Papallacta. Almost eighty species of birds have been identified in the area. The route climbs gradually through open pastures with views of the surrounding hills and the snowcapped summit of Antisana to the south. It follows the edge of the rushing Río Papallacta through some nice cloud forest, and then across swampy terrain to reach a pretty waterfall.

Access: The village of Papallacta is 55 kilometers (34 miles) east of Quito, along the road to Baeza. Five hundred meters (1600 feet) before (west of) the village, and 2 kilometers (1.2 miles) north along a side road, is the Termas de Papallacta Resort. There is a sign at the turnoff. Hourly buses from the Quito central bus station pass Papallacta on their way to several destinations in the Oriente (2 hours, $2); ask to be let off at the intersection for the thermal baths. It is a 30-minute walk uphill from this turnoff to the resort. Access to the trails is by a guard post to the right of the entrance to the pools.

Route: Take the path uphill from the parking lot, past the guard post to the information center, and farther uphill to meet the road again. Continue uphill along the road past some buildings on your left until you see a gate (also on your left) and the beginning of a trail signed with a footprint. Follow this trail north through several pastures. In **10 minutes** you will reach a wooden bridge crossing onto a small island (*la isla*) in the Río Papallacta, where you will find a picnic area. The island has some bushes and small trees, labeled with wooden signs.

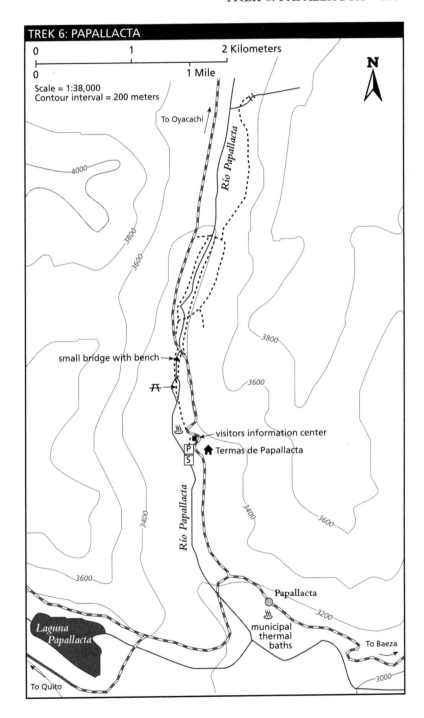

TREK 6: PAPALLACTA

0   1   2 Kilometers
0   1 Mile
Scale = 1:38,000
Contour interval = 200 meters

To Oyacachi

Río Papallacta

4000

3800

3600

3800

3600

small bridge with bench

3600

visitors information center

Termas de Papallacta

P
S

3400

3400

3600

Río Papallacta

3600

Papallacta

3200

municipal
thermal
baths

To Baeza

Laguna
Papallacta

To Quito

3000

N

Steaming-hot baths at Termas de Papallacta

Cross the island in **5 minutes** to its north end, where there is a fork. Two trails continue from here along both of the forested banks of the river. Take one in either direction to complete the loop. Along the east side is a wooden platform with benches overlooking the rushing rapids, a very pleasant spot. In **15 minutes** the two branches meet again at a small bridge with a bench along one side. One hundred meters (300 feet) farther up-river, the car road crosses the river on a larger concrete bridge.

Another trail starts by a gate on the east side of the road, halfway between the two bridges. Take this trail (which parallels the road going north) first through a cleared area and then into nice forest. In **15 minutes** you will reach a four-way intersection. One trail goes left down to a wooden footbridge back across the river; another continues north along the riverbank through a patch of forest with much bamboo; and a third branch goes east for a few meters, then turns to the north. Follow the third trail across a clearing with moss and ferns and into more cloud forest with mature trees clad in mosses, bromeliads, and other epiphytes. If you look carefully, you will find a variety of orchids here.

In **10 minutes** you will reach a fork. Continue along the left branch (to the north), climbing gradually through the forest and then dropping to a swampy area after **15 minutes**. Continue to the north, and enter a patch of forest. In another **15 minutes** the trail makes a sharp turn to the west; a few meters ahead it meets a smaller trail to the right. The main trail continues to the west, back to the river and the car road beyond. Take the smaller trail to the right, which maintains a northerly course. You will wind through forest ever closer to cliffs on your right, and passing some impressive boulders along the way. In another **15 minutes**, emerge from the forest onto a large open swampy area carpeted with moss. There are views of the rocky peaks and surrounding *páramo*. Continue to the north, stepping on the fern roots to avoid sinking in the mud. In **45 minutes** you will reach a waterfall at 3500 meters (11,500 feet), cascading down a rocky cliff to the east. Be careful: the wooden observation platform in front of the falls can be very slippery.

Return along the same trail you came on, to reach the main trail in **1 hour**. Then take the main trail west. In **5 minutes** it will lead to a wooden bridge across the river, where a small trail follows the east bank to the south. Cross to the west shore, where the trail splits. The right branch continues to the road. (This is an option for those with time and interest to continue farther north up the valley.)

To return to the thermal baths, take the left branch after the wood bridge and follow the riverbank south. In **45 minutes** you will reach another crossing, at the footbridge mentioned earlier. Do not cross here. The trail continues along the west bank of the river, high above the water (watch your step), to reach the concrete road bridge **15 minutes** later. Take the island trail to return to the entrance in another **30 minutes**.

Getting back: See "Access" above.

7 TOUCAN TRAIL

Rating: Easy, 16-kilometer (10-mile), 1- to 2-day trek.
Elevation: 1200 to 3000 meters (4000 to 9800 feet).
Map: IGM 1:50,000: CT-ÑII-E4 Calacalí.
Best time to visit: June through September are the driest months—but even then, an afternoon downpour is common. More frequent rain, fog, and mud are the rule at other times of the year.
Special gear: None.
Water: Found at the beginning and end of the route, but scarce along the main ridge-line portion (especially during the dry season). Best tank up at the start.
Hazards: Poisonous snakes in the lowlands.
Annoyances: Biting insects, including chiggers, in the lower portion of the trek. Take repellent.
Permits and fees: Foreign visitors pay a $6 fee to the Maquipucuna Reserve. At the time of writing, there was no formal entry fee at Yunguillas; however, a contribution to the community ecotourism project there is appropriate for those trekkers who do not take one of the local guides.

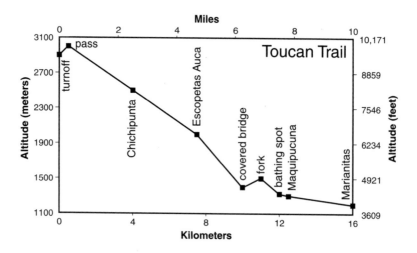

Services: The Yunguillas Community Ecotourism Project offers guides for this trek at a cost of $10 per day. The project also provides accommodations in Yunguillas for $15 per person, including three meals. Both guides and lodging must be arranged in advance. Contact Germán Collaguazo at (09)958-0694. Accommodations are also available at Maquipucuna, $45–65 per person, including three meals; reserve through their Quito office (see "Conservation Organizations" in Appendix A). **Provisions:** Bring provisions from Quito. Only basic items can be purchased in Calacalí, and nothing at all in Yunguillas. Meals are generally available at the restaurant in Maquipucuna, but large groups should call in advance.

Maquipucuna is a 4500-hectare (11,000-acre) private nature reserve situated northwest of Quito in a region aptly known as El Noroccidente. The reserve is surrounded by an additional 14,000 hectares (34,500 acres) of nominally protected forest which, although also used for agriculture, serves as an important buffer zone. The area can be reached by city bus from the capital, yet the cloud forest traversed by this trek rivals that of far more remote locations.

   More than 1000 species of plants have been identified here. The flora is exceptionally rich in epiphytes, such as orchids, ferns, and bromeliads. There are at least 45 species of mammals, including pumas, Spectacled Bear, agoutis, and deer. It is the birds and butterflies, however, that really make this walk a delight. More than 300 bird species have been catalogued, and the trekker is certain to be accompanied by their music throughout the hike. Among those easiest to observe are the many varieties of brilliant hummingbirds. A special treat, if you are lucky, is the brightly plumed

Plate-billed Mountain-Toucan (see below). The diverse butterfly species include the blue morpho, which can be seen along the lower parts of the walk floating through the warm air on large iridescent wings.

This trek, sometimes called the Camino Auca, was used for centuries by the Yumbos (aboriginal inhabitants of the area who have since vanished). The route follows the northeastern boundary of the Maquipucuna Reserve, descending along a ridge between the Río Santa Rosa and the Río Umachaca. The first part is on an abandoned vehicle road (now closed to cars by vegetation and several landslides), the remainder on narrow trails deep in the forest. It can all be walked in a single day with a light pack— if you leave early, move fast, and are prepared to spend the night at Maquipucuna should there be no transport out. An alternative is to take a tent and provisions for overnight. This allows you to travel at a more relaxed pace, as well as to enjoy the sights and sounds of the forest at dusk and dawn.

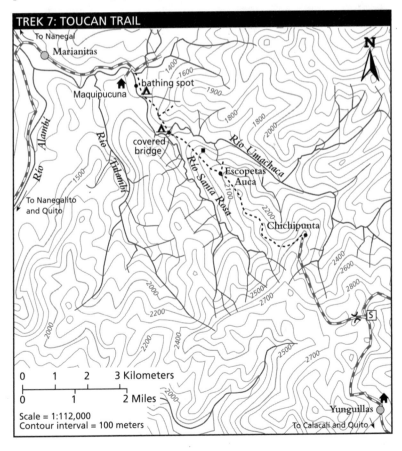

THE PLATE-BILLED MOUNTAIN-TOUCAN *by Lou Jost*

Ecuador's cloud forests come to life when the fog rolls in. Bird songs carry a long way through the mist, and one of the most far-carrying is the nasal, trumpet-like note that announces the fanciest bird in the cloud forest: the Plate-billed Mountain-Toucan. This big, blue-breasted, golden-backed toucan has patches of red and yellow around the tail, bare blue and yellow skin on its face, and a yellow plate on its mostly black bill. Such an elaborate *fiesta* of colors and shapes is seldom seen in the bird world.

These clownish birds are not hard to track down; they are full of curiosity and often come to observe the observer. When they find some-one intruding in their forest, they make a loud rattling sound with their beaks, bobbing their heads up and down in synchrony with the sound. Their movements make them easy to spot in the trees. Once their curiosity is satisfied, however, they will disappear back into the fog.

The Plate-billed Mountain-Toucan, which lives on the western slopes of the Andes between 1500 and 3000 meters (5000 and 10,000 feet), is one of three species of mountain-toucans that make their home in Ecuador. It is one of the so-called "Chocó endemics"—a set of species whose ranges are centered on the Chocó region of western Colombia.

Toucans' banana-sized beaks (their hallmark) are lightweight, hollow structures much less cumbersome than they look. Toucans use their beaks to reach out and pluck ripe fruits from branches that are too thin for them to walk on. Beaks also play a role in social interactions: rivals use them to fence with one another in mock sword fights. They are even used to reach into nest holes of other birds, to eat their eggs and chicks. (Contrary to popular belief, toucans are not exclusively vegetarian.)

Deforestation and hunting are the major threats to the Plate-

billed Mountain-Toucan, but in places where they are not hunted they can survive even in degraded forests. One of the best places in the world to see this species is the area near Maquipucuna.

Plate-billed Mountain-Toucan (Painting by Lou Jost)

Access: Take a bus marked Calacalí, traveling north along Avenida América in Quito (45 minutes, $.50); or a taxi to Calacalí ($12). At the town of Calacalí, you can hire a pick-up truck in the main plaza (if none is parked there, ask around) to take you to the village of Yunguillas (20 minutes, $3). Accommodations and guides are available at Yunguillas; stop here or ask to be taken past Yunguillas, 3.5 kilometers (2.2 miles) northwest to the first turn-off left, which leads to an area known as Guantug Pungo. Depending on the state of the road and the vehicle, you may be able to continue several more kilometers beyond this turnoff; the cost of transport will vary accordingly.

Route: Assuming you begin to hike at the turnoff, follow the dirt road west. In **15 minutes** of gentle climbing you will reach an unnamed pass at 3000 meters (9800 feet), the highest point of the walk. A couple of trails branch off beyond, but our trek continues along the vehicle road. At times it climbs for short distances, but it always continues to lose altitude overall as it swings gradually to the northwest (your general direction of travel for the entire trek).

One hour from the pass you will reach a small stream flowing across the road; there may be several others when it is raining, but be sure to take water here in the dry season. **Thirty minutes** farther is a large landslide—the first of several, and an insurmountable obstacle even to four-wheel-drive vehicles. Just past the slide, the trail climbs briefly to reach Chichipunta, not shown on the IGM map but marked by a small hand-painted sign. At this point the trail turns sharply southwest. The scenery begins to change from pastures and scrubby secondary growth to increasingly lush cloud forest filled with beautiful bird songs and fluttering butterflies.

Several more homemade signs follow, although none of the place names are shown on the IGM map. The next sign, in **30 minutes**, is for Chichisique. You will now be clearly on a ridge, which the trek follows northwest for most of its length, occasionally contouring along the northeastern flank. Palmito is the next sign, **30 minutes** farther. The ridge now becomes slightly narrower, although it is still wide enough to pitch a tent at various spots alongside the trail. The forest is very beautiful here and there are fine views down to the valleys of the Río Santa Rosa to the southwest and the Río Umachaca to the northeast.

In another **30 minutes** you will reach a sign for Apracana; **15 minutes** beyond, a sign reads "Escopetas Auca." At Escopetas Auca you will be back in pasture land and the trail will turn sharply north. In **5 minutes**, you will meet a smaller side trail that continues north, while our main trail regains its northwesterly course. **Fifteen minutes** farther you will emerge at what was once the end of the vehicle road, looking down to your right on a house and surrounding pastures.

Contour northwest through the pasture for **5 minutes** and, at its edge, you will reach a much narrower trail than the one you had been following. This trail, carved into a gully, continues to travel northwest but now drops more steeply through dense woods. In many places the track has been worn into the soft soil by years of use, and you will find yourself in gullies deeper than you are high. The walls are thick with moss and the trench barely wide enough to accommodate your backpack. The going is rougher here—but also very beautiful, as the sounds of birds and insects accompany you all the way. On a sunny day, butterflies are everywhere.

Along the descent you can hear the Río Umachaca below to your right, but it will take **2 hours** (and seem even longer) before you reach a covered wooden bridge over its crystal-clear waters, at an altitude of 1400 meters (4600 feet). The bridge is 100 meters (300 feet) up-river from the confluence of the Río Umachaca and the Río Santa Rosa. Just beyond the bridge, near the river's edge, is a small sandy area where you can camp or enjoy a well-deserved rest.

The trail climbs rather steeply from here before contouring around the 1500-meter (5000-foot) level, with many ups and downs along the way. You will remain mostly in the woods, with an occasional view down to the Río Umachaca Valley (now on your left). You will cross several small streams along this section. **Thirty minutes** past the bridge you will reach a fork. Take the left branch, which continues northwest and soon descends back toward the Río Umachaca. In **1 hour** you will emerge into pastures once again. There is a stream and flat terrain for camping here, but **20 minutes** farther are more ample grounds and a very nice spot for bathing in the chilly Río Umachaca.

Continuing north through pastures, the trail climbs slightly before joining a wider path **10 minutes** farther, and **5 minutes** farther still a vehicle road alongside the river. Follow the road west (left) for another **5 minutes** to reach the administration center and accommodations of the Maquipucuna Reserve.

Getting back: There is no regular transport from Maquipucuna, but you may be able to arrange a ride if there are visitors who have driven in. Otherwise, walk 3.5 kilometers (2.2 miles) west along the road (**1 hour**) to the village of Marianitas. Pick-up trucks can usually be hired in Marianitas (although there are only two of them) to take you to Nanegalito (not to be confused with Nanegal) on the paved road to Quito (30 minutes, $10). Buses to Quito pass through Nanegalito hourly throughout the day (1.5 hours, $1). There are also basic hotels and restaurants in Nanegalito, should you be stuck there overnight.

𝟪 GUACAMAYOS TRAIL

Research and editorial assistance by Kerry Alley
Rating: Moderately difficult, 10-kilometer (6.2-mile), 1- to 2-day trek.
Elevation: 1350 to 2200 meters (4400 to 7200 feet).
Maps: IGM 1:50,000: CT-OIII-C3 Cosanga, CT-OIII-E1 Sardinas.
Note that some contour lines near Sarayacu are incorrectly labeled on
the latter map.
Best time to visit: October through March tend to be drier; April
through September are very wet.
Special gear: None.
Water: Abundant.
Hazards: River crossings in the rainy season, and slippery logs.
Poisonous snakes at lower elevations.
Annoyances: Mosquitoes at night.
Permits and fees: In principle, foreign visitors pay a $5 fee to
Antisana Ecological Reserve, but there are no collection facilities along
this route.
Services: Baeza, 87 kilometers (54 miles) east of Quito and 28 kilometers
(17.5 miles) north of the trailhead, is a convenient place to spend the
night before this walk. There are several simple hotels and restaurants in
Baeza. To the south are: Archidona, 47 kilometers (29 miles) from the
trailhead, also with simple hotels and restaurants; and Tena, 58 kilometers (36 miles) from the trailhead, a provincial capital with all services.
Provisions: Basic supplies can be purchased in Baeza and Archidona.
Tena has well stocked shops with a variety of provisions, or you can
bring supplies from Quito.

The Cordillera de los Guacamayos (spelled Huacamayos on the IGM
map) is a range that rises east of the Cordillera Oriental and reaches 3044
meters (9987 feet). Located in the Antisana Ecological Reserve, it is famous
among biologists for its well-preserved cloud forest. Bird-watchers have
made this area an important stop to see some of its nearly fifty species of
tanagers, as well as Gray-breasted and Black-billed Mountain-Toucans.
The *cordillera's* name comes from the macaws (*guacamayos*) formerly found
here: the Chestnut-fronted Macaw and the Military Macaw. Botanists say
that the vegetation is every bit as fascinating. For the trekker, the experience of walking through this lush cloud forest is not to be missed.

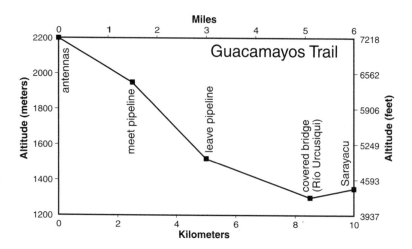

The trek starts in primary forest, at first under the canopy. Later a petroleum pipeline offers an experience similar to that of a canopy walkway, with views straight over and into the trees covered with bromeliads, orchids, and ferns. Small, colorful tanagers and other birds dart about. The second half of the trek goes through secondary forest and pastures, crossing several rivers. Views of the surrounding hills are breathtaking; even the developed portions are lush and green.

The trek requires a full day (6 hours) walking with light gear, without breaks. If you choose to do it in 2 days, increase the times indicated (the going is slower with a full pack).

Access: The trailhead is on the Baeza–Tena Road, 7.5 kilometers (4.7 miles) south of the village of Cosanga. From Quito, Papallacta, or Baeza, catch a bus bound for Tena or Coca; there are several throughout the day. The trail starts at the pass on the Cordillera de los Guacamayos, about an hour ride from Baeza (20 minutes past Cosanga). At the pass are a shrine to the Virgen de los Guacamayos and a set of antennas, just above the road. The path starts immediately behind the antennas and the guard's house.

Route: An obvious trail heads south. The first 2 kilometers (1.2 miles) are partially "paved" with rocks and logs. The path goes right through magnificent cloud forest. (If you are looking for just a taste of this splendid experience, consider walking only this section and returning to the antennas to catch a bus.) The path leads directly to the oil pipeline, reached in **1.5 hours**. It is right on the ridge line, and the swath that has been cleared for it offers broad views of spectacular untouched forest-covered mountains. This is a good place for bird-watching: its openness reveals

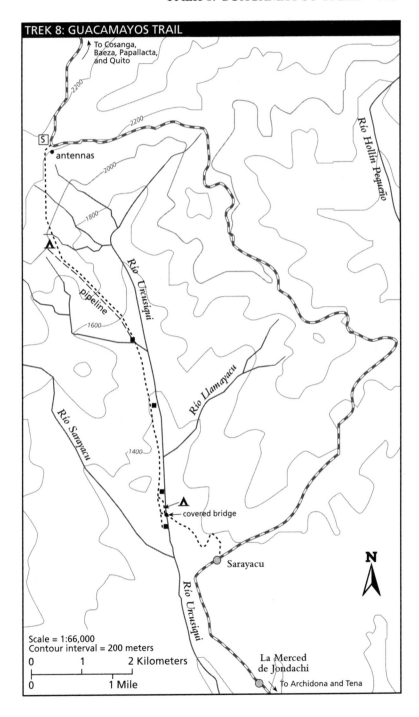

TREK 8: GUACAMAYOS TRAIL

To Cosanga,
Baeza, Papallacta,
and Quito

2200

2200

S

antennas

2000

1800

1600

pipeline

1400

Río Urcusiqui

Río Sarayacu

Río Llamayacu

Río Hollín Pequeño

covered bridge

Sarayacu

Río Urcusiqui

La Merced
de Jondachi

To Archidona and Tena

N

Scale = 1:66,000
Contour interval = 200 meters

0   1   2 Kilometers

0   1 Mile

birds otherwise hidden behind leaves. Up the pipeline are a couple of spots to put a small tent. (The closest water is almost 15 minutes back along the path you entered on.) Although this potential camping spot is close to the beginning of the trek, it is the best one in the forest and lets you spend the early morning bird-watching along either the path or the pipeline.

The route continues to the southeast, downhill alongside the pipeline on a log path *(empalizada)*. Walking on the logs is tricky—especially when they are wet. Fortunately, a small pipe running along the larger pipeline serves as a handrail. In **1 hour** you will come out of the forest into grassy clearings with several metal cabins (occasionally used by the oil company). The pipeline goes underground at this point. The path continues on the other side of a small unnamed river that runs east-west below the cabins. Continue briefly in the direction of the buried pipeline before going down right to the river. (Crossing this and other streams may be difficult after heavy rain.) Cross the river and look for the stony path that heads south through the lower end of the pasture. It will take **15 minutes** to reach the river, cross it, and get to the new trail.

The path is very rocky and a little hard on the feet; but hiking beside the trail can be so muddy (especially in the rainy season) that you will come to appreciate the rocky trail. After **25 minutes** through pastures and occasional patches of secondary forest, you will come to the first wooden one-story house. Keep an eye out for orchids around the streams here, and in the clumps of vegetation growing on dead trees. The trail continues south through forested and cleared patches; along the way you will get a couple of glimpses of the Río Urcusiqui on your left. This rather unusual Quichua name means Bum-Hill River.

In another **45 minutes**, you will reach an old wooden two-story house. A few minutes later, about 100 meters (300 feet) beyond the house (and within the same set of pastures), a faint animal track leads east (left) through the fields. It is easy to miss. Follow this faint path **15 minutes** toward and then along the Río Urcusiqui, until you come to a small covered bridge crossing the river. There is a nice spot to eat lunch, swim, or even camp along the Río Urcusiqui, before you reach the bridge. If you missed the turnoff and arrive at a third wooden house along the stony path, go back 5 minutes and look for a path heading straight to the river and bridge.

The obvious log path continues another **45 minutes** past the bridge to the southeast, through forest and the occasional pasture, before reaching the Baeza–Tena Road at the tiny hamlet of Sarayacu.

Getting back: There are no services at Sarayacu. You can return to Baeza, Papallacta, or Quito, or continue on to Archidona or Tena. Buses in either direction pass about every hour. Get out before sunset, as buses may be reluctant to stop after dark.

Kerry Alley fording a tributary of the Río Urcusiqui (Photo: Harry Jonitz)

Chapter 9
TREKS FROM LATACUNGA

Altitude, 2800 meters (9200 feet)
Population, 50,000

Latacunga, the capital of the province of Cotopaxi, is dominated by the spectacular volcano that gives this province its name. Although it receives its share of tourism, this remains an authentic Ecuadorean town with a well-preserved colonial feel. Most visitors come to climb Cotopaxi, see nearby indigenous markets, or enjoy a day trip to Quilotoa Crater Lake. These excursions are the mainstay of local tour operators. The area also offers great trekking potential.

Trek 9, Hostel Hopping to Quilotoa, is special in that it can be enjoyed with less gear than other multi-day hikes. Camp on this moderately difficult route if you wish, or lighten your load by staying at some of the colorful inns along the way. Shorter but more intense is Trek 10, Across Rumiñahui, which traverses a very scenic 4200-meter (13,800-foot) pass on this craggy extinct volcano.

9 HOSTEL HOPPING TO QUILOTOA

Research and editorial assistance by Kerry Alley
Rating: Moderately difficult, 25-kilometer (15.5-mile), 2- to 3-day trek.
Elevation: 2650 to 3900 meters (8700 to 12,800 feet).
Maps: IGM 1:50,000: CT-ÑIII-E1 Sigchos and CT-ÑIII-E3 Pilaló.
Best time to visit: May through September, December, and January are the driest months. October and November are only moderately wet, but February through April can be more so.
Special gear: Hiking boots.
Water: Available from small streams and local homes along the route.
Hazards: Since this trek goes through a populated rural area, be careful not to leave personal belongings unattended. Also watch out for some mean dogs (best to carry a walking stick).
Annoyances: None.

Permits and fees: A fee of $.50 is charged to pass through Quilotoa village. In principle, foreign visitors pay a $5 fee to Ilinizas National Park, but there are no facilities for collecting the fee along this route.
Services: Details of hostel accommodations are given in the route description.
Provisions: Latacunga is the nearest city with a wide range of shops. Basic provisions as well as very simple home-cooked meals are available in the villages of Isinliví, Chucchilán, Guayama, and Quilotoa. Hostels also provide meals. Fresh vegetables are available in season from the greenhouse in Itualó.

The Quilotoa region is a very popular destination among visitors because of its friendly people, colorful markets, wide variety of high-altitude agriculture, and stunning topography. The crown jewel of the area is Laguna Quilotoa, part of Ilinizas National Park. This crater lake is a sparkling emerald set in a 3-kilometer-wide (1.9-mile-wide), relatively new volcanic caldera. A rapid emptying of the underlying magma chamber caused the bulk of the mountain to fall in on itself about 800 years ago, releasing awesome quantities of ash, pumice, and other volcanic material detectable in the soil as far away as 150 kilometers (90 miles). Near the volcano, these deposits filled preexisting canyons hundreds of meters deep. The rivers subsequently reestablished their courses, leaving behind volcanic shelves high above the valleys.

You can trek from one hostel to another here without carrying a tent,

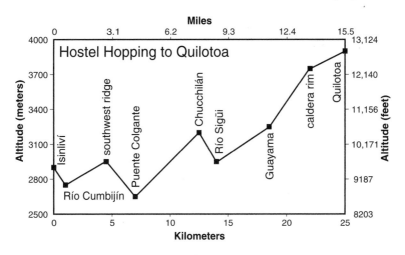

stove, and cooking supplies. (This is unusual for Ecuador.) If you choose to camp, however, there are ample possibilities along the way (but always ask for permission if you are close to a farm). The hostels are also convenient bases for day hikes to explore surrounding canyons, *páramo*, and cloud forest to the west. They are located in small towns and villages along the route; some are predominantly Spanish-speaking *mestizo* settlements, while others are mainly Quichua-speaking indigenous communities. The main economic activity of the region is subsistence farming; principal crops include potatoes, corn, broad beans, lupines, onions, squash, barley, and quinoa. Local crafts popular with tourists include primitivist designs painted on leather, as well as wooden masks. The town markets, held once a week, are very colorful and definitely worth a visit.

This trek begins in Isinliví; winds down, around, up, and over to the Río Toachi; and continues to the village of Itualó. From there you can continue through the town of Chucchilán, and then up, up, *up* to the rim of Quilotoa's caldera, passing canyons, rivers, farms, and more villages along the way. There are also many other options for trekking in this region. Most paths shown on the IGM maps are in moderately good condition.

Access: Buses from Latacunga to Isinliví leave from the *terminal terrestre* at 1100 (via Sigchos, 3.5 hours) and 1300 (direct, 2.5 hours), daily except on Thursday, when they leave from the Saquisilí market around 1100. The cost is $1.80.

Route: The trek begins in Isinliví, a small mestizo town tucked away along an old forgotten road. Here is Hostal Llullu Llama (baby llama), a nicely refurbished house with double rooms and great views ($8–$10 per person including supper and breakfast). Phone: (03)814-790. The trail starts beside the hostel and goes southwest down into the valley of the Río Cumbijín. In 15 minutes you will see the river. Do not continue to the bridge you see from here; instead, turn right 30 meters (100 feet) before it, at a small rocky outcrop, and take the path down to cross the Río Cumbijín at a different bridge. Then follow the trail along the southwest bank of the river, climbing gradually for 15 minutes.

The path then leaves the river valley and heads west through a green gap between hills. Several small paths lead to people's homes and fields. In **15 minutes**, soon after the trail starts to descend, look for a slightly smaller path to the west (left). The route continues west for **15 minutes**, offering views of the Río Toachi and arriving at a small, unnamed stream (a good place to collect water).

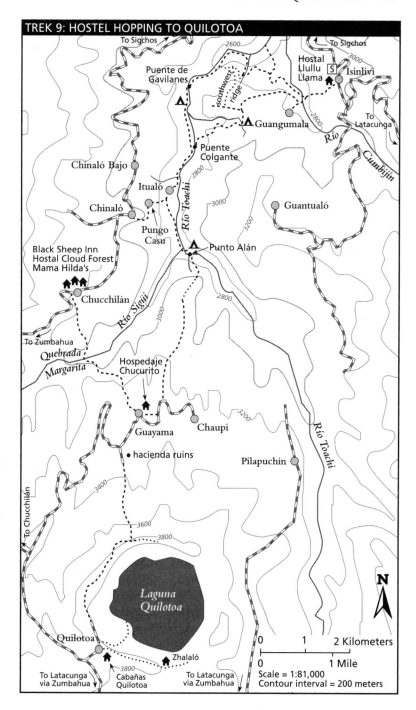

TREK 9: HOSTEL HOPPING TO QUILOTOA

To Sigchos
2600
To Sigchos

Puente de
Gavilanes

Hostal
Llullu
Llama

S Isinlivi

southwest ridge

To Latacunga

Guangumala

Río

Cumbijín

Puente
Colgante

Chinaló Bajo

Itualó

Río Toachi 2800

3000

Chinaló

3200

Guantualó

Pungo
Casu

Punto Alán

Black Sheep Inn
Hostal Cloud Forest
Mama Hilda's

Río Sigüi

2800

Chucchilán

3000

To Zumbahua

Quebrada
Margarita

Hospedaje
Chucurito

3200

Guayama

Chaupi

Río Toachi

hacienda ruins

Pilapuchín

To Chucchilán

3400

3600

3800

Laguna
Quilotoa

N

Quilotoa

3800
Cabañas
Quilotoa

Zhalaló

To Latacunga
via Zumbahua

To Latacunga
via Zumbahua

0   1   2 Kilometers

0   1 Mile

Scale = 1:81,000
Contour interval = 200 meters

Here you have a choice: either descend north into the Toachi Valley along the west side of the small stream, or climb through a sandy chute to the high road to Itualó. Locals usually take the low road, which meets the Río Toachi and continues upstream for 2 kilometers (1.2 miles), arriving at the Puente de Gavilanes (hawks' bridge), a felled eucalyptus tree with a delicate handrail. Cross here and continue upstream on the west side of the Río Toachi to the Puente Colgante (hanging bridge), where the alternative routes join. There are areas suitable for camping all along the Toachi Valley.

The scenic upper route, however, is recommended. After crossing the small, unnamed stream, follow the sandy chute. It climbs steeply; in **20 minutes** you will reach a high volcanic shelf with amazing views of the Toachi Valley. Here again there is a choice of routes. If you are short of time, cut down to the Río Toachi on a path headed west, which disappears a little over half-way down. Pick your way down along the edge of the fields (being careful not to walk through someone's yard). Then follow the Río Toachi upstream to the Puente de Gavilanes.

The best option, if you have the time, is to follow the small ridge that runs south from the volcanic shelf (not shown on the IGM map) to meet a larger ridge that climbs southwest. Follow the ridge top southwest, detouring only to avoid vegetation and cross fences. Eventually a faint path appears, leading south to a canyon rim with a clear trail running east-west along it. Climbing from the volcanic shelf to this point will take **30 minutes**. Take the trail east (left) for **10 minutes** to a major intersection; then take the right fork to descend into the unnamed canyon to the south. In the canyon, you will pass a spring with a trough carved out of the rock, where herdsmen bring their livestock to drink. There are places to camp nearby. To go down, into, and around this canyon takes **25 minutes**. Leaving the canyon, pass over a small ridge gaining new views of the Toachi Valley. In **5 minutes** you will come out on another volcanic shelf and find a small path going west down to the Río Toachi. It takes **30 minutes** to descend to the river; pause to admire the orchids growing on the walls of the sandy chute near the top.

At the Puente Colgante, rejoin the lower route described previously. Cross the bridge and continue upstream **20 minutes** to a tiny bridge crossing the bottom of an eroding gorge. Continue south along the Río

Photographing the Río Toachi Valley (Photo: Kerry Alley)

Toachi for another **5 minutes**, then climb the main path to Itualó. You will arrive at the central square in **15 minutes**. From Itualó you once again have a choice of routes: south direct to Guayama or southwest via Chucchilán, with the best choice of hostels along this trek; in either case you must first go through the center of Itualó.

If you choose to go south, there are good camping spots with water at Punto Alán, **20 minutes** farther up the Río Toachi (near its confluence with the Río Sigüi). Leave Itualó on a path heading toward the river, and use stepping stones to hop across the Río Sigüi. To continue to Guayama from Punto Alán, take a trail that starts by a clearing on the south side of the Toachi (which briefly runs east-west here), upstream from the confluence with the Río Sigüi. The path (not shown on the IGM map) is very faint at first. It switchbacks steeply upwards; take a welcome breather to admire the view of the confluence below, with Itualó and eventually Chucchilán in the background. In about **45 minutes**, you will reach the top and see rolling ridges and an abundance of agriculture. Head southwest cross-country up through a shallow valley for **30 minutes** until you come to a clear trail. Follow this trail south up the ridge for **45 minutes** until you see Guayama to the southwest and then come to an unpaved road. Turn west (right) toward Guayama and take a shortcut across the canyon that separates you from the village. This is a good place to admire the complex structure of the canyon walls.

If you choose to go via Chucchilán, leave Itualó Plaza taking the same path as above, and then the first fork west (right), a well-established trail that switchbacks up to Pungo Casu (30 minutes). At Pungo Casu, turn south (left) and continue 20 minutes to Chinaló, where you will meet an unpaved road. Turn left onto the road. Chucchilán is 30 minutes south. This small town, with both indigenous and mestizo population, is increasingly popular with tourists. The first hostel you reach, The Black Sheep Inn, is about one kilometer (0.6 mile) before town on the right and has an obvious sign. It is an ecologically friendly inn with good facilities and excellent vegetarian food. Phone: (03)814-587. The cost is $15–$18 per person including supper and breakfast. Just before town is Mama Hilda's, with clean rooms, hot water, and a cozy family atmosphere. Phone: (03)814-814; $8–$10 per person including supper and breakfast. Next door is Hostal Cloud Forest. Phone: (03)814-808; $7 per person including supper and breakfast. These hostels can fill up (especially on Saturdays), so try to reserve in advance.

In Chucchilán, continue to the west end of town. About 100 meters (300 feet) beyond the plaza, take a path heading initially south to the upper Río Sigüi (also called Quebrada Margarita), which you will reach in **30 minutes**. A small cement bridge crosses the river here, but getting to it is tricky due to landslides. After the bridge, a **10-minute** climb will bring you to the abrupt canyon wall; a switchback path climbs steeply, bringing you to the top in **30 minutes**. Turn east (left) to reach the Quichua village of Guayama in **20 minutes**. Hospedaje Chucurito (Familia Pilaguano) is beside the church in the middle of the village; this is a very basic, inexpensive establishment.

Continuing south from Guayama to Quilotoa, be careful of territorial dogs. From Guayama head out of the south end of town and continue southwest along the unpaved road for **15 minutes** to a fork. Take the left branch (southeast). In **5 minutes** you will pass an old, ruined hacienda building on the left. The road becomes a path that heads almost directly south up to the rim of Quilotoa's caldera. Aim for the lowest, sandiest part of the rim in front of you. It will take **1.75 hours** to reach the rim, and is thoroughly exhilarating when you at last see the glittering green waters below you. The lake is nearly 300 meters (1000 feet) below, and the caldera walls are lined with sharp outcrops and scree slopes interspersed with potato plants, grazing sheep, and goats.

It is possible to navigate down to the lake from here, but an easier route descends from the village of Quilotoa (where mules can be hired for the way back up). The village is **1 hour** counterclockwise around the rim of the caldera. Take the trail that goes outside the rim. You will lose sight of the lake. Quilotoa is a mainly indigenous village; here are Cabañas Quilotoa, a simple hostel with fireplaces ($7 per person, including supper and breakfast). **Thirty minutes** farther east (counterclockwise around the rim of the caldera) is Zhalaló—a nice restaurant ($8 per meal) with access to the lake and boats for exploring it; cabins are under construction. Quito phone: (02)246-7130.

Getting back: Pick-up trucks can sometimes be hired from Quilotoa village to Zumbahua ($10). Buses bound for Zumbahua and Chucchilán also pass along the main road, a short walk down from the village. You may also be able to hitch a ride for at least part of the way. (There is more traffic on Saturdays.) To walk along the road to Zumbahua (12 kilometers, 7.5 miles) takes about 3 hours. This town has a very interesting Saturday market and many daily buses to Latacunga.

10 ACROSS RUMIÑAHUI

Research by Miguel Cazar
Editorial assistance by Popkje van der Ploeg
Rating: Moderately difficult, 20-kilometer (12.5-mile), 2-day trek.
Elevation: 3000 to 4200 meters (9850 to 13,800 feet).
Maps: IGM 1:50,000: CT-ÑIII-C4 Machachi, CT-ÑIII-D3
Sincholagua. The IGM's *Mapa Ecoturístico del Volcán Cotopaxi* offers a
good overview of the area.
Best time to visit: June through September, and December through
January, are driest.
Special gear: Hiking boots.
Water: Available from streams along the route.
Hazards: Bulls.
Annoyances: None.
Permits and fees: A $10 entry fee is payable at the Cotopaxi National
Park entrance. There is a $3-per-person fee for using the park's camp-
ing area near Limpiopungo.
Services: The closest accommodation to Cotopaxi National Park is located
opposite the main road entrance, 1 kilometer (0.6 mile) west of the Pan-
American Highway. This hostel is called Cuello de Luna. Phone: (09)970-
0330; $17 per person including breakfast. In the park are camping areas
and two run-down shelters south of Limpiopungo. Refugio José Ribas,
Cotopaxi's mountain shelter ($14 per person), is not along this route.
Provisions: Best purchased in Latacunga.

Cotopaxi National Park is the most frequently visited in continental Ecuador. It takes its name from the perfectly cone-shaped snowcapped volcano.
Among the highest active volcanoes in the world (5897 meters, 19,348
feet), its scenic beauty is second to none. Northwest of Cotopaxi and still
within this 33,393-hectare (82,514-acre) national park is Rumiñahui,
another impressive volcano with several rocky peaks, the highest rising to
4722 meters (15,493 feet). A huge ancient eruption destroyed Rumiñahui's
cone, leaving a particularly craggy mountain. Rumiñahui means "stone
face" in Quichua, and is named for the Inca emperor Atahualpa's faithful
general. According to legend, after hiding Atahualpa's treasure in the
Llanganates, Rumiñahui found shelter at the foot of the mountain that
now bears his name, and from here continued his resistance against the
Spanish conquerors (see Trek 15, The Llanganates Experience).

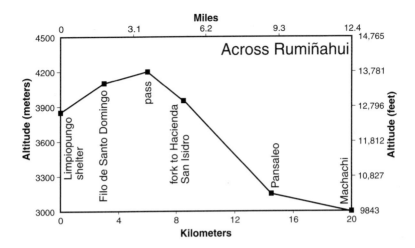

Cotopaxi's most recent eruption took place in 1902; evidence of the area's volcanic origin is everywhere. As you hike you will notice pumice stone, sand, and other volcanic debris. You will also see many typical *páramo* plants such as tussock grass, *chuquiragua*, large daisies growing close to the ground, club mosses, and little yellow flowers with "horns" called *cacho de venado* (deer's antlers). Trees include the polylepis, *quishuar*, and *cholán*. Cotopaxi National Park is also famous for its wildlife; it is home to the White-tailed Deer, Brocket Deer, rabbit, marsupial mouse, Andean Fox, llama, and many wild horses. Bird species include the condor, eagle, and several species of hummingbirds. Laguna de Limpiopungo is a small, shallow lake where you can observe many birds, including the Andean Gull and the Andean Lapwing.

This trek goes from the heart of Cotopaxi National Park, near Limpiopungo, over the southwest shoulder of Rumiñahui and down to the agricultural valley of Machachi. Along the way are magnificent views of Cotopaxi, the twin peaks of Ilinizas, several more distant mountains, and surrounding valleys. Machachi is an important dairy center and home of the *chagra,* the Ecuadorean cowboy. He can be seen riding in sheepskin or leather chaps, known as *zamarras,* and a woolen *poncho.* Ecuador's traditional mineral water, Agua Güitig/Tesalia, also comes from Machachi.

Access: To reach the starting point of the trek near Limpiopungo, take the main entrance to Cotopaxi National Park. This is located on the Pan-American Highway, 20 kilometers (12.5 miles) north of Latacunga and 25 kilometers (15.5 miles) south of Machachi. Pick-up trucks to the Limpiopungo camping area can be hired in Latacunga ($35), Machachi ($25), Lasso ($20), and sometimes right at the highway turnoff ($20). When taking a bus, be sure you do not get on an express between Latacunga and

Quito; it will not stop. Ask to be dropped off at the park entrance or the town of Lasso. It is a 20-kilometer (12.5-mile) drive from the highway turnoff to the Limpiopungo camping area. The ride takes about 40 minutes.

Route: Two kilometers (1.2 miles) past the visitors center and museum, just south of Laguna de Limpiopungo, there is a sign: "Area de Camping." Follow this sign north to reach a basic run-down shelter, with sites suitable for camping nearby. Close to the shelter is a water pipe where you can get water for the first part of the trek. Just beside the water pipe, a small trail heads northwest (the general direction of travel for the entire trek). Follow this trail along the western edge of a small unnamed *quebrada*. After **5 minutes** you will arrive at an irrigation canal. There is a concrete beam where you can cross. Continue in the same direction, following the west side of the *quebrada*; the views of Cotopaxi are magnificent. **Ten minutes** later you will arrive at a plain from where you can see the Rumiñahui massif in front of you. The trail becomes faint here, and you have to traverse the plain cross-country, heading northwest toward Rumiñahui. You will walk through a kind of volcanic desert with very scarce vegetation.

After **20 minutes**, you will arrive at the end of the plain. Descend from here toward the north, until you reach another small trail. In **15 minutes** this leads to the head of Quebrada Huertasacha, where three small gullies come together. Cross the *quebrada* where the branches join, and get water here. Continue northwest toward the ridge called Filo de Santo Domingo. It is a steep **45-minute** climb; zigzagging makes it easier. There are great views of several snowcapped peaks here: Cotopaxi, Sincholagua, and Antisana. A faint trail follows the ridge line; this is one of the access routes for climbing Rumiñahui. Full information is found in *Ecuador: A Climbing Guide* by Yossi Brain.

Our trek continues northwest, along the southwest flank of the ridge. Aim for the headwaters of Quebrada García Aucu. In **1 hour** you will reach some patches of woods at the base of Rumiñahui's cliffs. There are good camping possibilities and small clear streams coming from the mountain. Be sure to take water; it is scarce ahead. You will be just below Rumiñahui and have wonderful views of it. Club mosses, colorful gentians, and other dainty *páramo* flowers liven the landscape.

The route continues southwest, toward a pass between the southernmost of Rumiñahui's peaks (labeled as 4286 meters, 14,062 feet, on the IGM map) and the prominence called García Aucu. Look for a trail here; the climb is a bit difficult because it is steep and you will be walking on soft sand. It takes **30 minutes** to the pass. At 4200 meters (13,780 feet), this is the highest

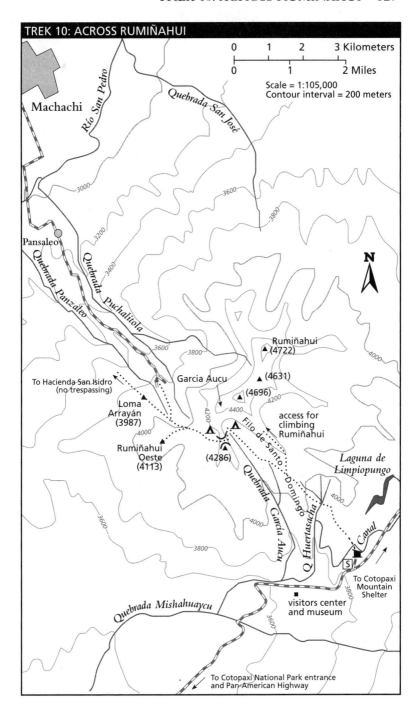

TREK 10: ACROSS RUMIÑAHUI

0   1   2   3 Kilometers

0   1   2 Miles

Scale = 1:105,000
Contour interval = 200 meters

Machachi

Río San Pedro

Quebrada San José

3000

3600

3800

Pansaleo

3200

3400

Quebrada Panzaleo

Quebrada Puchaliiola

N

3600

3800

Rumiñahui
▲ (4722)

▲ (4631)

To Hacienda San Isidro
(no trespassing)

Garcia Aucu

▲ (4696)

4000

Loma
Arrayán
(3987) ▲

4200

4400

4000

4200

access for
climbing
Rumiñahui

Rumiñahui
Oeste
(4113) ▲

▲ (4286)

Filo de Santo Domingo

Quebrada Garcia Aucu

Laguna de
Limpiopungo

4000

3600

4000

Q Huertasacha

Canal

3800

S

To Cotopaxi
Mountain
Shelter

3800

visitors center
and museum

Quebrada Mishahuaycu

3600

To Cotopaxi National Park entrance
and Pan-American Highway

Craggy slopes of Rumiñahui from the northwest

point of the trek, and it can be very windy. You can see the valley of Machachi to the northwest and the mountains of the Cordillera Occidental beyond: the Ilinizas, Corazón, Atacazo, and Pichincha. At your feet is a lovely polylepis forest, and beyond you can discern a clear trail. The first 100 meters (300 feet) of the descent are still sandy, followed by scree. In **10 minutes** you will reach a plateau, then descend to a second plateau **20 minutes** ahead. Here is some flat ground suitable for camping, and a trickle of water.

Traverse the plateau to the northwest and follow the trail you saw from above. In **15 minutes** you will reach a fork. The left branch goes toward Rumiñahui Oeste. Follow the right branch, which soon turns north. You can see Machachi in the distance, with Atacaso as a spectacular backdrop. In another **15 minutes**, take a smaller trail to the right, to reach the ridge between Quebrada Panzaleo and Quebrada Puchalitola. The larger trail on the left continues to Hacienda San Isidro, where trespassing is prohibited. The ridge between Quebrada Panzaleo and Quebrada Puchalitola gradually widens and it is easy to follow cross-country. The views of Rumiñahui's collapsed crater to your right and Ilinizas to the left are spectacular. Continue downhill for **1 hour** to reach a rough dirt road which you will follow north.

You have now left the national park behind and are hiking in a pretty rural area; cattle graze in lush pastures, and there are greenhouses where roses are grown for export. In **2.5 hours** you will arrive in Pansaleo, a small *mestizo* village. Cross the village and then continue following the small unpaved road that goes to Machachi. There might be some pick-up trucks from here, or walk another **1.5 hours** to Machachi. There are several simple hotels and places to eat here.

Getting back: Machachi is located on the Pan-American Highway. There are frequent buses north to Quito ($1) and south to Latacunga ($1).

Chapter 10
TREKS FROM BAÑOS

Altitude, 1800 meters (5900 feet)
Population, 15,000

Baños is the country's most popular highland resort, a favorite of Ecuadoreans and foreign visitors alike. Packed with hotels, restaurants, cafés, and tour agencies, this charming town has something for everyone—from hot springs to hot discos, a venerated basilica and an active volcano. Alongside horseback riding and mountain-biking, trekking is well established in Baños. There are strolls up to the cross at Bellavista, and to the nearby town of Runtún. (Occasional holdups have taken place along these trails.)

Baños has long been a gateway to Oriente. Tour operators here tend to specialize in jungle trips, although some can also organize highland trekking. Competition among the many agencies is fierce, and quality varies. Appendix A lists a few agencies in Baños; you are encouraged to shop around. If possible, try to get a personal recommendation from another visitor who has just returned from a tour. You can also purchase and repair backpacks in Baños; see "Camping Stores" in Appendix A.

The extensive tourist infrastructure, combined with its strategic location between two magnificent national parks (Llanganates to the north and Sangay to the south), makes Baños an ideal base for trekking. Our easy Trek 11, Valley of the Waterfalls, is a good way to start by taking in the grandeur of the Río Pastaza Valley. Following the Pastaza 110 kilometers (70 miles) southeast into the jungle brings us to the site of Trek 12, Cave of the Oilbirds. Moderately difficult and unusual among our hikes, it absolutely requires that you take a guide (an excellent opportunity to experience the native Shuar way of life).

Much closer to Baños on the north side of the Pastaza is Trek 13, the difficult Tapir Trail. Touching on the fabled Llanganates, this route follows trails "bulldozed" by Mountain Tapirs—engineers of the cloud forest. Also close to Baños, on the south side of the Pastaza, Trek 14 is a difficult and beautiful circumnavigation of the Tungurahua Volcano. Trek 15 is the Llanganates Experience, the most difficult in this book. Accessed from Ambato, west of Baños, it delves deep into the harshest and most pristine region of Ecuador's highlands.

|| VALLEY OF THE WATERFALLS

Rating: Easy, 8-kilometer (5-mile) day walk.
Elevation: 1550 to 1800 meters (5100 to 5900 feet).
Map: IGM 1:50,000: CT-ÑIV-D1 Baños (optional).
Best time to visit: November through February are the driest
months, but some rain and fog may occur at any time of the year. July
and August are wettest.
Special gear: None.
Water: Available from streams along the route.
Hazards: The bus ride back to Baños is safest during daylight hours.
Make sure you leave yourself enough time to return before nightfall.
Annoyances: None.
Permits and fees: None.
Services: There are some cabins at San Pedro near the end of the walk,
but they are not always open; there are also cabins at Río Verde and,
farther east, before Machay.
Provisions: Take lunch from Baños. There is a small restaurant at San
Pedro, but its opening hours vary.

The Río Pastaza, one of the great tributaries of the Amazon, has its source
at the confluence of the Patate and the Chambo Rivers, just west of
Baños. From here it hurtles east, cutting a deep gorge between the mountains. Along the way dozens of waterfalls tumble into the abyss from the
north and south rims of the canyon. The region has also been shaped

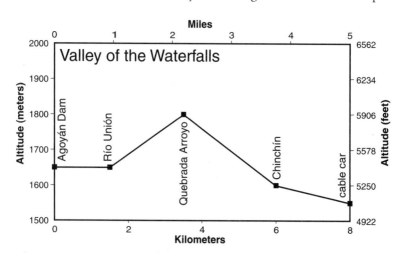

over the centuries by the volcanic activity of Tungurahua. Ancient lava flows and cataclysmic landslides have created unexpectedly flat platforms perched high above the rushing river.

This trek follows the southern rim of the Pastaza canyon east of Baños. It goes by some orchards and rural communities, as well as small patches of forest. Many colorful flowers dot the landscape: bright impatiens, hibiscus, hydrangeas, and daisies. Between February and May, magnificent magenta and white Sobralia orchids are everywhere. Fruit trees include tangerine, guava, and avocado; many ferns and tall grasses complete the scene. This is also a very good area for bird-watching. The more common species include Blue-and-white Swallows performing their aerobatics by the cliffsides, Green or Inca Jays, Blue-gray Tanagers, Mountain Caciques, and a variety of hummingbirds.

The views of the Pastaza canyon and waterfalls are awe-inspiring, yet this route is easily accessible. The walk ends with a breathtaking crossing of the Río Pastaza on a motorized *tarabita*, a primitive cable car that spans 400 meters (1300 feet), 150 meters (500 feet) above the river. If this is not for you, or you wish to finish sooner, you can end the walk at a pedestrian suspension bridge by the Manto de la Novia Waterfall (another spectacular crossing).

Access: The trailhead is on the Baños–Puyo Road, 4.5 kilometers (2.8 miles) east of Baños, just past the Agoyán Dam, where the paved road crosses the Río Pastaza on a large concrete bridge. Baños city buses marked *Túneles* leave from the corner of Eloy Alfaro and Luis A. Martínez every 20 minutes, between 0600 and 1800. The ride to the bridge takes 20 minutes and costs $.20.

Route: A good trail starts at the south (Baños) end of the bridge. It climbs at first, then contours and undulates, heading east along the southern bank of the Río Pastaza. Below you, the rocky riverbed is likely to be dry, as the water has been diverted to the Agoyán generating station. The trail is surrounded by colorful flowers; in **30 minutes** it reaches a fork, and the right branch climbs south along a ridge above the Ríos Unión or Guamba. Follow the left branch, which continues east along the Pastaza Valley; ahead where the canyon narrows are citrus orchards and some rural dwellings. **Five minutes** ahead, the trail crosses the Río Unión on a small log bridge. After crossing the river, do not take the first two clear trails (not shown on our map), which lead to private property. Instead, continue up-river along the rocks and take the third trail, which climbs east out of the Río Union Valley to a very flat plateau with citrus orchards and some houses. The trail passes to the south of these farms and crosses a small, unnamed stream **15 minutes** past the Río Unión. This area can get quite muddy.

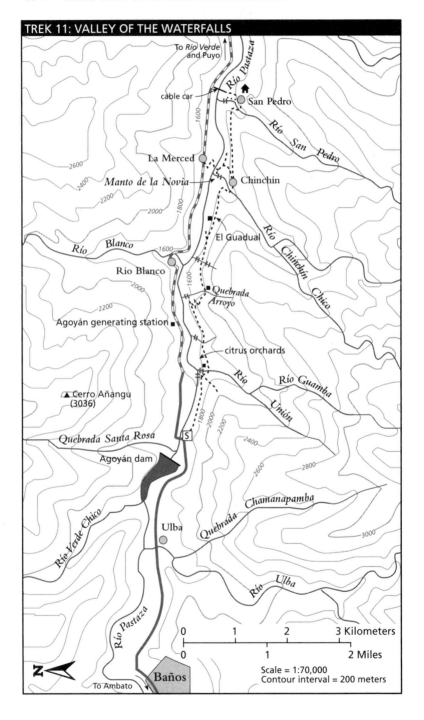

TREK 11: VALLEY OF THE WATERFALLS

To *Río Verde* and Puyo

Río Pastaza

cable car

San Pedro

Río San Pedro

La Merced

Manto de la Novia

Chinchín

El Guadual

Río Chinchín Chico

Río Blanco

Río Blanco

Quebrada Arroyo

Agoyán generating station

citrus orchards

Río Unión

Río Guamba

▲ Cerro Añangu (3036)

Quebrada Santa Rosa

Agoyán dam

Río Verde Chico

Ulba

Quebrada Chamanapamba

Río Ulba

Río Pastaza

Baños

To Ambato

| 0 | 1 | 2 | 3 Kilometers |

| 0 | 1 | 2 Miles |

Scale = 1:70,000
Contour interval = 200 meters

From here the route passes the base of steep cliffs on your right. Watch your step in this section, but also keep an eye out for small, purple *flor de Cristo* orchids on the rocks. In **15 minutes** the trail emerges at a pasture and begins to climb steadily, zigzagging up a steep slope. Before you reach the highest point on the trail, you will feel a brisk wind in your face and you may see the fog being propelled up the Pastaza Valley. To the west are nice views of the valley descending from Baños, and across the river is the Agoyán generating station, where the muddy brown waters of the Río Pastaza return to their course.

From here, the trail levels off and soon reaches Quebrada Arroyo, **30 minutes** from the start of the climb. Cross the stream and look for a small, muddy downhill trail (instead of following the main trail, which climbs and goes right through a house perched on the hill). Skirt around below the house, then regain the main trail. Gradually descend through a series of pastures separated by gullies with increasingly lush vegetation, including some nice tree ferns. On the opposite bank of the deep Pastaza gorge, toy cars and trucks snake their way along the narrow Baños–Puyo Road, precariously perched on the steep cliffside. In **15 minutes**, the village of Río Blanco and the river of the same name (a white ribbon of water dropping into the muddy Pastaza) come into sight on the north side of the valley. **Ten minutes** ahead, you will cross a small, unnamed stream that comes from a waterfall in the cliffs above.

The trail now descends, and shortly there is a fork. Take the right branch, which goes above the pasture into an area with more greenery. Notice how the vegetation is gradually changing; there are now more broad leaves and vines. The trail undulates through the forest; in **30 minutes** it emerges at another flat balcony over the Pastaza, with a few farms. This spot is known as El Guadual, after a small stand of *caña guadúa* (a large bamboo), which grows just east of the farms. In addition to citrus, the crops now include bananas and sugar cane. The trail continues to undulate through the vegetation, gradually descending; in the distance to the east, you can see a suspension bridge across the Río Pastaza. In **20 minutes** you will reach a fork. Take the right branch, which turns south and drops to the Río Chinchín Chico. Cross the river on a small bridge and climb out of the river valley. You will soon see a larger trail; take it downstream (to the northeast) toward the village of Chinchín, **15 minutes** away.

Chinchín is the access to the magnificent Manto de la Novia (Bridal Veil) Waterfall and to the pedestrian suspension bridge across the Río Pastaza. To access these, take the left-hand trail at the soccer field, just past the school. This wide trail, surrounded by colorful impatiens, zigzags down to the swing bridge in **20 minutes**. Before reaching the bridge it meets another trail going east, parallel to the river. To get to the base of the falls, continue west past the bridge for **5 minutes**. (It is quite muddy here.) There are great views of the falls from the bridge and also from the trail on the north shore of the Río Pastaza. The climb to the hamlet of La Merced on the Baños–Puyo Road takes **20 minutes**.

To continue along the south shore of the Pastaza, climb back to Chinchín (**30 minutes**). (The lower trail mentioned previously is overgrown and becomes impassable.) From Chinchín, take the right-hand trail from the east end of the soccer field. It again goes through undulating country with a few crops and a little forest. You will reach the village of San Pedro in **45 minutes**. There is a restaurant to the left of the trail, from which you can go down a rough side trail to a waterfall on the Río San Pedro in **10 minutes**. There are also some cabins to the right of the trail, but these are not always open. From San Pedro, follow the trail that turns north; it will lead you in **10 minutes** to the *tarabita*. It is a wonderful ride across the Pastaza, with views of the San Pedro Waterfall and the Pastaza below. The little cable car is powered by a modified truck engine ($.50 one way; open 0800 to 1800). It takes you to the Baños–Puyo Road.

The plethora of waterfalls continues down river; the best known is the Pailón del Diablo, accessed from Río Verde, 3 kilometers (1.9 miles) east of the *tarabita*. Another 2.5 kilometers (1.6 miles) beyond is Machay, with several more nice cascades.

Getting back: There is frequent bus service on the Baños–Puyo Road. Buses will pick you up either by the *tarabita* or at La Merced. From the *tarabita*, it takes 30 minutes to Baños and costs $.25. Remember to return to Baños by daylight, and try to sit on the left side of the bus to admire the cliffs above which you have just walked.

Robert crossing the Río Pastaza in a motorized tarabita

12 CAVE OF THE OILBIRDS

Research by Luís and Elisabeth Reyes
Editorial assistance by Popkje van der Ploeg

Rating: Moderately difficult, 17-kilometer (10.5-mile), 2- to 3-day trek, including the cave visit and a full-day guided walk in the jungle (not shown on our map).

Elevation: 650 to 800 meters (2150 to 2600 feet).

Map: IGM 1:50,000: CT-OIV-E3 Nueva Huamboya (Veinticuatro de Mayo), optional.

Best time to visit: February through April are generally driest, but there can be heavy rain at any time of the year.

Special gear: Rubber boots are indispensable, as are a mosquito net and insect repellent. Take three different light sources into the cave: a headlamp, a flashlight, and candles, as well as extra batteries, a lighter, and matches. A 10-meter (30-foot) length of rope is helpful for climbing to the higher level of the cave. A hammock may be useful for sleeping at the Mukucham home.

Water: There are several small streams along the route.

Hazards: The greatest hazard is flash flooding of the Río Tayuntza, the river that runs through the cave. Navigation in the rainforest is very difficult, and taking a local guide is imperative for this trek. Poisonous snakes are also a hazard.

Annoyances: Mosquitoes, sand flies, mud.

Permits and fees: The cave is on the property of the Mukucham family. They charge an entrance fee of $5 per person.

Services: You can sleep in one of the traditional Shuar huts of the Mukucham family ($1 per person per night, bedding not provided). Meals are not provided either, but you can purchase manioc and plantain. Near the trailhead, at the Shuar community of Centro Consuelo (also called La Punta), there are small food stalls where you can buy simple meals. Cristóbal Mukucham, a local guide, charges $8 per day to take a small group to the cave or through the forest.

Provisions: Puyo and Macas are both well-supplied jungle cities with a full range of services. At Centro Consuelo, you will find only the most basic provisions.

The Amazon jungle hides many secrets which the rainforest people are, at times, willing to share with visitors. Among these is the Cueva de los

Tayos, Cave of the Oilbirds, the highlight of this trek. The Oilbird, locally known as *tayo* or *guácharo*, is a large nocturnal bird that lives in colonies of several hundred. Oilbirds leave their caves only at night, in search of palm and other fruits. Their ability to echolocate inside the dark caves is common among bats, but unique to this species of bird. The high fat content of the fruits they eat makes Oilbird chicks very fatty, hence their name.

Several caves in the Ecuadorean Oriente are called Cueva de los Tayos. This one is located in tropical rainforest halfway between Puyo and Macas, close to the Río Pastaza, an important tributary of the Amazon. Although many regions of the Ecuadorean Amazon have been deforested, this area still boasts primary rainforest within easy access of a main road. The abundant vegetation includes huge trees, vines, heliconias with their bright flowers, and epiphytes such as bromeliads. Among the animals

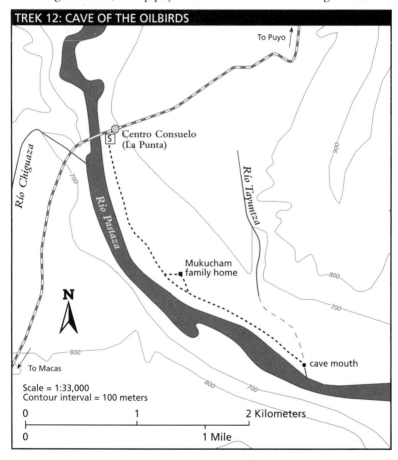

TREK 12: CAVE OF THE OILBIRDS

To Puyo

Centro Consuelo
(La Punta)

Río Chiguaza

Río Pastaza

Río Tayuntza

Mukucham
family home

N

To Macas

cave mouth

Scale = 1:33,000
Contour interval = 100 meters

0   1   2 Kilometers

0   1 Mile

that live in this area are monkeys, sloths, anteaters, armadillos, parrots, and toucans. The chances of seeing many animals on your trek are pretty low, but you will hear the birds and see some footprints. You can also observe many insects, including beautiful butterflies and colorful centipedes.

The area south of Puyo is home to the Shuar people, still known for their former tradition of shrinking the heads of their enemies. This custom has not been practiced for the past two generations, but the Shuar continue to take their territorial rights very seriously. Any visit to their land must be arranged under their auspices. If you visit an indigenous family, they will expect you either to share your meals with them or to bring gifts (even though you are already paying for accommodation and guiding). The Cueva de los Tayos is on the land of the Mukucham family, some thirty strong. The older members speak no Spanish, only Shuar. The cross-cultural exchange is as interesting as the cave and forest.

Access: The trek starts at Centro Consuelo (La Punta), halfway between the cities of Puyo and Macas. Here is a large and spectacular suspension bridge over the Río Pastaza. There are a few buses a day from Baños to Macas, and many more that go only as far as Puyo. From Puyo you can take a Macas-bound bus: 2.5 hours to the bridge, $2.25, several departures throughout the day. Buses cannot cross the suspension bridge, so all passengers alight here anyway, walk across, and continue their journey on vehicles that wait on the other side.

Route: At Centro Consuelo, on the east (Puyo) side of the Río Pastaza, 30 meters (100 feet) before the bridge, a wide trail heads southeast, parallel to the shore of the great river. You will go by a couple of houses and in **15 minutes** arrive at a spot with construction materials for a new bridge that one day will replace the current suspension bridge. Continue southeast; after **30 minutes** the trail gets narrower and more muddy. Continue to follow the course of the Río Pastaza through secondary rainforest with a predominance of bamboo and heliconia. (You cannot see the river all the time, but you will certainly hear it.)

After **1.25 hours** you will reach a fork where one trail continues south, following the Río Pastaza, and another goes east to the home of the Mukucham family. Follow the east trail (to your left) for **30 minutes**. Along the way you will pass small agricultural plots growing manioc, papaya, and corn. Once you arrive at the Mukucham home, ask for Cristóbal, the eldest son. He speaks Spanish and can guide you not only to the Cave of the Oilbirds, but also in the surrounding rainforest. (You should not go alone to either.)

From the Mukucham home, once again follow the shores of the Río Pastaza southeast. There are nice views of the wide river and forest along the banks. Most of the time you will walk on sand and stones. After **2 hours** climb to the east, toward some big rocks to your left. It takes **10 minutes** to cross these rocks and arrive at the mouth of the cave.

The cave is spacious, 3 meters (10 feet) across and 4–5 meters (13–16 feet) high. In it flows the Río Tayuntza (1.5 meters, 5 feet wide), which comes from the north and empties into the Río Pastaza. You will first descend into the cave on stones, but later the footing is solid rock. Soon you will notice the noisy presence of the Oilbirds. They communicate by a screaming call that sounds like a saw. They also emit clicks for echolocation. When intruders interrupt the normal silence in the cave, the birds fly in circles and then return to their roosts. The Oilbirds are inoffensive; try not to disturb them.

You can follow the river inside the cave for about 1 kilometer (0.6 mile), walking upstream in the water. The water level varies: it is often about knee high, but there are some pools where it gets deeper. After **1.25 hours** you will begin to hear the sound of a small waterfall. If you want to see it, you will either have to continue in the river (the water is quite deep at the base of the falls; it may reach your neck) or have the guide fix a rope and climb to a second level of the cave (2 meters or 6.5 feet up). After passing the waterfall you can continue for **15 minutes** more, until you reach a big rock that blocks the cave. Return the same way you came.

Getting back: From the Mukucham family home, follow the trail you came on, back to Centro Consuelo. There you can catch a bus to Puyo or Macas.

Mukucham family in front of their home (Photo: Luís Reyes)

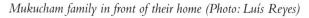

13 TAPIR TRAIL

Rating: Difficult, 14-kilometer (8.7-mile), 3- to 4-day trek.
Elevation: 2200 to 3700 meters (7200 to 12,140 feet).
Maps: IGM 1:50,000: CT-ÑIV-B3 Sucre, CT-ÑIV-D1 Baños; IGM
1:25,000: CT-ÑIV-B3d Los Llanganates. Note that, as elsewhere in the
Llanganates, some topographic features do not appear on these maps.
Best time to visit: October to March are the driest months; April to
September are usually very wet.
Special gear: A machete or pruning shears may be useful, as well as a
fishing rod.
Water: Available on route.
Hazards: Navigation on this route is difficult, especially in poor weather.
Annoyances: Mud; biting insects, especially sand flies.
Permits and fees: In principle, foreign visitors pay a $5 fee to
Llanganates National Park, but there are no collection facilities on this
route.
Services: Local guides and porters are usually available in El Triunfo;
pack animals are not suitable for this route. There are no accommoda-
tions in El Triunfo or Viscaya, but you can ask for permission to stay at
the school or to camp nearby.
Provisions: Baños is the most convenient place to shop. Only basic
supplies are available in El Triunfo and Viscaya.

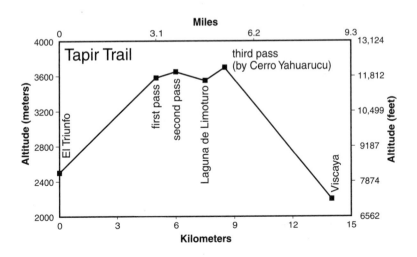

Many of the trails in the cloud forest were originally made by the Mountain Tapir (see sidebar at the end of this trek description), rather than by man. In areas of little human traffic, it is easy to be fooled and mistakenly take a tapir trail; you will notice when it dead-ends at a cozy home under a tree. In higher areas with dense scrub forest, tapir trails are true tunnels traveling long distances through the thick vegetation. Parts of this trek follow tapir trails, some of which are relatively untouched. If you are taller than a tapir (and most adults are), then be prepared to take off your pack and crawl under the branches. Once you are there, do not miss the opportunity to admire the abundance of life around you: mushrooms, orchids, ferns, and mosses, as well as countless insects making their way from one leaf to the next.

The valley of the crystal-clear Río Verde Chico, with easy access from Baños, is the setting for this trek. It touches on the southernmost reaches of Llanganates National Park (see Trek 15, The Llanganates Experience). The hike starts at the village of El Triunfo and follows Quebrada de Plata (one of the tributaries of the Río Verde Chico) up to its headwaters in the Cordillera de Los Llanganates (part of the Cordillera Oriental). The route then traverses an area of páramo to reach a pretty lake known as Laguna de Limoturo or Laguna de Viscaya. The descent is along Quebrada de Valencia, another tributary of the Río Verde Chico, through more beautiful *páramo,* scrub, and cloud forest, to arrive at the village of Viscaya. Although there is a good deal of logging in this area, some lovely forest remains. If you wish to do a trek with less navigational challenge, then you can climb to the lake from Viscaya and return the same way.

Access: One daily bus (around midday) and a few pick-up trucks in the morning leave Baños for the 22-kilometer (14-mile) trip to El Triunfo (1 hour, $.75). They stop along the main Baños–Puyo Road, just east of the bus terminal. Ask around, as the schedule varies from day to day.

Route: In El Triunfo take the street going east past the church; in **5 minutes** it climbs to the high school. Cross the schoolyard and continue **5 minutes** beyond it, east along a wide trail to the south shore of Quebrada de Plata. A good trail climbs gradually from here, through secondary forest along the south shore of the river. In **20 minutes** it crosses to the north shore, where it climbs steeply before leveling off to follow the north shore for **15 minutes.** Then it crosses back to the south shore. Just beyond the second crossing, a small trail branches off to the left and leads immediately to a pretty waterfall. The main trail continues climbing and in the course of the next **15 minutes** crosses the river four more times, so you end up back on the south shore. **Ten minutes** beyond, you will

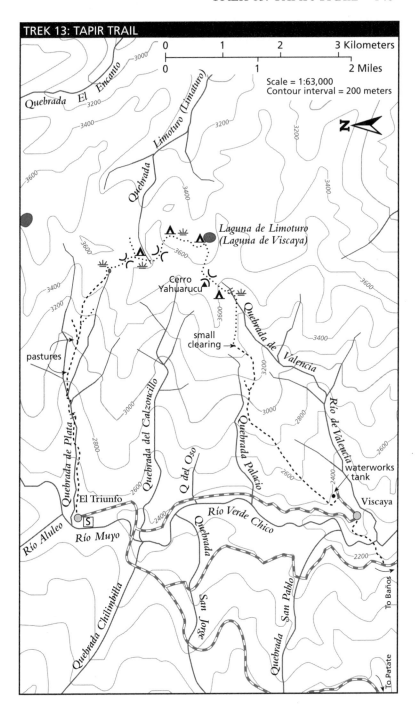

TREK 13: TAPIR TRAIL

0   1   2   3 Kilometers

0   1   2 Miles

Scale = 1:63,000
Contour interval = 200 meters

Quebrada El Encanto

Quebrada Limoturo (Limoturo)

Laguna de Limoturo
(Laguna de Viscaya)

Cerro Yahuarucu

small clearing

pastures

Quebrada de Valencia

Quebrada del Calzoncillo

Quebrada de Plata

Quebrada Palacio

Río de Valencia

waterworks tank

El Triunfo

Q del Oso

Viscaya

Río Aluleo

Río Muyo

Río Verde Chico

Quebrada Chilimbilla

Quebrada San Jorge

San Jorge

Quebrada San Pablo

To Baños

To Patate

reach the junction of two main branches of the river; this spot is locally known as La Y. Take water here for the climb ahead.

From the junction of the rivers the trail climbs more steeply east along a ridge, through secondary forest; there are many orchids and birds. A few small clearings along the way offer good views back to the valley of El Triunfo. In **5 minutes** you will reach a pasture and, **1 hour** later, a larger one. The trail splits here; take the right branch, which continues to climb east along the ridge line. In **15 minutes** a small trail branches off to the right; continue straight along the main trail following the ridge line east. The route then turns southeast along the southern flank of the ridge, climbing steadily through nice cloud forest and later scrub. You will reach a flat spot at 3450 meters (11,300 feet) in **1.5 hours**. The trail ends here.

Just beyond is a very small pond surrounded by a swampy plain (one of the sources of the Río de Plata). Go clockwise around the pond, then cross the plain southeast and look for a small trail in the scrub (the first tapir trail). Head southeast through the forest for **45 minutes**, to a saddle at 3580 meters (11,746 feet). A faint trail drops from the saddle, south to a large boggy plain (**20 minutes**). There is flat ground for camping here and a small stream at the south end of the plain. A faint trail continues northeast along the edge of the bog and then down toward the upper Quebrada Limoturo (Limaturo on the IGM map), the headwaters of the Río Verde Grande—but this is not our route.

Follow the west edge of the bog south; in **10 minutes** you will reach the small stream mentioned above. Cross it and head southeast to the edge of the bog. Look for a tapir trail that climbs south and then southeast along a small forested ridge, **10 minutes** away. (If you reach an open grassy slope in just a few minutes, then you have gone too far west.) The tapir trail climbs steeply through thick forest and in **40 minutes** reaches a very small grassy clearing. Continue climbing (and crawling) through the forest; in **1 hour** you will suddenly emerge from the brush to an open saddle at 3650 meters (11,976 feet). A faint trail descends east and then southeast from the saddle, traveling through straw and *sigses*. In **20 minutes** it ducks back into brushy forest, still headed southeast, and becomes steep and muddy. In **45 minutes** it emerges from the bush onto a small bog. Watch your step here; it is very swampy. There is some slightly higher ground suitable for camping on the north side of the bog. A small stream to the east is difficult to access for water.

Continue south over the bog toward a low, wooded east-west ridge (**20 minutes**). You will cross this ridge as you travel south. There are some tiny deer trails here, but no one clear tapir trail (where is he when you most need him!)—so bashing through the brush is unavoidable. On the far side of the ridge, only a couple of hundred meters (but **1 to 1.5 hours**) away, is an open, grassy slope. Climb this slope gradually southwest, then turn southeast at the base of a low hill. You will reach Laguna de Limoturo in **20 minutes**. This is a very pretty lake surrounded by low, forested hills. There are nice camping spots along the edge, trout in the lake, and (unfortunately) some trash.

From the west shore of the lake, look for a trail climbing west through the tussock grass. This is at last a little easier to follow (except in the fog). When you reach the first small bog, skirt it on the right. After **20 minutes** the trail climbs more steeply, zigzagging to reach a straw-covered plain in another **15 minutes**. This area has been trampled, and the trail is lost; look a bit south to find another good trail amid the tall grass. It climbs steeply southwest and in **30 minutes** reaches a pass at 3700 meters (12,140 feet), southeast of Cerro Yahuarucu.

From the pass, a steep muddy trail descends southwest to a small

Waterfall in Quebrada de Plata

boggy plain overlooking the headwaters of Quebrada de Valencia (**45 minutes**). This is a lovely spot suitable for camping. The views are magnificent: southwest to Tungurahua Volcano and the wide Río Patate Valley, and southeast to the forested cliffs and irregular summits of the range you have just crossed. The trail continues to drop steeply southwest; soon it enters nice forest, then crosses the Quebrada de Valencia stream just below a pretty waterfall. (If you are following the route in the opposite direction, look for this waterfall; it will help you find the trail headed up to the pass.) Going downhill, the trail emerges at a much larger plain (also boggy) **30 minutes** ahead. Here it becomes indistinct and meanders west for **25 minutes** over the soggy *páramo*.

Just before the stream of Quebrada de Valencia plunges vertically southwest off the end of the plain, the trail crosses it and soon enters the forest on your right. It climbs gradually west and then contours west on the slope north of Quebrada de Valencia. There are some fallen trees and lots of huge grass to contend with along the way, but the forest—with its tall trees richly laden with moss and epiphytes—is especially beautiful. In **1.5 hours** you will reach a small clearing on the ridge line separating Quebrada de Valencia from Quebrada Palacio. A well-defined trail now descends southwest through the more open forest. You greet it with mixed feelings: happy for the improved path, but sad to leave behind the realm of the Mountain Tapir.

In **1 hour** a large trail branches off to the north; continue traveling west. (If you are going in the opposite direction—up to the lake—be sure to take the less-obvious branch east here.) From here down, the trail gets even wider and very muddy. Several large parallel branches descend in ever-deeper mud. In **30 minutes** the trail veers southwest, and you will see more and more evidence of logging and human destruction. In **45 minutes** of steady descent, you will reach the first pastures and have nice views southwest to Tungurahua and the Río de Valencia, headed for its junction with the Río Verde Chico. It is another **1.5 hours** down to Viscaya, with more lovely views along the way. After crossing a small stream, the trail emerges by a cement waterworks tank. Here it meets a dirt road; follow the road right, **5 minutes** to the center of Viscaya.

Getting back: In addition to occasional pick-up trucks, there is one early-morning bus from Viscaya to Baños (1.5 hours, $1). Or, in 45 minutes you can walk from Viscaya to cross the Río Verde Chico at a pedestrian bridge and up to the Baños–El Triunfo Road. Here you can catch the vehicles that run more frequently from El Triunfo to Baños (30 minutes, $.50).

THE MOUNTAIN TAPIR *by Craig C. Downer*

Among the many wonders of the Andean cloud forest is the Mountain Tapir, a mammal usually found at elevations above 2000 meters (6500 feet). Also known as the Andean tapir, this herbivore is one of four species of tapirs that exist today. (Three make their homes in Latin America.) Tapirs have a long history and have changed little since the days of their ancestors, 30 million years ago. Their closest modern relatives are the horse and the rhinoceros. One characteristic of tapirs that may have contributed to survival of the species is their prehensile snout—a miniature "elephant's trunk" used for foraging, spraying water, and perceiving predators. Their diet consists of a variety of trees, shrubs, ferns, epiphytes, grasses, and fruits.

Mountain Tapirs are stout and very strong: an average adult weighs 150 kilograms (330 pounds) and stands 90 centimeters (35 inches) high at the shoulder. They have a coat of soft, thick, dark brown or black fur (well-adapted for cold temperatures) with white around their lips and ears. The young also have white spots and lines on their bodies for camouflage. Mountain Tapirs are excellent climbers and traverse the most vertical and entangled patches of forest. They can also be seen in *páramos* (where they go in the dry season) and have even been spotted in snowfields above 4000 meters (13,000 feet).

The number of Mountain Tapirs has shrunk drastically in recent years. Estimates suggest there are probably fewer than 2500 left in Colombia, Ecuador, and northern Peru. The Mountain Tapir's home, the middle to high northern Andean cloud forests and *páramos* of South America, is among the world's most threatened ecosystems. Additionally, tapirs are hunted for their meat, fur, hooves, and snout; the last two are used as folk remedies.

It is not easy to spot a Mountain Tapir in the wild. You need binoculars and experience—or plenty of luck. Their characteristic large three-toed prints are simpler to find, as is their dung (similar to horse dung, but bigger) and the unique tunnels they bulldoze through thick vegetation.

14 AROUND TUNGURAHUA

Rating: Difficult, 25-kilometer (15.5-mile), 4- to 5-day trek.
Elevation: 1700 to 3700 meters (5600 to 12,100 feet).
Maps: IGM 1:50,000: CT-ÑIV-D1 Baños, CT-ÑIV-D3 Palitahua;
IGM 1:25,000: CT-ÑIV-D1c Volcán Tungurahua.
Best time to visit: December through February are the driest
months, June through August the wettest (when rain can be constant
and the mud very deep).
Special gear: A 20-meter (60-foot) length of rope is recommended
for lowering packs over small ledges during the steep descent. A fishing
rod and machete or pruning shears are optional. If Tungurahua is active
but the route is safe, take a small disposable mask to protect your
mouth and nose from volcanic ash.
Water: Abundant year-round throughout the route, except for the
ridge-line descent.
Hazards: Volcanic activity can make this route dangerous or block
access to the trailhead at Palitahua. In June 2001, after this trek was
researched, there were landslides in the area above San Antonio. Inquire
locally before undertaking the trek.
Annoyances: Sand flies and ticks; take repellent.
Permits and fees: In principle, foreign visitors pay a $10 fee to Sangay
National Park, but there are no facilities for collecting the fee along
this route.
Services: None.
Provisions: Baños and Riobamba have well-stocked shops with a
variety of provisions.

Tungurahua is an active volcano with a small glacier near the summit. Its
most recent period of activity began in October 1999, following an 80-
year lull. Tungurahua's perfect cone rises to 5023 meters (16,480 feet)
above sea level, within sight of Baños. The eastern slopes of the volcano
are part of Sangay National Park and boast a variety of landscapes and
ecosystems, ranging from bare black volcanic sand, through austere *páramo*,
to lush cloud forest.

Large ridges radiate out from the volcanic cone, and the intervening
valleys are drained by a complex system of rivers. This convoluted topography is interspersed with expanses of flat *páramo*, the site of several lakes

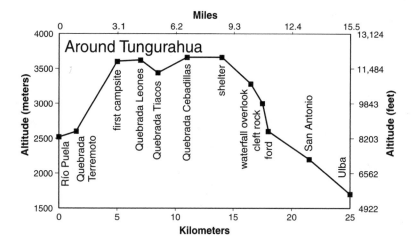

and ponds. To the south of Tungurahua lies another colossus, El Altar. Its multiple glaciated peaks reach 5320 meters (17,455 feet), while the thickly forested curtain of the Cordillera de Las Flautas forms the eastern geographical boundary of the area. To the north lies the deep canyon of the Río Pastaza, and to the west its tributary, the Río Chambo. The entire watershed drains east to the Amazon.

This trek circumnavigates Tungurahua counterclockwise from the southwest to the northeast, passing between it and El Altar. With at least one of the mountains frequently in sight, the views in good weather are stunning. Tungurahua will be a constant companion over your left shoulder. The region's forests are filled with polylepis trees, some of which have grown to an enormous size. They seem enchanted (and are certainly enchanting), with their long beards of moss harboring many bromeliads and orchids. Animals include many birds (condors may sometimes be seen), rabbits, Andean Fox, deer, and Mountain Tapir. There are trout in Laguna Minsas.

Access: You can hire a pick-up truck in the main plaza of Baños to take you to the Palitahua thermal baths, a well-known local landmark (1 hour, $10, but see "Hazards" above). There is no public transport along this route and no traffic for hitchhiking. From Riobamba, Cooperativa Bayushig buses run from the Terminal de Baños (corner Espejo and Cordovez) to Palitahua village (45 minutes, $1). You must then walk an additional 3 kilometers (1.9 miles) to the trailhead.

Route: Beginning at the bridge over the Río Puela (the access point for the thermal baths), follow a good dirt track along the north shore of the river. Note that this is not the same trail that leads to the baths; the latter is cobbled and climbs steeply to the north. **One hour** of gentle climbing will bring you to the Quebrada Terremoto, a reliable water source where you can tank up for the thirsty slog ahead. **Fifteen minutes** farther are some farm buildings and a fork marked by a homemade sign, *"prohibido pescar en la naranja"* (fishing prohibited at la naranja). Take the left branch.

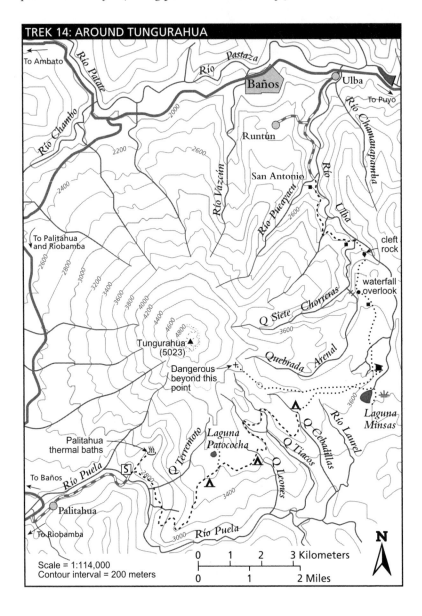

TREK 14: AROUND TUNGURAHUA

Scale = 1:114,000
Contour interval = 200 meters

The trail continues to ascend, at first zigzagging gradually through a fragrant stand of eucalyptus, then becoming steeper and continuing up a slope of mixed woods and pasture. After **45 minutes**, you will reach a second fork by a small stream. Go right. Still climbing hard, the trail now emerges into open pastures offering fine views over the Río Puela Valley, with its many spectacular waterfalls.

More steady climbing brings you to a tunnel of overhanging vegetation, **1.5 hours** past the second fork. Just beyond this tunnel is a third fork; follow the left branch north, alongside a large open pasture. Another **1.5 hours** over a more gentle grade, through a patch of lush cloud forest that slowly dwindles to bushes and tussock grass, lead to several potential campsites around 3500 meters (11,500 feet). There is a small stream for water here, just west of the main trail.

Half an hour farther uphill is another fork (easy to miss because of the thick, low bushes). The left branch climbs to Laguna Patococha, a pretty pond at 3660 meters (12,000 feet) with a few ducks and superb views of Tungurahua. It makes a nice 1-hour side trip, but the area is not recommended for camping because it can be windswept and muddy (and the shallow pond water is dirty).

Our trek continues along the right branch, soon reaches a minor fork (keep right), and climbs for **30 minutes** to an open ridge top with fine views of the Cordillera de las Flautas, the plains and valleys below. Descending gradually, in **15 minutes** you will reach another fork. Take the right branch, and **15 minutes** ahead the trail reaches Quebrada Leones. You will find water and good camping opportunities on either side of the stream.

For the next **30 minutes**, the trail contours through low brush, crossing two more small streams, before descending to yet another fork. Take the left branch. The route climbs hard for **30 minutes** and then plunges steeply into the canyon of the Quebrada Tiacos. This slope is clad in pristine polylepis forest, thick with moss; occasionally you will glimpse the valley floor far below, as well as Tungurahua towering overhead. The steep descent to a tributary of Quebrada Tiacos takes **1 hour**. After crossing this stream, the trail climbs briefly and then drops to the bottom of the main *quebrada*, requiring another **15 minutes**. All of the surrounding slopes are too steep for camping.

From the bottom of Quebrada Tiacos (best take water here), the track climbs for **1 hour** through more steep, forested slopes before emerging onto flat, open country. Here the scenery begins to change, as the boggy *páramo* is covered only in cushion plants adorned with tiny bright flowers. There are several small ponds, and it can be very muddy in the wet season. **One hour** past the east rim of Quebrada Tiacos, the trail crosses the shallow Quebrada Cebadillas—little more than a stream meandering over the moorland. Camping is possible here.

From Quebrada Cebadillas the trail climbs gently and becomes less distinct. After passing north of the headwaters of the Río Laurel (visible below you, to your right), it disintegrates into multiple cattle tracks. One such track, heading west, climbs a high ridge and is a good option for a side trip (see details below). To continue on our route, follow a compass bearing east here through undulating *páramo* until you can see the large Laguna Minsas below (**45 minutes** past Quebrada Cebadillas).

From the high ground, you should be able to see both the lake and a small shelter with a tin roof, 1 kilometer (0.6 mile) north of Laguna Minsas. Small tracks go over a low ridge and down toward the lake, the surroundings of which are too boggy for camping. Along the main route, another **30 minutes** of cross-country travel to the northeast will bring you to the shelter. A clear trail appears only after the little wooden building is well in sight. There is a small side trail from the shelter to a nearby gully (the water supply).

The shelter, situated at the edge of a forested ridge, offers only a dirt floor, four walls, and a roof—but there is plenty of ground for camping nearby. This spot makes a good base for side trips. (Even in this remote area, it is best not to leave your gear unattended.)

You can make a short and easy side trip back to Laguna Minsas. Follow the main trail southwest from the shelter, then east over a low ridge (30 minutes each way). Many small trails crisscross the boggy surroundings; you can watch the Andean Ducks here, fish for trout, or take in magnificent views of Tungurahua and El Altar over the water.

A full-day side trip (6 hours return) to one of the ridges arising from Tungurahua's cone affords outstanding views of the surrounding countryside, including El Altar and your entire route so far, but see "Hazards" above. The unnamed ridge separates Quebrada Tiacos to the southwest from Quebrada Arenal to the northeast. In good weather the ridge is clearly visible when you look west from the shelter, and cross-country travel to the base of the ridge is straightforward. From here a faint trail climbs the ridge line—at first through forest, then over grassland, and finally on volcanic sand to a height of 4150 meters (13,600 feet). It is not safe to continue farther. The walk brings you close to the many waterfalls thundering down Tungurahua's sheer cliffs.

One hundred meters (300 feet) west of the shelter, the main trail turns north into the forest to begin its long descent, dropping gently at first and passing through a combination of woods and open country where the track is not distinct. You will cross a ravine with a stream **30 minutes** past the shelter. Another **30 minutes** through similar surroundings bring you to the edge of a dense forest and a steeper descent. The trail is again clear here, and the polylepis trees large and spectacular. You feel like you are in an enchanted forest.

Thirty minutes beyond the start of the steep grade are a private shack, a few tilled fields, and a stream. Be sure to take as much water as possible here, since there is none on the seemingly endless ridge-line descent that follows. The trail suddenly becomes almost invisible; it turns sharply left and continues to drop, bearing northwest through the forest for **45 minutes** until it reaches the rim of a huge canyon with views of a spectacular 200-meter (650-foot) waterfall. This is Quebrada Arenal just above its confluence with Quebrada Siete Chorreras: perhaps the most beautiful spot on the entire trek. (Fatal overhangs are camouflaged by the dense vegetation, so be very careful when taking those unforgettable photos.)

The trail, now a little better, follows the rim of the canyon north

Two-hundred-meter waterfall in Quebrada Arenal (Photo: Lou Jost)

before taking to a ridge line. Although gentle at first, it becomes increasingly steep until you will find yourself on a 50 percent grade, along a pencil-thin ridge, amid very dense forest. The trail passes over several ledges that can be safely negotiated without a pack. (Use a rope to lower your gear beforehand.) Landmarks are difficult to identify among the claustrophobic vegetation; one exception is when the trail passes through a cleft in a huge rock at 3000 meters (9800 feet), **2.5 hours** beyond the waterfall. There is just enough room to pitch two small tents here, but no water; this is the only possible campsite along the steep descent.

From the rock, the trail continues down very steeply, dropping 400 meters (1300 feet) in as much linear distance. Fallen trees at times will force you off the ridge line; be sure to regain it as soon as possible. After **2.5 hours** (which may seem like an eternity), the trail leaves the ridge to continue dropping sharply along its west flank. It reaches the Quebrada Siete Chorreras **1 hour** later, just above its confluence with the Río Ulba. You will feel as though you have at last "arrived"—but you will find nowhere to lie down, let alone camp! The river must be forded here; it is usually calf-deep, but it may swell quickly after heavy rain.

On the west shore, 5 meters (15 feet) down river from the crossing, the trail scrambles up over the rocks of an old landslide (now covered in secondary growth); it then contours northwest and reaches a fork **45 minutes** from the river. Take the left branch to reach a private shack and farm in another **15 minutes**. The site has water—200 meters (650 feet) farther along the trail, just before it leaves the property—and space for camping, but you must ask permission first.

The trail is very good beyond this point, contouring for **30 minutes** to reach a rocky gully and stream. Another **30 minutes** of gentle descent bring you to a fork. Take the right branch. From here the trail descends more steeply, zigzagging down a cleared slope, with fine views over the Río Ulba Valley. After another **30 minutes** you will reach the roadhead at San Antonio, at the confluence of the Ulba and Pucayacu Rivers.

Getting back: There are a few farms and occasionally vehicles at San Antonio, which might give you a ride to Ulba or Baños, but it is more likely that you will have to walk. Follow the dirt road for 30 minutes downhill to its intersection with a larger gravel road that descends from Runtún. Take this gravel road to the right, downhill for another 30 minutes to the main Baños–Puyo Highway at the village of Ulba. From here, city buses run to Baños every 30 minutes from 0700 to 1900 (10 minutes, $.20); taxis run until approximately 2200 ($1).

15 THE LLANGANATES EXPERIENCE

Rating: Very difficult, 7- to 14-day trek. The distance shown on this book's map is approximately 35 kilometers (21.7 miles) round trip, but both hiking distance and time will vary considerably depending on conditions.
Elevation: Approximately 3350 to 4200 meters (11,000 to 13,800 feet), depending on your route.
Maps: IGM 1:50,000: CT-ÑIV-B1 San José de Poaló, CT-ÑIV-B3 Sucre; IGM 1:25,000: CT-ÑIV-B3b Cerro Hermoso.
Best time to visit: November and December are the only months with a reasonable chance of good weather. Even at this time, however, conditions can be very severe. See the hazards described below.
Special gear: Rubber boots are indispensable for the boggy terrain. A machete or pruning shears may be helpful in forested areas.
Water: Everywhere except ridge tops.
Hazards: Trekking in the Llanganates is recommended only for the very experienced and well equipped. The area presents many challenges and hazards. The first is **weather.** The Llanganates combine textbook conditions for hypothermia: cold, windy, and especially very wet. You must have adequate gear.

The second challenge is **navigation.** The terrain is extremely irregular, and many of its complex features are not shown on IGM maps nor on our map. In addition, thick fog frequently obliterates all landmarks and can roll in very suddenly. The area is filled with indistinct trails

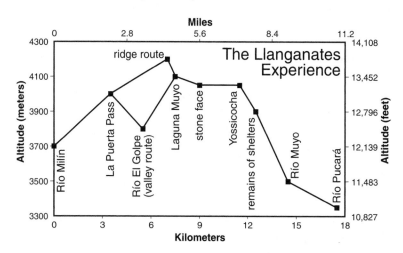

(most made by animals) that constantly fade in and out. Most people get seriously lost more than once during a trek in the Llanganates. IGM maps, compass, and strong navigation skills are all indispensable; a GPS is highly recommended. Taking a qualified guide (especially for your first visit) is a very good idea. Note, however, that the place names used by guides are often very different from those shown on IGM maps. The trekking times listed below must be multiplied several-fold in poor weather.

The third hazard is **vegetation.** Areas below 3800 meters (12,500 feet) are clad in dense brush. Above this elevation thrives a species of bambusoid grass locally known as *pintos* or *flechas* (arrows). This unusual plant grows especially tall and dense near streams, forming an almost impenetrable barrier. The tips of its leaves are needle-sharp and can cause serious eye injury.

The fourth challenge is **isolation.** There is no population in or near the Llanganates (which is unusual for Ecuador). In the event of an emergency, any assistance will be several days of hard hiking away. Trekkers must therefore be completely self-sufficient.

Annoyances: Many biting insects after rain; ticks in lower areas.

Permits and fees: In principle, foreign visitors pay a $5 fee to Llanganates National Park, but there are no facilities for collecting fees along this route.

Services: Guides and porters can usually be hired in the town of Píllaro, in the nearby village of Poaló, or in El Triunfo. Arrangements must be made on-site, at least two days in advance. In Píllaro, you can make contacts through your hotel; in Poaló, Sr. Noé Granda (who lives at the corner of the soccer field) can be a valuable source of contacts and information; in El Triunfo ask for Segundo Rodríguez. Due to the very boggy terrain, pack animals are not used in the Llanganates.

Provisions: Ambato, one of Ecuador's main commercial cities, is the nearest major center for all supplies. Píllaro is a large town with many shops offering a wide selection of basic items.

In densely populated Ecuador, crisscrossed by roads and trails and dotted with villages, the Llanganates provide a very unusual experience. Situated roughly between the Cotopaxi and Tungurahua Volcanoes, this magnificent hinterland offers the wildest trekking in the country. The area's Paleozoic bedrock—sculpted for eons by the forces of uninterrupted glaciation—presents a convoluted landscape of highly irregular ridges, endless bogs, and hundreds of unnamed lakes.

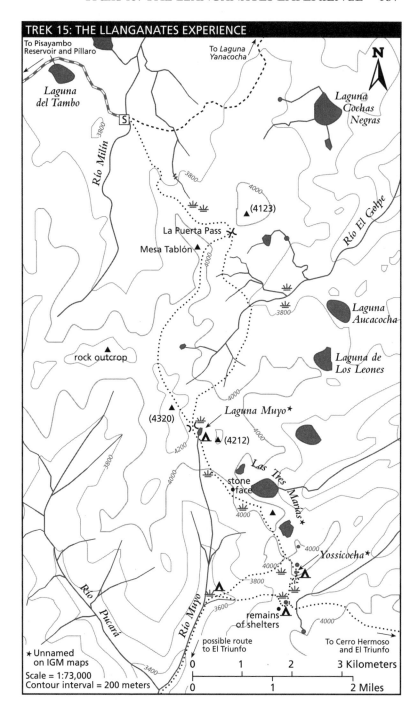

TREK 15: THE LLANGANATES EXPERIENCE

Here, more than anywhere else in the Ecuadorean Andes, the humidity that rises from the eastern jungle suddenly condenses as it meets cold mountain air and becomes a blanket of impenetrable fog, a curtain of driving rain, or a wall of sleet. The area is constantly wet and therefore the source of many important rivers plunging south and east from the highlands around 4000 meters (13,100 feet), through great valleys and gorges, toward the Amazon basin.

Protected by this constant and extreme humidity, the vegetation of the Llanganates is pristine (see "A Living Sponge" later in this trek description). Unlike almost everywhere else, potential colonists have been unable to burn off native plants in order to make way for grass to support cattle. The area's harshness in general has proven a superb defense against human incursion and destruction, leaving intact its great natural beauty, unique flora, and abundant fauna. Deer, Mountain Tapir, Andean Fox, Spectacled Bear, and exquisite hummingbirds are all common here. Seemingly endless expanses of cushion plants, mosses, and in places *frailejones* populate the vast high bogs, while *flechas* (see "Hazards," above) and tall grass fill highland slopes and line streams. Dense cloud forests descending to jungle clothe the many valleys that drop from the heights of the Llanganates.

The harshness and isolation of the region have also clothed it in mystery. Foremost among Llanganates mysteries is its legend of cursed treasure: the remains of the fabulous fortune offered the *conquistadores* by the last Inca ruler, Atahualpa, in exchange for his freedom. The Inca was betrayed and killed by the Spaniards before his ransom could be fully paid, and by far the largest part of the treasure was allegedly later hidden in the Llanganates by Atahulpa's general, Rumiñahui (literally "stone-face"), one of Ecuador's national heroes. Many generations of Llanganates treasure hunters have perished or gone mad in their quest, and the topic retains a cult following to this day. Those interested in further details are referred to *Sweat of the Sun, Tears of the Moon* by Peter Lourie.

In view of all these natural and supernatural hazards, many a potential trekker might ask, "Why go?" Our answer: Go to the Llanganates because they are exceptionally beautiful and present the ultimate trekking challenge in Ecuador. Go, however, to *experience* the mists and mysteries of the Llanganates, rather than to rigidly follow a specific route or reach a specific goal. Here, even more than elsewhere, the journey itself and a safe return are the goal.

Access: There are frequent buses from Baños to Ambato. Take a bus from the Ingahurcu neighborhood of Ambato to the town of Píllaro.

Buses leave when full throughout the day from the corner of Colón and Unidad Nacional near Parque La Merced (30 minutes, $.30). The excitement of the trip begins right here, as the bus winds its way over the steep slopes of the upper Río Patate gorge. Píllaro has two simple hotels and several basic eateries near the park. Spend the night here to arrange for guides and porters (ask at your hotel), or simply to get a fresh and early start the next day. Pick-up trucks run throughout the day from Píllaro market to the village of Poaló (30 minutes, $.35), where guides and porters may also be hired. Pick-up trucks from Píllaro can likewise be hired for the 42-kilometer (26-mile) ride past the Pisayambo Reservoir and Laguna del Tambo, to the trailhead: a small concrete bridge over Río Milín, where the road becomes impassable to vehicles (2 hours, $15).

Route: Immediately after crossing the Río Milín, leave the road and follow a series of poor trails southeast over the *páramo*, then along the crest of a low ridge. The waterfall to your left drains a bog for which you are headed, but the cascade is not shown on the IGM map. Climb along the ridge, looking back occasionally for fine views of the many lakes that dot the broad plateau stretching to the shores of the Pisayambo Reservoir. **Thirty minutes** from the road, as the ridge becomes steadily steeper, contour along its eastern (left) flank and then regain the ridge line. Still traveling southeast, you will reach a much higher part of the ridge in another **30 minutes**. Turn east, contouring under high walls to your right. In **15 minutes** you will cross a low saddle and, turning southeast again, reach the western edge of the bog mentioned above. Follow this edge of the bog southeast for **30 minutes** and, as the flat terrain begins to rise, turn south to gradually climb through your first *flechas*. In **30 minutes** you will reach a broad pass at 4000 meters (13,124 feet), situated between Mesa Tablón and the peak labeled 4123 meters (13,528 feet) on the IGM map. This pass is fittingly called La Puerta, "the door" or gateway to the Llanganates.

There are fine views from La Puerta in clear weather, back north and west from where you have just come, and south along the route(s) you are about to follow. Below you to the southeast (left) lies the very large and boggy valley of the upper Río El Golpe. To the southwest a wide but convoluted ridge extends from Mesa Tablón to the next pass on the route, 4 kilometers (2.5 miles) away. (It can be a very long 4 kilometers indeed!) Choose either the ridge line (which is the preferred route in good weather but difficult and dangerous in dense fog or high winds) or an alternate route through the valley. Walking southwest along the ridge, you will reach the base of a large, unnamed, rectangular outcrop of rock in

2 hours. Here, cattle trails climb very steeply west to the top of the outcrop; do not follow them. Instead, contour south toward a saddle and then descend southeast along the base of high walls on your right. In clear weather you will see a lake below, on your left. Keep well above the lake and look for a ravine climbing steeply south (right). Follow the ravine up to a larger valley running northeast-southwest. Climb south out of this valley to the top of a ridge and then descend south to a saddle. Climb south again to reach a notch just northeast of the point labeled 4320 meters (14,174 feet) on the IGM map, **2 hours** past the base of the rectangular outcrop mentioned above.

From here you will descend, steeply at first, bearing 160 degrees. Continue in this direction over a small, flat, boggy area, to reach in **30 minutes** a gully which drops steeply southeast. Descend through the gully; it opens onto a steep tussock-covered slope. Drop southeast along the slope to reach a pass with an unnamed lake (which the authors call Laguna Muyo) in another **30 minutes.** The lake is situated at 4100 meters (13,452 feet) between the peaks labeled 4320 and 4212 meters respectively (14,174 and 13,820 feet) on the IGM map. Note that these reference points appear on two different (adjacent) topo sheets.

If you decide on the valley route, descend gradually south and then southeast from La Puerta for **1.5 hours** over the undulating tussock. Do not drop too far down into the huge bog- and vegetation-filled valley; rather, aim to cross the upper Río El Golpe at 3800 meters (12,500 feet), at a point where the river cuts through two low ridges that approach it on either shore. The grass and *flechas* are very high and thick on both banks, but fortunately only for a short distance; then you will be in the open. Climb gradually south and then southwest along the east shore of the upper Río El Golpe, moving steadily away from the main stream, and crossing several side streams along the way. The vegetation alternates between open areas with tussock or cushion plants and stands of *flechas*, and in **3.5 hours** you will reach the approach to the unnamed pass and Laguna Muyo, described in the previous paragraph.

The lake has a small outflow to the south (not shown on the IGM map); this is a source of the Río Muyo, one of the many valleys descending south from the high Llanganates toward the Río Pastaza basin. The views are superb in clear weather. Cross the outflow and begin to contour southeast along the western flank of the ridge. There are several spots suitable for camping in this area, although they are all soggy. There is also a fantastic array of *páramo* vegetation along the way: a great variety of large green cushion plants adorned with tiny bright yellow and purple flowers; slightly larger pink and purple gentians; lurid orange and mauve club mosses, and a few velvet-leafed *frailejón* relatives.

After **15 minutes** of contouring southeast below the ridge line, you will reach the first of several flat, boggy areas. Always skirt these on their southeast (left) side. In another **30 minutes** along the same undulating southeast course, after a steep climb, you will reach a most evocative sight: a 10-meter-high (33-foot-high) stone face emblazoned on the side of

Daisy climbing out of the Río Muyo

the ridge. (Is this the indomitable Rumiñahui?) Along the way are other unforgettable sights in clear weather, south to the massive snow-covered volcanic cones of Tungurahua, El Altar and Sangay, all in a row. From the stone face, climb more steeply southeast, go by some more boggy areas, and reach the broad ridge top in **20 minutes**. The ridge undulates; in **15 minutes** it becomes narrower and offers additional splendid views in all directions, with three lovely lakes (locally called Las Tres Marías) far below to the north and east.

Ten minutes beyond, the ridge begins to climb steeply east on the slopes of an unnamed conical hill. Contour south here, then drop to a notch at 4000 meters (13,124 feet) in **15 minutes**. Cross over to the eastern slope of the ridge, then drop slightly and contour south again high above the southernmost of Las Tres Marías for **30 minutes**. (Watch your step here, as the thick *flechas* hide sheer drops on your left.) The route then begins to rise to another notch at 4000 meters (13,124 feet), from which you will gradually drop south over undulating terrain to reach a very scenic pond in **20 minutes**. It is unnamed; the authors call it Yossicocha, in memory of friend and colleague Yossi Brain (author of *Ecuador: A Climbing Guide*). There are several good places to camp here.

Follow the east (left) shore of Yossicocha past its small outflow. The ground begins to drop suddenly, and a very poor trail zigzags south down the steep slope, thick with brush. In 45 minutes it reaches a broad, flat saddle 150 meters (500 feet) below the pond. Continue south across the flats, then for 15 minutes climb a low ridge to reach another level bog with a muddy lake in the middle. Follow the east (left) edge of the bog. If you wish to approach Cerro Hermoso (4571 meters, 14,997 feet, the highest summit in the Llanganates) and exit via El Triunfo (near Baños), then you must continue east. There is not enough space to describe this route here, but it is found on our website, *www.trekkinginecuador.com*. If you do not wish to approach Cerro Hermoso, skirt clockwise around the bog for **20 minutes** to its south side, where some sporadically used camping areas are tucked in among the low hills. This is a good site and has the remains of several rudimentary shelters.

By now you have been introduced to the Llanganates and can plan the remainder of your trek accordingly. Your choices include the Cerro Hermoso-El Triunfo route mentioned above, and retracing your steps to the Río Milín, perhaps returning via the upper Río El Golpe Valley if you came on the ridge from La Puerta pass, or vice versa.

The most experienced and daring trekkers might wish to explore the virgin valley of the upper Río Muyo, but be warned: *this is very difficult and potentially hazardous.* First, note the inconsistency between the IGM maps 1:50,000 CT-ÑIV-B3 Sucre and 1:25,000 CT-ÑIV-B3b Cerro Hermoso regarding the nomenclature of the upper Río Muyo. The former map gives the name Río Muyo to a western branch originating in the *páramos* of Achirihuín, Jaramillo and Pucará, while the latter calls this Río Pucará, implicitly naming the more easterly branch Río Muyo. The following description and the map in this book are based on the latter: CT-ÑIV-B3b Cerro Hermoso.

From the remains of the rudimentary shelters, head north for **30 minutes** over some low hills and gullies covered with *flechas*, to reach the broad valley that descends west to the Río Muyo. From high ground you can clearly see the flat, open triangular area that surrounds the intersection of the valley you are about to descend westward, and the Río Muyo Valley descending from north to south. Seeing and reaching, however, are two very different things. As the valley drops west, it rapidly becomes clogged with very thick, tall stands of *flechas*, especially by stream banks. Lower down, the *flechas* are interspersed with trees to form an almost impenetrable barrier. Even more than a machete, gravity will assist you on the way down, but after the first difficult bits try to climb back up through the dense vegetation. *If you find this too difficult, do not proceed downhill.* You will have to climb 250 vertical meters (800 feet) through this dense forest on your way back up. There are a very few open boggy patches along the way, but it will take **6 hours** of steady slogging through thick brush to reach the flat valley floor of the Río Muyo. There you will find many camping possibilities—all soggy.

This area is truly pristine and should be treated with corresponding respect. You will see a great deal of Mountain Tapir prints and droppings and, if you decide to proceed downstream along the Río Muyo, you will have only tapir trails to follow (see "The Mountain Tapir" in Trek 13). In principle, a route can be envisaged along the east shore of the Río Muyo to join the human trails that climb the river valley from the village of El Triunfo toward Cerro Hermoso. El Triunfo is "only" 13 kilometers (8 miles) linear distance and 1100 meters (3600 feet) vertical drop away yet, in 3 tough days, the authors made less than 2 kilometers (1.2 miles) linear and 200 meters (650 feet) vertical headway. We had not quite reached the Río Pucará when we turned back! This is a magnificent wilderness and a delight to explore, but also *very difficult and potentially hazardous going:* alongside, in, and at times precariously high above the river.

Plan on returning upstream the same way you came. To climb out of the Río Muyo Valley, start very early in the morning and stay on the north side of the valley you descended. The vegetation will try to force you due north, but you must maintain a course northeast up the increasingly steep slope through dense forest. It is very difficult going indeed. There are only one or two small clearings along the way, and in fog you will be totally dependent on your instruments for orientation. After **5 hours** of grueling ascent through the forest, you will reach a more open and level area at 3800 meters (12,500 feet), which provides a balcony over the wide valley to the south (right). From here follow a small and thickly forested ridge farther uphill and northeast. In **3 hours** it emerges into open *páramo* at 3850 meters (12,600 feet). Several flat spots will be barely suitable for camping; not all have water.

Carefully avoiding the last few fragments of forest, head east over a series of low ridges to reach the edge of a large flat bog in **2 hours**. The going at last becomes easier. Contour north above the bog for **1 hour** and then climb for **30 minutes**. You will meet the route you followed days earlier, near the notch between the contour above the southernmost of Las Tres Marías and Yossicocha. You will feel as though you have "emerged"—but you will still be several days of strenuous hiking from any human settlement.

Getting back: It is a very long 42 kilometers (26 miles) of road walking from the bridge over the Río Milín back to Píllaro. There is no traffic at all along this route, so arrange to be picked up by the same vehicle that took you in. (Be sure to give yourself at least one extra day to meet your ride.) If you are stuck, you can try to inquire at the guard post of the Pisayambo Dam. They have communications and can sometimes (but not always) arrange transport.

A LIVING SPONGE *by Craig C. Downer*

The treeless, wet *páramo* is a unique and relatively young biome (bioclimatic zone) of the northern Andes. It can be described as a giant "living sponge" composed of a sumptuous blend of grasses, mosses, club mosses, sedges, cushion plants, ferns, horsetails, lichens, and a variety of herbs and shrubs—all adapted to harsh winds and cold temperatures. The sunflower family is the most diverse of the flowering plants here, and especially characteristic are the statuesque composite *Espeletia*, known in Spanish as *frailejón*. This elegant, woolly-leafed, generally columnar perennial, primarily found in the *páramos* of Colombia and Venezuela, occurs as an isolated population in the Llanganates (its southernmost known distribution). More than forty-four species of this *páramo*-endemic genus have been named, from sessile forms to prodigies rising spectacularly more than 15 meters (50 feet) in height!

Because of the cold temperatures, dead vegetation is not quickly decomposed in the *páramo*. It becomes peatlike and may form incipient soils in topographic depressions or on more level mountain crowns. Also, because of the cold, more minerals remain dissolved in *páramo* waters. This is because they are not absorbed by roots to the degree they would be at lower elevations, with their higher temperatures and more rapid plant metabolisms. Furthermore, below-freezing nighttime temperatures retard the release of water to lower elevations, as does the water's absorption by the spongy vegetation and slowly decomposing peat. These and other factors allow the high *páramo* to act as a living sponge that wisely stores, enriches, and equitably distributes its precious nutrient-bearing waters to all lower elevations. The water courses through a complex interconnected system of *páramo* lakes and gurgling underground passageways, leading to brilliantly cascading streams and rivers of the forested Andean slopes. Its delivery, as if upon demand, helps mitigate the effects of droughts and floods alike.

Living sponge highlands, such as the Llanganates, absorb, purify, and supply vast quantities of water and waterborne minerals to the Andean cloud forests and Amazon rainforests (some of the most biologically diverse ecosystems on Earth) as well as to agricultural and population centers. The conservation of these *páramos* is therefore indispensable to the survival of most living creatures in Ecuador—undoubtedly including man.

Chapter 11
TREKS FROM GUARANDA

Altitude, 2600 meters (8550 feet)
Population, 35,000

Situated on the western slopes of the Cordillera Occidental, far from conventional tourist routes, Guaranda is a hidden gem. The city is so tranquil and traditional that a 9 P.M. siren marks the end of the evening stroll in the central plaza—and most folks promptly trot off to bed. The province of Bolívar, of which Guaranda is the capital, offers a great deal to explore. Of particular interest is the transition zone from the cold highlands to the *subtrópico*, warm valleys that descend toward the Pacific coast. There are not many tour agencies in Guaranda, and no commercial treks. It is a wonderful place from which to strike out on your own.

Trek 16, Great Cascade Trail, is special in a number of ways. Although it covers a good deal of both horizontal and vertical distance, it is nonetheless easy, mostly downhill on a good trail. This trek also combines lovely scenery with a glimpse of remarkably successful community development projects. Moderately difficult Trek 17, Forgotten Footsteps, retraces one of the early trade routes between Ecuador's highlands and coast, through picturesque and untouristed countryside.

GREAT CASCADE TRAIL

Rating: Easy, 20-kilometer (12.5-mile), 2- to 3-day trek.
Elevation: 900 to 3750 meters (2950 to 12,300 feet).
Map: IGM 1:50,000: CT-NIV-D2 San José de Camarón.
Best time to visit: July through September are the driest months, February to April the rainiest.
Special gear: Clothing for both warm and cold conditions.
Water: Available from streams along the lower part of the route, but best to tank up at the beginning for the upper part.
Hazards: Poisonous snakes in the lowlands.
Annoyances: Biting insects in the lowlands, ticks in the dry season; take repellent.

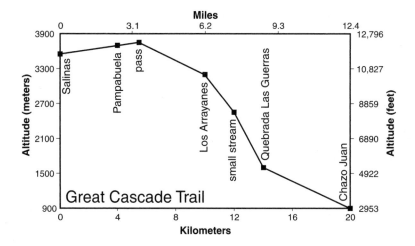

Permits and fees: The town of Salinas charges visitors a $.50 entry fee.
Services: Salinas offers the following two hotels: The community-run
El Refugio has comfortable rooms with private bath for $4 per person
(cheaper in dormitory). Phone: (03)981-266. Across the street is the
simpler Hostería Samilagua for $2 per person.

For guides or pack animals, inquire at the hotel or the Centro de
Turismo Comunitario on the plaza. Phone: (03)981-574. Guides may
also be hired in Chazo Juan, at the low end of the trek, for the walk up
to La Chorrera waterfall; ask around the village. There are simple
accommodations for visitors at La Granja, 500 meters (1600 feet)
southwest of Chazo Juan along the road to San José de Camarón, and
very basic rooms at the *hospedería* in town. There are simple hotels and
restaurants in Echeandía. (Amparito is the best.)

Provisions: Buy most of your staples in Guaranda. Salinas produces a
number of quality foods that provide a welcome supplement to your
trekking provisions. These include excellent cheeses, salami, dried
mushrooms, chocolate, and jams, all of which can be purchased at the
Centro de Comercialización, two blocks from the plaza. There is also a
bakery in Salinas.

In the region of this trek, the slopes of the Cordillera Occidental drop
dramatically from cold, windswept *páramo* at almost 4000 meters (13,100
feet) above sea level, to lush subtropical lowlands at elevations below
1000 meters (3300 feet), in less than 20 kilometers (12.5 miles) linear

distance. Lofty ridges and deeply incised river valleys offer stunning views in clear weather. These views are enhanced by the otherwise-unfortunate fact that much of the native cloud forest has been cleared for pasture (especially in the upper sections).

Tumbling over this abrupt topography are several lovely waterfalls, none more striking than the 300-meter (1000-foot) cascade called La Chorrera, which the trek skirts for much of its length. You will first glimpse this splendid torrent from well above the falls; the impressive sight and sound will accompany you throughout the day's walking. There are camping possibilities with a view of La Chorrera, and you can swim in the cool, clear waters of its stream; but there is at present no safe route to the base of the waterfall itself. The lower parts of the trail have more vegetation; hence many birds and butterflies appear as you descend and the climate warms. Towering above you in these lower sections are almost-vertical valley walls clothed in the last remnants of native forest.

The social environment of this trek is as interesting as its natural beauty. Levels of development and prosperity rare in most of rural Ecuador are easily noticeable here: fine herds of dairy cattle in the highlands, large tracts of land reforested with pines, and many thriving community projects in the towns and villages. In addition to being friendly, many of the folks you meet along the trail seem unusually comfortable with outsiders. The terms *gringo* or *mister*—so common in some other areas—are seldom heard. A quiet confidence and optimism can be felt throughout the region. For the remarkable history of the Salinas area, see the "A Model for Community Development" sidebar at the end of this trek description.

Access: Buses from Guaranda to Salinas run Monday to Friday at 0600 (departing from the upper end of Plaza Roja by the Verbo Divino school), 0700 (from Parque Montufar, corner General Salazar and Sucre), and 1300 (from Plaza 15 de Mayo). All take 2 hours and cost $1. Service is less frequent on Saturday and Sunday; inquire locally. You can also hire a taxi or pick-up truck in the Plaza Roja of Guaranda to take you to Salinas (1 hour, $10). If you wish to begin the trek in Los Arrayanes rather than in Salinas, then arrange for the pick-up to take you the additional 10 kilometers (6.2 miles). Negotiate the price in advance. There is no bus service to Los Arrayanes, but if you wish to stay in Salinas first you can usually hire a pick-up there as well ($20). You may sometimes be able to get a ride along the road from Salinas to Pampabuela and Arrayanes, but there is very little traffic.

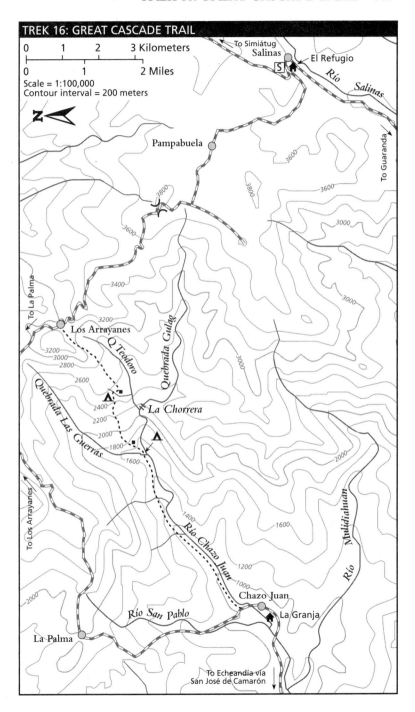

TREK 16: GREAT CASCADE TRAIL

0   1   2   3 Kilometers

0   1   2 Miles

Scale = 1:100,000
Contour interval = 200 meters

N

To Simiátug
Salinas
El Refugio
Río Salinas
To Guaranda

Pampabuela

3600
3800
3000
3600
3800
3000

To La Palma

3400
3200
3000
2800
2600
2400
2200
2000
1800
1600

Los Arrayanes
Q. Teodoro
Quebrada Gulag
La Chorrera

Quebrada Las Guerras

To Los Arrayanes

Río Chazo Juan
1400
1200
1000
1600
2000

Mulidiahuan
Río

Chazo Juan
La Granja

Río San Pablo

La Palma
2000

To Echeandía vía
San José de Camarón

Route: The authors suggest starting in Salinas unless you are short on time or wish to avoid road walking in the highlands. It is worth spending a day in Salinas to acclimatize and enjoy nearby day walks or to visit the local community projects. Take water from Salinas for the first part of the trek.

The trek begins by heading southwest along the unpaved road to Pampabuela, the lower (left-hand) of the two roads that start next to the El Refugio Hotel. (Ask which is the correct road.) After a few minutes of level going (with nice views over the Río Salinas and glimpses of town nestled under the base of impressive cliffs), the road gradually swings northwest and begins to climb gently toward Pampabuela. Pastures hemmed with planted pines will surround you, and early in the morning you will likely meet many *campesinos* bringing their milk to the Salinas dairy. Many carry the buckets on their backs, some use mules, and a particularly innovative soul has fitted a llama with a special cargo saddle for milk cans. Keep an eye out for it!

It is an easy **1.5 hours** to the small village of Pampabuela, which has its own satellite dairy. The road passes to the left of the village and continues to climb gradually, now to the west. In **20 minutes** you will reach an intersection; take the unpaved road on your right, which in **5 minutes** heads north to a broad pass. At 3750 meters (12,300 feet), this is the highest point of the trek. The road now drops gradually, north and west, winding its way down the upper slopes of the Cordillera Occidental and offering superb views in clear weather. The vegetation changes almost imperceptibly, from the straw so typical of the high *páramo*, to bushes and a few small broad-leaved trees. In **1.75 hours** you will reach the even-smaller village of Los Arrayanes along a series of hairpin bends in the road. If you are low on water, ask for some in the village.

Fifty meters (150 feet) past the church in Los Arrayanes a trail begins on your left, descending to the southwest; this will be your general direction of travel for the remainder of the trek. (The unpaved road also continues to Chazo Juan via La Palma, but this is a much longer route.) Follow the trail as it drops—gently at first, then more steeply, through thicker vegetation that now separates the pastures. Fog is common here, but when it clears the views are marvelous. **Two hours** of increasingly steep descent along the trail bring you to a house and **5 minutes** beyond it, a small stream. There are some flat spots for camping in the pasture to your right after crossing the stream, but be sure to ask permission if anyone is around.

The deep valley of Quebrada Teodoro lies to your left, and soon you will begin to hear the sound of the great waterfall called La Chorrera, drifting in and out as the trail winds its way ever lower. **Forty-five minutes** later you will get your first good view of this mighty cascade (formed by the waters of Quebrada Gulag tumbling into Quebrada Teodoro)—a highlight of the trek. Here a steep meadow on your left makes a good spot for a rest and some photos. Descending past a few isolated houses, the route now takes to the ridge line separating Quebrada Teodoro to the south from Quebrada Las Guerras to the north. This is the steepest part of the walk, but the trail is quite good. In **1 hour** you will reach a patch of flat ground with a house, some smaller adjacent structures, and superb views of La Chorrera and other waterfalls tumbling into Quebrada Teodoro.

María Mercedes Ramos milks her cow with a view of La Chorrera.

The trail continues to descend. In **45 minutes** you will reach a pasture at the confluence of Quebrada Teodoro and Quebrada Las Guerras, where they form the Río Chazo Juan. There are yet more wonderful views of the waterfalls here, and many good places to camp. The scene in late afternoon light (if there is no fog) is especially breathtaking. It is tempting to try to approach the base of La Chorrera either from here or from the house above, but this cannot be done safely because of dense forest and steep cliffs. It is best to admire the spectacle from afar.

The trail crosses Quebrada Las Guerras (only ankle deep in the dry season, but subject to flooding after heavy rain), becomes wider, and descends more gently. It roughly follows the north shore of the Río Chazo Juan through lush subtropical vegetation with many bright flowers. There are several nice spots where you can descend to the river for a chilly dip or just to stretch out on the large boulders. After crossing a couple of small side streams (which can also swell in the wet season), in **2.5 hours** the trail rejoins the unpaved road from La Palma and Los Arrayanes, just outside the little town of Chazo Juan.

Take the road left, south across a concrete bridge, and into Chazo Juan. If you wish to stay at La Granja (see above), walk through town and an additional 500 meters (1600 feet) southwest along the road to San José de Camarón. La Granja is marked by a sign on your right.

Getting back: There is at least one pick-up truck daily, early in the morning, from Chazo Juan through San José de Camarón to Echeandía (45 minutes, $.50). There are ten daily buses from Echeandía up to Guaranda, as well as frequent connections to the lowland cities of Babahoyo and Guayaquil.

A MODEL FOR COMMUNITY DEVELOPMENT

In 1970 Salinas was remarkably poor even by the standards of rural Ecuador. The hamlet consisted of a few straw huts perched on the cold *páramo*. Its residents subsisted almost exclusively by drying salt from nearby mineral springs. In the ensuing thirty years, however, Salinas has become a model of sustainable development, boasting over a dozen different successful community enterprises. Sustainability and diversification are both elusive goals in Ecuadorean community work, but by far the most exceptional feature of Salinas has been its apparent ability to pass the projects' prosperity along to inhabitants of the area.

Much of the credit for this extraordinary success has been attributed to Padre Antonio Polo, a Salesian missionary priest from Italy, who first arrived in 1971. Many of Padre Antonio's early projects foundered; but thanks to the assistance of various volunteer collaborators (particularly the Swiss cheesemaker José Dubach), a successful dairy cooperative was eventually established. There are tiny satellite dairies in villages throughout the Salinas area, where *campesinos* bring the daily milk production of their few cows. The milk is pasteurized and a simple white curd produced. Once every few weeks the curd is taken to the central dairy in Salinas, where it is ripened into a variety of excellent European-style cheeses that are sold throughout Ecuador. They are arguably among the best cheeses in the country.

Aided by Padre Antonio's knack for conceiving new projects, Salinas was able to spin off the success of its dairy. The whey from cheesemaking is returned to *campesinos* who use it to raise pigs. The pork is processed into high-quality salami and sausages. Reforestation with pine trees resulted in edible mushrooms growing among their roots. These mushrooms are harvested and dried for sale. Wool from the area's flocks is spun into fine yarn; crafts are produced by an artisans' cooperative; and tourism is attracted by the region's natural beauty and its intriguing history. Inspired by this success, neighboring lowland communities have gotten into the act by making use of their own local resources. Excellent jams are produced from tropical fruits by cooperatives around Facundo Vela, north of Salinas. Mozarella and provolone cheese are the local specialties in Chazo Juan, where accommodations have also been built for tourists.

The level of hygiene in the various cottage food industries is remarkably high, and the importance of cleanliness in general seems to have become part of the region's mentality. Yet Salinas is by no means perfect; it is not free of rivalry or inequality, nor is its future sustainability guaranteed. It is, however, the most successful example of community development in Ecuador, well worth visiting as much for a glimpse of its many thriving projects as for its lovely natural surroundings.

17 FORGOTTEN FOOTSTEPS

Rating: Moderately difficult, 15-kilometer (9.3-mile), 2- to 3-day trek.
Elevation: 1200 to 3300 meters (3900 to 10,800 feet).
Maps: IGM 1:50,000: CT-NIV-D2 San José de Camarón, CT-NIV-D4 Guaranda Oeste.
Best time to visit: July through September are the driest months, February to April the rainiest.
Special gear: None.
Water: Available from streams and rivers along the route.
Hazards: Poisonous snakes in the lowlands. Occasional holdups have been reported along the Guaranda–Echeandía vehicle road, and nighttime travel is not recommended. The trails off the road are safe, and folks along this route are particularly friendly and helpful. Dogs can be nasty, however, so carry a walking stick.
Annoyances: Biting insects in the lowlands, ticks in the dry season; take repellent.
Permits and fees: None.
Services: Pack animals can be arranged in San Juan de Llullundongo. Señor Fausto Lara (house diagonally across from the health center) is a reliable muleteer who knows the area well. Messages for him may be left with Señor Gonzalo Naranjo in Guaranda. Phone: (03)980-867. Call several days in advance; only Spanish is spoken. Echeandía has simple hotels and restaurants; Amparito is the best.
Provisions: Guaranda is the place to shop. There are no supplies in San Juan de Llullundongo. Illuví has two very small shops with soft drinks and candy. Echeandía is a small regional center, where shops are well stocked with basic items.

The province of Bolívar was an important crossroads between the highlands and coast from pre-Inca times until the construction of the railroad in the early twentieth century. Bolívar's ridges and valleys are still crisscrossed by many trails bearing witness to the active trade that once flowed through the region (originally borne by caravans of llamas and later by mules and oxen). Early Spanish chronicles speak of fresh fish being rushed from the coast to the Inca emperor's table in Quito, and local residents still tell of their grandparents transporting every imaginable kind of merchandise along these trails. Many well-known travelers also took this route—people like

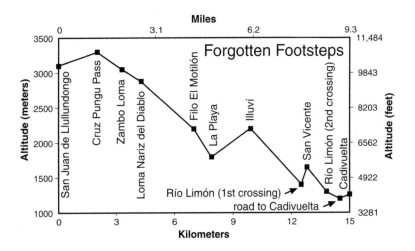

Simón Bolívar, Alexander von Humboldt, Richard Spruce (see "The Cascarilla Story" at the end of this trek description), and Edward Whymper, all of whom wrote fascinating chronicles of their arduous journeys.

While some of the old tracks have been abandoned, and others lie beneath modern roads, many of the trails are still there and still used by local inhabitants and their animals. This trek follows part of one of the trails that joined the city of Guaranda with the port of Ventanas, on the river of the same name, where goods destined for Guayaquil and the world were once loaded onto steamers. It goes from a 3300-meter (10,800-foot) pass to the *subtrópico*, warm and humid foothills where sugar cane, citrus, bananas, and *cascarilla* are grown. The transition through different climatic zones is interesting: as you descend, the vegetation becomes more lush, butterflies and birds more abundant, and your sweat glands more active. The humidity of the lowlands rises toward the mountains, making fog very common. Although the area has been populated for many years and most of the native forests were replaced by pastures and orchards, small pockets of cloud forest remain in the steeper gullies. Despite it once having been a crossroads, residents of this area are not used to seeing many contemporary trekkers, so you may be the object of friendly curiosity.

Access: The trek starts in the village of San Juan de Llullundongo, 12 kilometers (7.5 miles) by road from Guaranda. A truck can be hired in Guaranda's Plaza Roja ($3 for the 20-minute ride). On Saturdays, trucks provide passenger service to San Juan for $.30 per person—but they can get very crowded. An alternative is to take a city bus from Guaranda to the town of Guanujo and walk 6.5 kilometers (4 miles) to San Juan. To do this, take a dirt track from the upper part of Guanujo down to the Río Atandagua (marked Río Salinas on the IGM map). After crossing the bridge, take the first left on the road; then, past the village of Atandagua, take the right fork to San Juan.

Route: Follow the main street of San Juan uphill past the soccer field on your right. At the top of the street, take the left fork downhill. Follow this trail, which bears northwest through pastures. After dropping slightly, it gradually climbs to the pass called Cruz Pungu (3300 meters, 10,800 feet) **1 hour** from the entrance to San Juan.

Descending from the pass, the trail is soon surrounded by pretty flowering bushes. In **5 minutes** it reaches a fork; take the left branch. **Five minutes** later there is another fork; this time go right. In **10 minutes** you will meet a larger trail amid boggy ground; go right again here, alongside a flat pasture. The trail then descends more steeply through trenches worn by centuries of traffic, to reach a ridge top with views of a dirt road just below you to the north. (This road comes from San Juan.) The main Guaranda–Echeandía Road can also be seen in the distance to the north. The trail zigzags down the side of the ridge to meet the road from San Juan in an area called Zambo Loma, **30 minutes** past the boggy area mentioned above. Follow the road to the left for 500 meters (1600 feet) or **10 minutes**, then continue on a trail to the right. The vehicle road continues west toward the hamlet of Guanto Cruz (not shown on the IGM map).

After leaving the road, the trail at first follows the ridge line and then drops steeply to the northwest. It narrows as it cuts into the rocky cliff of Loma Nariz del Diablo (Devils Nose Hill). **Forty-five minutes** past the Guanto Cruz Road, you will meet a side trail coming down from the left. Follow the main trail right; it continues to descend northwest and then due west. **Thirty minutes** farther, it reaches the top of a ridge known as Filo El Motilón. Here, a branch of the trail drops steeply to the right, toward the confluence of Río La Playa and Quebrada Tambo Real. Continue on the left branch, which bears west. Follow the Motilón ridge line for another **10 minutes** before turning sharply left to begin a steep zigzag descent through thick bamboo, along the southern flank of the ridge. The trail here is much narrower and overgrown with vegetation. In **30 minutes** you will reach a spot known as La Playa (The Beach) at 1800 meters (5900 feet), at the confluence of Río La Playa and Quebrada Ospituche.

There are several good spots to camp in the vicinity (and of course abundant water). One recommended camping area is just across Quebrada Ospituche. Ford this small stream and follow a faint trail uphill until you

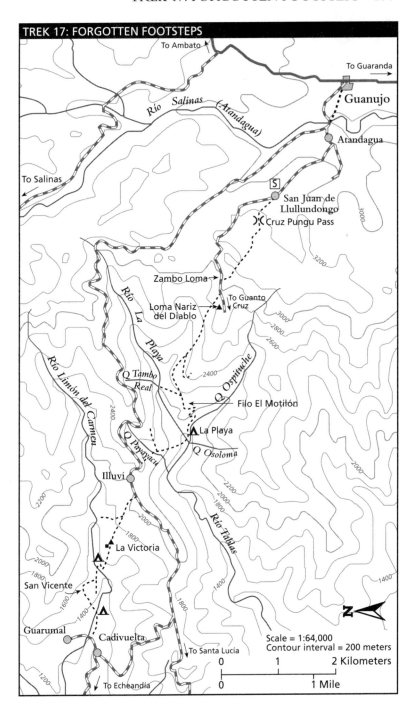

TREK 17: FORGOTTEN FOOTSTEPS

To Ambato

To Guaranda

Guanujo

Río Salinas (Atandagua)

Atandagua

To Salinas

S

San Juan de Llullundongo

Cruz Pungu Pass

3000

3200

Zambo Loma

To Guanto Cruz

Loma Nariz del Diablo

Río La Playa

3000

2800

2600

2400

Q Tambo Real

Q Ospituche

Filo El Motilón

La Playa

Río Limón del Carmen

2400

Q Payayacu

Q Osoloma

2000

Illuví

2200

1800

2000

Río Tablas

1800

2200

1800

La Victoria

1400

San Vicente

2000

1800

1600

1400

1400

Guarumal

Cadivuelta

To Santa Lucía

N

Scale = 1:64,000
Contour interval = 200 meters

0   1   2 Kilometers

0   1 Mile

To Echeandía

1200

Rustic dining: restaurant on the road west of Illuví

reach a large clearing on level ground (sometimes grazed by cattle). Water is also available from Quebrada Osoloma, 250 meters (800 feet) west of the clearing. All these drainages are very steep upstream. The level of their rivers can rise quickly after heavy rain; in the dry season they are usually between calf and knee deep.

To continue, carefully ford the Río La Playa about 100 meters (300 feet) upstream from the confluence of Quebrada Ospituche. On the north shore, the trail starts in a small opening in the vegetation. (It is not obvious and veers immediately to the left.) From the river's edge, the main trail zigzags northward up the steep slope through thick bamboo. It will take **20 minutes** to reach a barbed-wire fence with a primitive gate. Through the gate is a cultivated field; and the trail continues through the crops and then to the right of them, to reach a small side stream in another **20 minutes**. For the next **30 minutes** you will climb north and contour west through nice vegetation. Gaps in the foliage provide fine views down to Río La Playa (known as the Río Tablas downstream), as it cuts through successive perpendicular ridges often shrouded in mist. When you reach a fork, take the left branch downhill for **10 minutes** to reach a second, larger, and very pretty side stream called Quebrada Payayacu (or Payacyacu). From here the trail continues to climb steadily, at first surrounded by vegetation and later through pastures. In **30 minutes** you will reach a few houses and the main Guaranda–Echeandía Road, just east of the village of Illuví, at 2200 meters (7200 feet).

Illuví is scenically perched on a ridge between the watersheds of the Río La Playa and the Río Limón del Carmen; there are two small stores and, 1 kilometer (0.6 mile) west of town, a rustic restaurant selling home-baked bread and serving good simple meals. Walk along the road to the west for **20 minutes**, past Illuví as far as the restaurant. Here a trail drops steeply to the right, zigzagging amid pastures on the northern slope of the ridge. In **30 minutes** you will reach an area called Calitero and a fork. Take the left branch and descend more gradually for **30 minutes** to the north-west, toward a ridge with three successive knolls (on which you can see a few houses). Continue along the ridge to the west alongside pastures to the third knoll, known as La Victoria, in another **30 minutes**. From this point the trail again descends steeply, and the pastures gradually give way to more luxuriant vegetation. You will reach the shores of the Río Limón del Carmen (1400 meters or 4600 feet) in **30 minutes**. There are some small clearings to pitch a tent here, but the ground can be soggy.

A one-log bridge crosses the river. On the north shore the trail climbs steeply, and in **15 minutes** you will reach a barbed-wire fence and a fork. Take the upper trail, which continues to climb through pastures. In another **15 minutes** you will reach a grassy hill where there are fine views in clear weather. Continue uphill in a northerly direction; the trail then levels off, turns west, and drops to cross a small stream, **15 minutes** ahead. This area, known as San Vicente, can be very muddy. Continue up the west side of the stream through more pastures. Just after passing a house in another **15 minutes**, the trail takes to a ridge running southwest. It passes near two more houses and in **45 minutes** drops steeply, once again to the shores of the Río Limón del Carmen, at 1300 meters (4250 feet). The banks of the river are clad in pretty rainforest. There is another simple log bridge across the river here and, on the other side, a few small clearings where you can pitch a tent.

Favián Naranjo tends the family still near Cadivuelta. Home-brewed cane liquor is a well-known product of the subtropics of Bolívar.

The trail climbs gently on the south shore and then contours west, following the river downstream to meet a rough dirt road in **30 minutes**. To the right, the road crosses the river again (there is yet another small log bridge just upstream from the main ford) and goes to the hamlets of Guarumal and Cadiloma, where there are remnants of the area's *cascarilla* forests. This can be a 2- to 3-hour side trip. Otherwise, follow the road to the left, past a pretty waterfall, and climb to the Guaranda–Echeandía Road at Cadivuelta in **30 minutes**.

Getting back: There are ten daily buses in each direction between Guaranda and Echeandía. Flag them down vigorously to make sure they stop. It is a 1-hour ride from Cadivuelta to Echeandía ($1); to Guaranda 2 hours ($2). The last bus to Echeandía passes Cadivuelta around 1730, the last bus to Guaranda around 1600. Echeandía is a pleasant, quiet town.

THE CASCARILLA STORY

Among the many historical travelers to cross the subtropics of Bolívar was the Victorian botanist Richard Spruce. The account of his 1860 journey stands out not only for its fine description of the region's flora, but also because it reveals one of the earliest documented cases of genetic piracy in Latin America. Today, genetic piracy is an especially controversial issue.

More than two centuries before Spruce, the conquering Spaniards had learned from the natives of Ecuador about the medicinal properties of the bark of the *cascarilla* tree, cinchona or red bark, which is still the source of quinine used to treat malaria. Since then, the Spanish Crown held the monopoly of selling this precious remedy in Europe, often at exorbitant prices. During the heyday of British empire-building in malaria-ridden India and Africa, obtaining an alternate source of quinine became a matter of national strategic interest. Richard Spruce was therefore dispatched by Her Majesty's government on a genuine cloak-and-dagger mission, to smuggle cinchona seeds and seedlings out of Ecuador, so they could be planted in Ceylon and Jamaica.

After sailing up the Amazon to reach Ecuador, Spruce eventually traveled from Ambato to Guaranda along the Royal Road of Trek 22. He then took the trail described here to the subtropics of Bolívar, where he found *cascarilla* trees near Limón, some 3 kilometers (2 miles) east of Cadivuelta. Spruce wrote:

We set forth from Guaranda on the 17th of June, the direction of our route being first northerly, as far as the adjacent village of Guanujo, and then to the north-west to the pass of Llullundengo.... Having surmounted this, we entered on the most precipitous and dangerous descent I have ever passed. The track leads straight down a narrow ridge [fortunately, the current trail contours more gently].... The track in the precipitous ascents and descents is mostly a gully worn in the soft loamy soil by the transit of men and beasts, to the depth in some places of 10 feet [3 meters], and so strait [narrow] that the traveller, to save his legs from being crushed, must needs throw them on his horse's neck.... [T]here is a considerable depth of black tenacious greasy mould [loose soil], worn by the equable steps of beasts of burden into transverse ridges (called camellones, from their resemblance to humps on a camel's back)....

The *camellones* are there, as are many other elements of Spruce's vivid description. Malaria remains an important disease throughout the tropics of the world, and a few Bolívar locals continue to use a remedy of *cascarilla* bark soaked in home-brewed cane liquor, the latter being another well-known product of the area. The sun has set over the British Empire, but gin and tonic, the international version of the Ecuadorean folk remedy, seems destined for immortality.

For further details of the *cascarilla* story see *The Fever Trail* by Mark Honigsbaum or the original writings of Richard Spruce in *Notes of a Botanist on the Amazon and Andes,* edited by Alfred Russell Wallace.

Chapter 12
TREKS FROM RIOBAMBA

Altitude, 2750 meters (9000 feet)
Population, 120,000

Riobamba likes to call itself *corazón de la patria*, the nation's heartland, and for good reason. Situated near the geographic center of the country, it is the very essence of Andean Ecuador. The city is surrounded by numerous highland indigenous communities and five massive snowcapped volcanoes. Riobamba is an important regional center, the capital of the province of Chimborazo, and the hub of the country's once-famous railroad.

The chilly cobblestone streets of Riobamba welcome their share of tourists. Most come to ride the remnants of the railway over the Devils Nose, or to climb one of the summits over 5000 meters (16,500 feet). The proximity of Sangay National Park, the Chimborazo vicuña reserve, and other splendid natural areas also make Riobamba an ideal base for highland trekking. Agencies here are very well set up to organize treks. The Inca Trail from Achupallas to Ingapirca is perhaps the most heavily visited in Ecuador.

Northeast of Riobamba, Trek 18, Volcano Watching, is an easy but exciting hike—especially when Tungurahua is spewing fire. The brute force of ancient volcanic activity is evident along Trek 19, a moderately difficult and popular hike to the crater of El Altar, located east of the city. To the southeast, far off the tourist track, are the Atillo and Osogoche Lakes of moderately difficult Trek 20. This area offers grand scenery and an opportunity to experience the authentic highland native way of life.

To the west, on the opposite side of Riobamba, are two other moderately difficult treks, both in the shadow of Ecuador's highest summit: Chimborazo. Popular Trek 21, Vicuña Trail, crosses the Continental Divide north of Chimborazo, at 4400 meters (14,450 feet), before descending to visit a fauna reserve for this rare species. The less-frequented route of Trek 22, Royal Road, traverses the Cordillera Occidental on the southern flanks of Chimborazo, following an ancient highway almost into downtown Guaranda.

Back on the east side of Riobamba, in Sangay National Park, are three difficult and very worthwhile treks. Trek 23, Hot Springs in the Cloud Forest, offers a rare treat: a warm soak in luscious surroundings at the end of the trail. Trek 24, Black Rock of Cubillines, and Trek 25, High Lakes and Ridges, explore the *páramo*-clad hinterlands south of El Altar. These real cross-country routes connect with each other, as well as with Trek 23 to the east and Trek 19 to the north, offering the possibility of a multiweek excursion.

18 VOLCANO WATCHING

Rating: Easy, 15-kilometer (9.3-mile), 2- to 3-day trek.
Elevation: 2800 to 3900 meters (9200 to 12,800 feet).
Map: IGM 1:50,000: CT-ÑIV-C2 Quero.
Best time to visit: Throughout the year.
Special gear: If Tungurahua is active, take a small disposable mask to protect your mouth and nose from volcanic ash. These are easily available in pharmacies and hardware stores.
Water: This trek crosses a populated rural area. There is not much ground water—and what little there is, is not clean. You should therefore take water with you and ask residents for tap water along the way.
Hazards: Volcanic activity; check alerts before undertaking this trek (see "Internet Sites" in Appendix A).
Annoyances: None.
Permits and fees: None.
Services: There is one simple hotel in Pelileo.
Provisions: Get supplies in Riobamba. There are none in Santa Fé de Galán.

It is difficult to describe the emotions you feel when the brute force of an erupting volcano is displayed right in front of you. All your senses are on alert as you wait in the still night. When an explosion occurs, everything happens at once: the cannon-shot sound, fireworks shooting into the air, red-hot boulders tumbling down the side of the mountain, your pulse racing wildly. The daytime experience is no less impressive, with mushroom clouds of steam and ash being heaved several kilometers up into the sky.

"*Mama*" Tungurahua (5023 meters, 16,480 feet) is one of Ecuador's most active volcanoes, with a history of eruptive periods lasting from months to years, and occurring approximately once every century. The

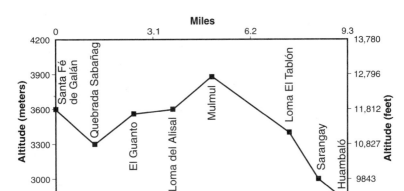

most recent period of activity began in October 1999, following 80 years of dormancy. Periodic explosions have been spaced several minutes to hours apart, with incandescent rocks, ash, and steam being expelled. There have also been less frequent episodes in which an incandescent glow (like a halo) can be seen in and above the crater. Neither lava flows nor pyroclastic flows (a dangerous mixture of very hot gas and ash) have taken place. Life in the communities around the volcano has been disrupted, some have been evacuated, and small amounts of volcanic ash have fallen over a large area. At the same time, volcano watching has become Ecuador's latest attraction.

The western slopes of Tungurahua are dramatically steep, dropping almost 3000 meters (10,000 feet) in only twice as much linear distance, to the valley of the Río Chambo. On the opposite bank of the Chambo is Cerro Igualata, a *nudo* (transverse massif linking the central and western cordilleras) reaching 4430 meters (14,535 feet). The eastern flanks of Igualata (itself a dormant volcano) also drop suddenly into the Chambo Valley, but its upper slopes are quite gentle, creating a balcony that overlooks Tungurahua. Our trek follows this balcony north along the east side of Igualata, among cultivated fields and small rural communities. Along the way, evidence of past and present volcanic activity is everywhere (see "The Mother of All Landslides" at the end of this trek description).

Whether Tungurahua is active or dormant, the magnificent views of this and other peaks, the deep canyon of the Chambo, and a glimpse of rural life in central Ecuador make this trek worthwhile.

Access: The starting point of the trek is the village of Santa Fé de Galán, at 3600 meters (11,800 feet), 26 kilometers (16 miles) northeast of Riobamba via Guano. There are five daily buses from Riobamba, at 0600, 1000, 1200, 1400, and 1600. They depart from the gas station at the corner of Av Sucre and Febres Cordero, near the Mercado Dávalos (1.5 hours, $.70).

Route: The populated rural area covered by this trek is crisscrossed with many small dirt roads, and it is easy to get lost. The best way to navigate here is to regularly ask locals how to get to the next village along the route. The first lookout is 2 kilometers (1.2 miles) northeast of Santa Fé de Galán, on the road to Palestina. It is a **30-minute** walk to this lookout, a grassy spot where the road makes a sharp turn to the right. There are superb views of Tungurahua right in front of you. To the south are the glacier-covered peaks of El Altar, and farther south the black rock of Cubillines (sometimes sprinkled with a little snow).

From this lookout the terrain drops very steeply, east to the Chambo Valley and north to Quebrada Sabañag (labeled Quebrada Guilles on the IGM map). To continue north, return toward Santa Fé de Galán. Follow the road back west; when you reach the intersection for Santa Fé de Galán, continue straight instead of turning left. At the next intersection turn right (north). This is **30 minutes** from the lookout.

The next village along the way is El Guanto, on the north side of the deep Quebrada Sabañag. Follow the road north toward Loma de Galán. In **15 minutes** it makes a sharp turn left. Leave the road here as it begins a large detour west in order to cross the deep *quebrada* ahead. A poor trail starts here behind a farmhouse; it continues to the northeast and later due north through tilled fields and pastures, down the very steep slopes of Quebrada Sabañag. In **45 minutes** you will reach the stream at the bottom, where there are a few eucalyptus trees and a small wooden bridge.

The trail continues north, at first climbing steeply 200 meters (650 feet) up and out of the *quebrada* and then more gradually alongside cultivated fields. In **45 minutes** you will reach a dirt road. Follow it north and then northeast past a series of intersections, toward the center of El Guanto, **15 minutes** ahead. As you climb higher, you will have good views of the antenna-topped summit of Igualata to the southwest and, to the northwest, the imposing silhouettes of Chimborazo and Carihuayrazo.

From El Guanto, you can either turn east and descend through a broad valley called Hierba Buena, or continue northeast to contour around Hierba Buena on higher ground. Both routes lead in **1 hour** to a gently curved

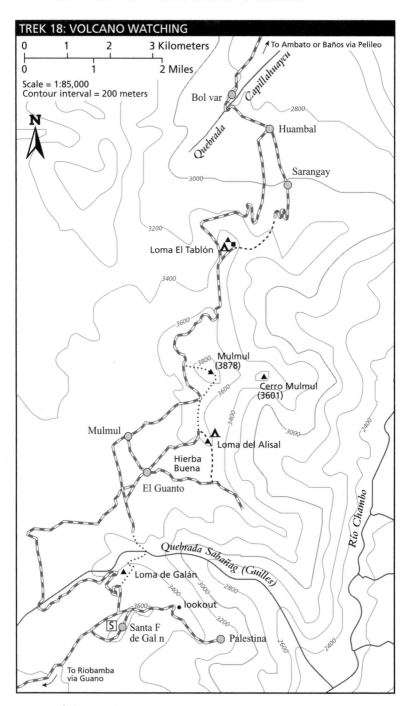

TREK 18: VOLCANO WATCHING

ridge called Loma del Alisal, which has a trail along its top and several flat spots for camping. There is no water or wind shelter here, and at 3600 meters (11,800 feet) it can be quite cold. By way of compensation, however, you will be directly across from Tungurahua—11 kilometers (6.8 miles) from the crater as the crow flies, with stunning views of its volcanic activity. Between you and the volcano lies the Río Chambo, 1400 meters (4600 feet) below. You can also admire six major summits from Loma del Alisal. Clockwise from the west they are: Chimborazo, Carihuayrazo, Cerro Hermoso (in the Llanganates), Tungurahua, El Altar, and Cubillines.

Your next goal is Mulmul, the highest point in this area. Mulmul is shown on the IGM map at a height of 3878 meters (12,724 feet). It should not be confused with the town of Mulmul to the southwest, nor Cerro Mulmul (3601 meters, 11,815 feet), which is 1 kilometer (0.6 mile) due east. A faint trail leads north along the ridge top of Loma del Alisal, arriving in **30 minutes** at a notch in the ridge, right at the base of Mulmul. A number of pretty bushes grow here, including many colorful lupins. A dirt road here contours west around the base of Mulmul, but it is far more satisfying to climb Mulmul for beautiful views from the top. As you get higher, you can look right into the crater of Tungurahua and—in addition to all the mountains mentioned above—you can now see the distant snowcapped peaks of Cotopaxi and Ilinizas in the north.

There is a surveyor's benchmark at the summit of Mulmul. The climb from the notch takes **45 minutes**.

Descend along the western flank of Mulmul until you reach the dirt road in **15 minutes**. Follow the road north toward Loma El Tablón. Walk downhill for **1 hour** to a fork; take the right branch (northeast) to climb for **10 minutes** to Loma El Tablón. There are antennas and a few small buildings on this flat-topped hill at 3400 meters (11,155 feet); you can camp with permission from the guard (no fee, but contributions of food or a

"Mama" Tungurahua erupting in December 1999 (Photo: Alois Speck)

small tip are appreciated). The site offers more spectacular views of Tungurahua, its crater, and the surrounding valleys.

From Loma El Tablón, head east on a trail that soon turns north along a ridge and descends toward the village of Sarangay. In **30 minutes** you will reach a dirt road that zigzags down to Sarangay, **15 minutes** ahead. Continue north through Sarangay to the town of Huambaló in another **30 minutes**.

Getting back: From Huambaló there are several buses a day to Pelileo, where there are more views of Tungurahua, basic services, and frequent bus connections to Ambato or Baños.

THE MOTHER OF ALL LANDSLIDES

Consider some of the cataclysmic history of Tungurahua as you walk alongside it. A previous version of the volcano, known to scientists as Tungurahua II, occupied roughly double the volume of the current structure. Tungurahua II most likely had larger glaciers than the present volcano, and its western slope was equally steep. Approximately 3000 years ago (very recently in geologic terms), a large eruption caused the entire western flank of Tungurahua II to collapse into the Chambo Valley. The resulting landslide occupied an estimated 8 cubic kilometers. The concise notation belittles this impressive volume, equal to 8 billion cubic meters, 283 billion cubic feet, 20 trillion gallons, or 80 trillion liters!

The central part of this tremendous landslide collided with a ridge of Igualata immediately across the Chambo Valley, forming a bench some 400 meters (1300 feet) above the valley floor. Another part of the landslide traveled up the Chambo River for 21 kilometers (13 miles) from the crater, leaving deposits up to 200 meters (650 feet) thick (which can easily be seen along this trek). Present-day towns and villages on both sides of the Chambo Valley occupy platforms built up by the landslide.

A second cataclysm ensued when water and ice-saturated parts of the original landslide began to move downslope; yet another occurred when the repressed waters of the Río Chambo, which had formed a very large lake, eventually breached the dike formed by the first two landslides. Following such a traumatic series of events, it seems that Tungurahua rested for approximately 700 years. It is all the more impressive that in the ensuing 2300 years, another volcano of the dimensions of the current Tungurahua has been built up. Further details are given in *Tungurahua Volcano, Ecuador* by Minard Hall et al (see Appendix B).

19 CRATER OF EL ALTAR

Rating: Moderately difficult, 20-kilometer (12.5-mile), 3- to 4-day trek.
Elevation: 3100 to 4300 meters (10,200 to 14,100 feet).
Maps: IGM 1:50,000: CT-ÑIV-C4 Guano, CT-ÑIV-D3 Palitahua,
CT-ÑIV-F1 Volcán El Altar; IGM 1:25,000: CT-ÑIV-D3c Cerros
Negros, CT-ÑIV-F1a Laguna Pintada.
Best time to visit: December through February are the driest months.
April and May are the wettest, when the plains can be extremely soggy
and the mud very deep. July and August are coldest.
Special gear: None.
Water: Abundant year-round throughout the route.
Hazards: Bulls, avalanches, and extremely rare flooding.
Annoyances: Mud.
Permits and fees: Foreign visitors pay a $10 fee to Sangay National
Park at the ranger station outside Candelaria.
Services: Hacienda Releche, located at the trailhead outside Candelaria,
offers a variety of useful services. Phone: (03)949-761 on-site, (03)960-848
in Riobamba. Services include comfortable accommodations at the
hacienda ($6 per person) and meals available if requested in advance (or
you can pay extra to use the kitchen facilities). They also run the
Collanes shelter, with simpler accommodation and facilities (same
prices as above). Arrangements must be made in advance to use the
shelter. Horses and mules for riding or hauling gear to the Collanes
shelter can be arranged at the *hacienda*.
Provisions: Baños and Riobamba have well-stocked shops with a
variety of provisions. Only a very few basic items are available in
Candelaria.

El Altar is called *Capac Urcu* (Chief Mountain) by local indigenous inhabitants, and for good reason. Before the cataclysmic eruption that collapsed the western wall of its crater in prehistoric times, El Altar may have
been the highest mountain in Ecuador (and possibly one of the highest
in the world). What remains today is no less impressive: an open *cirque* 3
kilometers (1.9 miles) in diameter, with a turquoise-green lake at its base,
surrounded by sheer cliffs rising 1000 meters (3300 feet) to a horseshoe
of glacier-topped summits. There are nine main peaks, all bearing religious names. El Obispo (the bishop) on the south face is the highest at

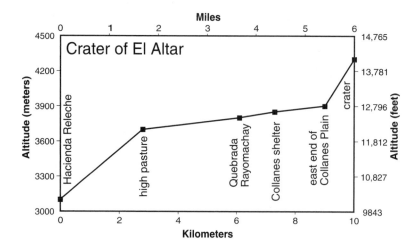

5319 meters (17,452 feet), followed by El Canónigo (the canon) on the north face at 5259 meters (17,255 feet).

The Ecuadorean Andes are dotted with many extinct volcanic cones, but none is as awe-inspiring (and at the same time as accessible to trekkers) as that of El Altar. The Collanes Plain (also called Collantes) was carved by glaciation subsequent to the collapse of the crater, and is equally worthy of admiration. This 2-kilometer-long (1.2-mile-long), gently sloping meadow is crisscrossed by meandering streams that gleam silver in the afternoon sun. Fog drifts incessantly over the landscape, jealously revealing its mysteries in bits and pieces, as condors glide majestically overhead. Crystal-clear moonlit nights provide a distinct and equally unforgettable image of the *cirque,* while avalanches rumble down the immense cliffs day and night, echoing throughout the crater.

In October 2000, after this trek was researched, an exceptionally large avalanche fell into the crater lake. The resulting "tidal wave" is estimated to have splashed 50 meters (160 feet) over the top of the normal outflow and roared across the Collanes Plain in less than one minute, wiping out everything in its path. The Collanes shelter was destroyed but subsequently rebuilt, and trekkers have returned. The plain currently presents a lunar landscape of bare boulders, and the woods at its east end are mostly gone.

Access: The trek begins and ends in the little village of Candelaria, which has daily bus service from the Terminal de Baños, corner Espejo and Cordovez, in Riobamba. There is usually one bus early in the morning and another in the afternoon (1.5 hours, $1); confirm schedules in

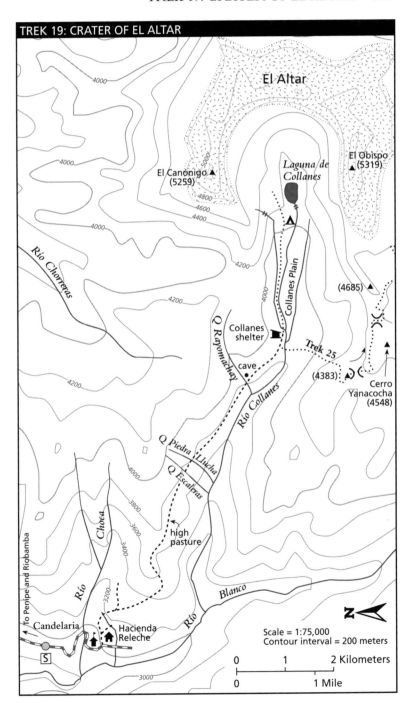

TREK 19: CRATER OF EL ALTAR

El Altar

El Canónigo ▲ (5259)

El Obispo ▲ (5319)

Laguna de Collanes

Río Chorreras

Q Rayomachay

Collanes Plain

(4685) ▲

Collanes shelter

Trek 25

cave

(4383)

Río Collanes

Cerro Yanacocha (4548)

Q Piedra Llucha

Q Escaleras

high pasture

Choca

Río

Río Blanco

To Penipe and Riobamba

Candelaria

Hacienda Releche

Scale = 1:75,000
Contour interval = 200 meters

0   1   2 Kilometers

0   1 Mile

advance. Every half hour there is a bus from the same location in Riobamba to Penipe (45 minutes, $.75).

From Penipe pick-ups can be hired to Hacienda Releche, at the trailhead past Candelaria (45 minutes, $10). Or you can walk along the road the 12 kilometers (7.5 miles) uphill from Penipe to Hacienda Releche in 3 to 4 hours.

Route: From Candelaria, walk **30 minutes** south along the road (which crosses the Río Choca) to Hacienda Releche. Just before the *hacienda* is the ranger station where you pay your park entry fee. If you have heavy gear, consider hiring pack animals. The walking times indicated below will depend more than anything else on the depth of the mud on the trail. Fortunately, you will quickly forget the rigors of this notoriously slippery slog once the peaks of El Altar come into view.

From Hacienda Releche, follow the broad trail that heads east and climbs steeply uphill alongside fenced pastures. There are two major forks at the start of the walk, both marked with arrows. Take the first fork left and the second one right; the remainder of the route is easy to follow. The trail at first winds up into the hills above the *hacienda,* bringing the valley of the Río Blanco, its fields and pastures, into view. After crossing a stream, the trail turns south and contours above the Río Blanco Valley for 1 kilometer (0.6 mile) before turning gradually east once again to enter the narrower valley of the Río Collanes.

Two hours after leaving the *hacienda,* you will reach a large, high pasture overlooking the intersection of the two valleys. From here the trail becomes narrower and muddier, contouring over tussock grass between 3700 and 3800 meters (12,150 and 12,450 feet) along the north side of the Collanes Valley. Several side streams, including the Quebrada Escaleras and the Quebrada Piedra Llucha (naked rock), are crossed along the way, making for an undulating track. At each bend you will get an additional enticing glimpse of the *cirque* of El Altar.

Three hours after the high pasture you will reach Quebrada Rayomachay, which can flash flood and become temporarily impassable after heavy rains. If you are headed out to Candelaria, just east of Quebrada Rayomachay is a cave where you can take shelter in a storm or while waiting for the water level to fall. It is **1 hour** more from the cave to the beginning of the Collanes Plain—in all, **6 to 7 hours** to walk up from Candelaria.

The muddy trail ends at the Collanes shelter, a cluster of straw-thatched huts located at the northwest end of the broad plain. There is also good camping just east of the huts, offering superb views of El Altar in clear weather. This is a good base for exploring the area; you can take side trips to the surrounding hills and connect here with Trek 25, High Lakes and Ridges. The climb south to the unnamed summit marked 4383 meters (14,381 feet) on the IGM map takes about 2 hours up and offers particularly fine views in clear weather.

From the shelter it is **1.5 hours** to the eastern edge of the Collanes Plain. Here, a patch of *fical* woods was severely damaged by flooding in 2000, and camping is now recommended higher up along a sparsely forested ridge that climbs eastward toward the crater of El Altar. This area offers fine views over the vast expanse of the Collanes Plain to the west and glimpses of Altar's cirque to the east. Many waterfalls tumble over the nearby cliffs.

It is **1 hour** of easy going up along the crest of this ridge (on the north side of the outflow of Laguna de Collanes, El Altar's crater lake) to an area of old moraine now covered with tussock grass. Here the pitch becomes much steeper and the scrambling more difficult, but an additional **1 hour** will bring you to the edge of a plateau at 4300 meters (14,100 feet) that covers the northwest quadrant of the crater. In clear weather there are superb views of the *cirque* and Laguna de Collanes (also known as Laguna Amarilla). **One hour** more will take you across the plateau to the snowline at the base of the granite cliffs, with countless views along the way. You can also carefully make your way down to the

Collanes shelter before the October 2000 floods

shore of the lake. The plateau is extremely soggy, and the crater is not suitable for camping. It is better to enjoy a day hike from Collanes.

Getting back: Two buses a day run from Candelaria to Riobamba, usually around midday and in the afternoon. Irregular pick-up trucks run from Candelaria to Penipe, from which there is frequent bus service to Riobamba. See "Access" above.

HOW DO YOU TELL THE SEX OF A VOLCANO?

Scientists remain uncertain about the exact date and circumstances of El Altar's massive crater collapse, but the native people of Ecuador have their own explanation. They begin by ascribing a personality—and a gender—to each and every mountain.

How do you tell the sex of a volcano? Just look. The *chuquiragua*, a small bush with bright orange flowers, grows only on the slopes of male volcanoes, while females are devoid of this plant. The significance of this botanical correlation is unclear, but there is universal agreement about the gender of Ecuador's major summits. Chimbo-razo is male and often dubbed *taita*, which means "father" in Quichua, while its companion to the northeast is called *"Mama"* Tungurahua.

El Altar is another male volcano. Local legend has it that this young upstart had his designs on Tungurahua, thus infringing on Chimborazo's long-standing relationship with her. *"Taita"* Chimborazo, the largest and most powerful of Ecuador's mountains, would not stand for such effrontery. He lifted an enormous club and smote El Altar's crown, producing the great gash in its crater.

As you walk through the gaping wound in the crater of El Altar, look back for a glimpse of Chimborazo. High above the wrinkled plains and valleys they dominate, Ecuador's volcanoes inhabit a world of their own. This insight was perhaps embellished by native lore, but a cloudless day is certain to convince any trekker of its validity.

The chuquiragua: *a favorite of the Chimborazo Hillstar hummingbird*

20 ATILLO AND OSOGOCHE LAKES

Research by Miguel Cazar
Editorial assistance by Popkje van der Ploeg
Rating: Moderately difficult, 22-kilometer (13.7-mile), 2- to 3-day trek.
Elevation: 3500 to 4200 meters (11,500 to 13,800 feet).
Map: IGM 1:50,000: CT-ÑV-A4 Totoras.
Best time to visit: The dry season is December through April.
December and January are the driest months, when the weather can be
very clear—but occasionally it can still rain. During the rest of the year,
rain and fog are very common.
Special gear: None.
Water: Take enough water for the first part of the trek in Atillo. After
the pass there are some streams with clear water.
Hazards: The fog can be very dense in this area, hiding steep slopes
and cliffs as well as complicating navigation.
Annoyances: None.
Permits and fees: There are no official entrance fees for this area.
Local people, however, might ask for a contribution when you pass
through their communities.
Services: Accommodations in the area are very basic but authentic. In
Atillo Chico and Totoras you can spend the night in a *choza,* a humble
thatched shelter. Dora Paña—a knowledgeable native guide—runs
Restaurant Los Saskines in Atillo Chico, and offers accommodation ($2
per person). If you want to stay in Totoras, ask for Pedro Cajilema or José
Ortega; they charge $1 per person to sleep in their *choza.*

Pack animals are easy to find in Atillo. (Horses are more common
here than cars.)
Provisions: The nearest city for shopping is Riobamba. In Atillo you
will find only a small shop with very basic supplies, but you can obtain
local trout and cheese here (and both are very good).

This trek through remote *páramo* takes you to some of the most beautiful
highland lakes of Ecuador. Far from tourist routes and flanked by very
traditional native communities, the *lagunas* near Atillo and Osogoche offer unique and spectacular scenery. The trek offers a magnificent overview of the lakes. In clear weather you can see both Chimborazo and
Sangay. The latter is Ecuador's most remote volcano—snowcapped and

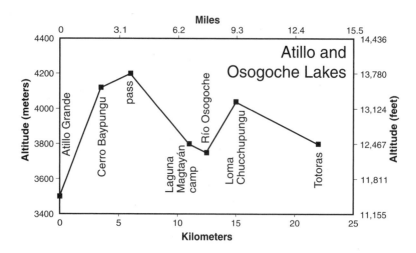

in constant activity. On the route you are surrounded by typical *páramo* vegetation such as gentians and club mosses; with a little luck you may catch a glimpse of the endangered Andean Condor.

There are more than sixty lakes in the vicinity of Atillo and Osogoche. The fog, which often shrouds this area, gives them a mysterious feeling. It is perhaps not surprising that local people recount a number of legends about the lakes. According to their oral history, the small island in the northern part of Laguna Colay once was a prison of the Puruha nation. Any prisoner who tried to escape would drown in the icy waters. Another legend (which has yet to be scientifically studied) is the so-called "tribute of the birds" in the Osogoche lakes (Lagunas Magtayán and Cubillín). Locals say that every year, in early September, thousands of small songbirds locally known as *cubibigs* fly over the lakes on their migration south. Many fall into the water and die, in what has been interpreted as a mass suicide.

Most of the trek is cross-country, but there are some animal tracks to follow and the low vegetation, dominated by tussock grass, facilitates navigation in clear weather. The area is thinly populated, and you may meet a few herdsmen or farmers. The people are friendly but rather reserved; they are not used to seeing outsiders.

Access: From Riobamba there is one daily bus to Atillo (the name is used for both Atillo Chico and Atillo Grande). It leaves from the corner of 10 de Agosto and Benalcázar at 1500 (1430 on Sundays, 4 hours, $2); to get a seat, be there at least an hour in advance. You will arrive in Atillo around nightfall, so you will have to spend the night there and start hiking the next day.

Route: The trek starts in Atillo Grande, 1 kilometer (0.6 mile) south of Atillo Chico. Ask for the Caspicara School, and from there follow the main unpaved road toward Macas. After **10 minutes** take a small dirt road south (right) to cross the Río Atillo. In another **10 minutes** the road leads to a trout farm (where you can buy good fresh trout). At the back of the farm, cross the small Río Cachi and follow a trail south; the trail disappears after only 100 meters (300 feet).

You will now be standing at the foot of Cerro Baypungu (4120 meters, 13,500 feet), which lies to the south (and which you are about to climb). The northeast flank of this mountain is covered with a forest of young pine trees. Climb to the right of the pines. (You may wish to zigzag, because the ascent is quite steep.) Your first goal is a ridge above the valley of the Río Cachi, from where you can see the river below. This ridge at first climbs south and later turns southwest. Follow the tussock-covered terrain toward the summit; it will take **3 to 4 hours** (depending on your stamina) from the trout farm to the top of Baypungu. Standing on the summit, you will have a wonderful view northeast over the lakes near Atillo and, if the weather is clear enough, past them in the same direction to Sangay. To the east and southeast are more lakes, Iguan Cocha and Pucacocha, and to the west Quebrada Bolsa Huaycu. To the northwest is Chimborazo. The vegetation here is low but very pretty, with a great variety of tiny bright flowers.

Continue climbing south toward the next set of craggy summits known as Los Sasquines. In 1 hour you will reach level, boggy ground at the base of the crags. Skirt the bog on its east (left) side and then turn west to cross it. There are some spots suitable for camping here and you can get water from small streams flowing into Quebrada Bolsa Huaycu. After you cross the bog, head for a pass between the summits labeled 4348 and 4377 meters (14,266 and 14,361 feet) on the IGM map.

There is some confusion about the names here, but locals may refer to these as Cerro Achipungu and Los Sasquines, respectively. It will take **30 minutes** to reach the pass at 4200 meters (13,800 feet); there you can look down, south, to the largest lakes around Osogoche: Magtayán and Cubillín.

Beyond the pass are more places to camp, with a small stream for water. Our route begins an easy descent along sheep trails, southwest to the valley of the Río Osogoche. At first you will be high above Laguna Magtayán; then you can either head southwest toward the village of Osogoche Grande, or track a little to the east toward the lakeshore.

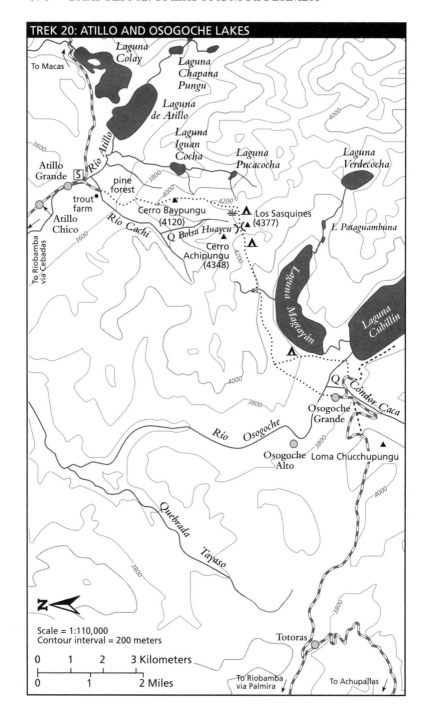

There are nice camping possibilities along the latter route, **3 hours** beyond the pass.

Follow the shore of Laguna Magtayán south, then continue south toward Laguna Cubillín. Before reaching this larger lake, cross a small bridge over the Río Osogoche, **45 minutes** past the camping spots. Immediately after crossing the bridge, turn west and follow a good trail for **30 minutes** to reach the small, unpaved road that connects Osogoche Grande with Totoras. The road walk west to Totoras will take **3 to 4 hours**; you can take a few shortcuts where the road winds its way out of the Río Osogoche Valley, up the slopes of Loma Chucchupungu.

Getting back: A daily bus from Totoras to Riobamba leaves at 0500 (3 hours, $1.40). During the rest of the day there is very little traffic, but you might be able to get a ride with a pick-up truck. They can drop you off at the Pan-American Highway (1 hour), where you can catch any northbound bus to Riobamba.

Laguna Colay (Photo: Miguel Cazar)

21 VICUÑA TRAIL

Rating: Moderately difficult, 22-kilometer (13.7-mile), 2- to 3-day trek. Several worthwhile side trips are available along the way, and there is an alternate route out. The combination of these options may add 1 or 2 days to the trek.

Elevation: 3550 to 4400 meters (11,700 to 14,450 feet).

Maps: IGM 1:50,000: CT-ÑIV-C1 Chimborazo, CT-ÑIV-C2 Quero. The IGM's *Mapa Ecoturístico de los Volcanes Chimborazo y Carihuayrazo* provides a general overview.

Best time to visit: July and August are the driest months, but also the coldest. December is sometimes nice. Rain and fog are common at other times of the year.

Special gear: Be prepared for snow and below-freezing temperatures overnight.

Water: Plentiful in streams along most of the route.

Hazards: Bulls.

Annoyances: None.

Permits and fees: In principle, foreign visitors pay a $10 fee to the Reserva de Producción Faunística Chimborazo, but there are no facilities for collecting the fee along this route. The community of Mechahuasca charges a fee of $1 per person for traveling through their lands. They also expect an additional contribution if you spend the night there.

Services: Posada La Estación, located at the start of the trek in Urbina, offers a variety of useful services. This pleasant converted railway station is a convenient place to spend the night before heading out. Accommodations are $6 per person, meals $5; the Riobamba telephone is (03)942-215 for reservations. They can also provide pack animals. Daniel Villacís, who lives in the village of 12 de Octubre, 3 kilometers (2 miles) north of Urbina, and 2 kilometers (1.2 miles) west of the Pan-American Highway, is also a reliable muleteer who knows the area well.

Provisions: The starting point of this trek is between Ambato and Riobamba. Both cities have well-stocked shops. There are no shops at Urbina, Mechahuasca, or 12 de Octubre.

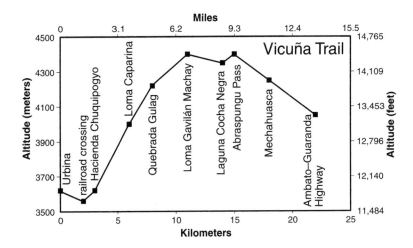

The sight of Chimborazo rising to 6310 meters (20,703 feet) above sea level is among the most impressive in all the Andes. Since the earth bulges near the equator, this snowcapped giant is not only the highest mountain in Ecuador, but also the highest in the world if measured from the center of the planet. Its base is approximately 20 kilometers (12.4 miles) in diameter, and it is widest from east to west. Chimborazo is an extinct volcano. Volcanic debris on its western flanks forms the *arenal*, a harsh, high semidesert comparable to the *altiplano* of Bolivia. Eight kilometers (5 miles) northeast of Chimborazo is its relatively diminutive companion, Carihuayrazo, another extinct volcano that reaches "only" 5018 meters (16,464 feet). Its several peaks have been heavily eroded by glacial activity, giving Carihuayrazo a particularly craggy appearance.

Between Chimborazo and Carihuayrazo lies the broad valley of the Río Mocha. The vegetation here is that of a relatively dry *páramo*: tussock grass on the hillsides, a variety of cushion plants in the valley floors, bushes such as the *chuquiragua* and the *sacha chocho* (wild lupin), and very few stands of *fical* trees. Birds found here include the *curiquingues*, snipes, and several species of hummingbirds. There are many rabbits and a few deer, but the highlight of the mammalian population are definitely the vicuñas, llamas, and alpacas (see "Vicuñas and Other Camelids" at the end of this trek description).

This trek follows the valley of the Río Mocha up-river, along the north flank of Chimborazo to the Continental Divide; views along the way are magnificent in clear weather. From the pass between the two mountains, you can either continue northwest to the vicuña reserve at Mechahuasca and exit at the Ambato–Guaranda Road, or make a loop and return along the south flank of Carihuayrazo, following the Río Mocha from its source to the village of 12 de Octubre, near the starting point at Urbina.

Access: Urbina is located approximately halfway (25 kilometers, 16 miles) between Ambato and Riobamba along the Pan-American Highway. Take a bus from either city (frequent service) and tell the driver you are going to Urbina. Get off the bus at a dirt road marked with a sign, "Posada La Estación–Urbina." Walk west along the dirt road; in 1.2 kilometers (0.75 mile) you will reach a cobbled road and the old railroad station (at 3619 meters or 11,874 feet, the highest point on the Ecuadorean railway). Next to the station house stands a lone pine tree, an unmistakable landmark.

Route: From the station at Urbina, follow the cobbled road southwest, gently downhill for **30 minutes**. Just after the road crosses the railway tracks, and before the village of Santa Rosa de Chuquipogyos, take a dirt road to the right; it will climb gradually to the north, through onion, potato, and barley fields. You will have excellent views of the east face of Chimborazo here, to spur you on for the "grunt" ahead. In **30 minutes** you will reach the Hacienda Chuquipogyo on your right, and a fork. Take the left branch, which climbs more steeply to the west (still through cultivated fields). You will reach another fork in **20 minutes**. Our route again continues along the left branch, climbing to the west directly toward Chimborazo. You are 9 kilometers (5.6 miles) away from the mountain here, but it feels as though you could reach out and touch the shimmering ice-cream cone of its glaciers. In **20 minutes** you will cross a metal gate by a small stream. The road now turns north and climbs harder toward Loma Caparina, a ridge top at 4000 meters (13,100 feet), which you will reach in **30 minutes**.

As you look up at Chimborazo, you can now see some impressive brick-red rock formations, highlighted by the white snow. By this point the tilled fields have given way to tussock-covered *páramo*. Keep following the road, which at Loma Caparina will turn west again. You will reach an intersection in **15 minutes**, with a trail going to the left and a small road to the right. Do not take either; instead, continue straight along the main road. **Five minutes** ahead you will reach another minor fork; take the right branch. Passing a few small ponds to your right (north), you will arrive at the edge of Rumipamba Grande in **30 minutes**. Rumipamba

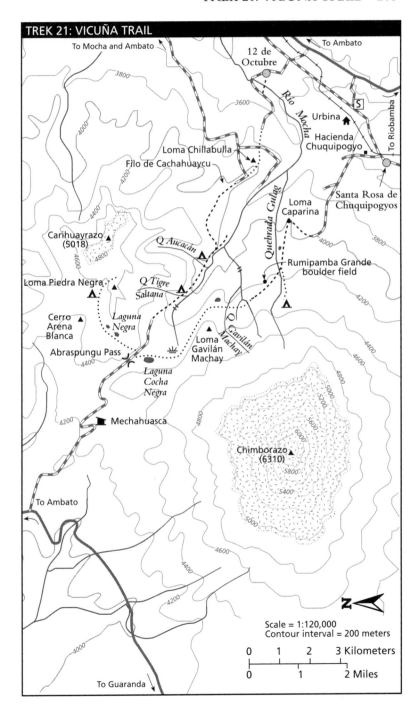

TREK 21: VICUÑA TRAIL

To Mocha and Ambato

To Ambato

12 de Octubre

Río Mocha

Urbina

S

To Riobamba

Hacienda Chuquipogyo

Loma Chillabulla

Filo de Cachahuaycu

Loma Caparina

Santa Rosa de Chuquipogyos

Carihuayrazo (5018)

Q Aucacán

Rumipamba Grande boulder field

Loma Piedra Negra

Q Tigre Saltana

Quebrada Gulag

Cerro Aréna Blanca

Laguna Negra

Gavilán Machay

Abraspungu Pass

Loma Gavilán Machay

Laguna Cocha Negra

Mechahuasca

Chimborazo (6310)

To Ambato

To Guaranda

Scale = 1:120,000
Contour interval = 200 meters

0   1   2   3 Kilometers

0   1   2 Miles

means boulder field in Quichua, and indeed there are many large stones strewn about this broad plain.

Five minutes ahead you will reach Quebrada Gulag, which runs with silty melt-water from the glaciers of Chimborazo. There are ample spots for camping **20 minutes** up the *quebrada*, which heads west toward a glacier of Chimborazo. Take your water from one of the small, clear streams nearby (some of these may dry up during July and August), rather than from the milky main drainage. From the campsite you can make an interesting 3- to 4-hour side trip, walking cross-country to the head of the *quebrada* and possibly up to the toe of the glacier (depending on conditions at the time).

To continue on our trek, return to the road in **20 minutes** and, after crossing Quebrada Gulag, follow the road northwest across the Rumipamba Grande plain. Here it deteriorates into a rough track, which can be very muddy in the rainy season. In **45 minutes** you will reach the first of three branches that make up Quebrada Gavilán Machay, **15 minutes** later the second one, and in another **10 minutes** the third branch (which has the clearest water). From this third stream, the trail climbs hard for **5 minutes** to a pretty pond in a bowl surrounded by flowering vegetation. There are spectacular views here of Carihuayrazo over the water, Chimborazo looming large overhead, and back toward Rumipamba Grande.

The trail continues along the left (west) shore of the pond in a northerly direction and becomes less distinct. It drops slightly at first, then climbs steadily along the tussock-covered slopes of Loma Gavilán Machay. **Twenty minutes** from the pond you will reach this ridge at 4400 meters (14,450 feet). From here, descend steeply for **20 minutes** along a rutted path and then continue northwest, crossing several low perpendicular ridges. In **30 minutes** you will reach a swampy basin—the source of the Río Mocha—where the path is again less distinct. Stick to the edge of the straw-covered hills and watch your step here, to avoid sinking waist-deep into the orange mud. Spectacular cliffs tower above you at the base of Chimborazo; to the northeast are more nice views of Carihuayrazo.

Take the trail north along the western edge of the swamp. It climbs and in **20 minutes** reaches Laguna Cocha Negra. Follow the eastern shore of the lake and continue north for another **20 minutes** to meet a dirt road at the Abraspungu Pass. This is the Continental Divide, at 4400 meters (14,450 feet). Water flowing west reaches the Pacific Ocean through the Río Guayas in less than 150 kilometers (93 miles); that flowing east is carried almost 3500 kilometers (2200 miles) to the Atlantic by the Amazon River. From the pass, the main trek follows the road northwest; you can also make a 5- to 7-hour side trip here to the base of a glacier on Carihuayrazo, or loop back in 1 to 2 days to the village of 12 de Octubre along the north side of the Río Mocha. These alternative routes are described below.

Following the main route, you will enter communal lands as soon as you begin your gentle descent northwest along the road. Here you are likely to see native shepherds with flocks of sheep, llamas, alpacas, and cattle. With a little luck, you will also be able to spot the first vicuñas. After **1 hour** of easy road walking, you will reach a metal gate and a fork immediately beyond it. Follow the left branch for 250 meters (800 feet) to some buildings on the left. These were the Mechahuasca headquarters for the vicuña reintroduction project. There is tap water here, and you can camp or stay in the buildings (now run by the local community); someone with a key will come as soon as they notice you. Groups of vicuñas can often be seen in the valley to the southeast of the buildings.

From the metal gate, the right branch of the road continues to descend through parched landscape—the beginning of the *arenal* of Chimborazo. It passes a few homes and, after crossing a small stream in **30 minutes**, reaches two newer buildings. These are also shelters, but were not in use at the time of writing. Continue on the road past the shelters. At the first fork go left; at the second fork, by a stone corral, go right. In **30 minutes** you will reach the paved highway that connects Ambato

Snow-capped summits of Chimborazo and Carihuayrazo: between them lies the Río Mocha Valley

and Guaranda. There is a large orange sign here reading "Reseva de Producción Faunística Chimborazo."

Abraspungu Pass to Carihuayrazo: If you wish to make this side trip toward Carihuayrazo, then take the road from the pass southeast for about 500 meters (1600 feet) or **10 minutes**. Leave the road and follow a small valley uphill to the northeast. There is no trail here; once you emerge from the valley, use your compass to follow a bearing of 45 degrees. (Note that dense fog can obliterate all landmarks.) Climb gradually in this direction over a few bare ridges, always keeping the black rock of Loma Piedra Negra to your right. **Thirty minutes** from the road you will pass a small lake, Laguna Negra. Take water here, then climb for **20 minutes** to another even smaller unnamed pond. Past the pond, turn east and climb for another **20 minutes** toward the saddle between Loma Piedra Negra on your right and Cerro Arena Blanca on your left. After crossing the saddle, you will find a small trail that leads east in **15 minutes** to a flat area suitable for camping, at the base of the black cliffs of Loma Piedra Negra. The only water here is from stagnant ponds. At 4540 meters (14,900 feet), this is one of the base camps used by climbers headed for Carihuayrazo. It has wonderful views of the mountain's western face, with a waterfall tumbling from glaciers towering above the cliffs. The area has a great variety of cushion plants and some high-altitude birds, including snipes. A faint trail leads from above this campsite to a pass between Loma Piedra Negra and the massif of Carihuayrazo (reached in **1 hour**).

Abraspungu Pass to 12 de Octubre: The south flank of Carihuayrazo above the Río Mocha Valley offers a good way to return to the Ambato–Riobamba Road. From the Abraspungu Pass, follow the road southeast. It descends gradually and narrows, no longer passable by vehicle. To the south are views of Laguna Cocha Negra and the swampy basin that is the source of the Río Mocha (behind which the glaciers of Chimborazo loom high above massive cliffs). The road eventually becomes a track and descends gradually over a series of gentle switchbacks to Quebrada Tigre Saltana, reached in **1.5 hours**. After crossing the stream of Quebrada Tigre Saltana, there is a flat area on your left (suitable for camping) and nice views of a waterfall at the head of the Río Mocha Valley.

From here the trail continues to descend gradually, following the valley of the Mocha. It goes through a small stand of trees and later through more open, tussock-covered *páramo*. There are small streams near the trail; if it has been raining they overflow, making the path quite muddy. In **1 hour** you will reach Quebrada Aucacán. After crossing this stream on a footbridge, you can find another area suitable for camping a few meters downstream. Take some water here, as there are fewer streams ahead.

From Quebrada Aucacán the trail climbs through tussock grass. There are nice views of a 100-meter (300-foot) waterfall in Quebrada Gavilán Machay, on the south side of the broad Río Mocha Valley. In **30 minutes** you will reach a fork. Take the left branch, which climbs more steeply to the northeast toward a ridge called Filo de Cachahuaycu or Sachahuaycu. The trail gradually swings around to the southeast before it reaches the top of the ridge. In **1 hour** it becomes a dirt road. This road will lead you to the town of Mocha—but that requires 10 kilometers (6.2 miles) of very circuitous walking. Instead, when the road makes a sharp left turn, continue cross-country to the southeast, to the top of Loma Chillabulla or Chillobullo (**1 hour** after the trail becomes a road). This point offers fine views in all directions. Descend the eastern slopes of Loma Chillabulla,

cross another dirt road, and reach a third dirt road. This takes **30 minutes**. Follow this road for **45 minutes**, at first down to a footbridge over the Río Mocha and then up to the village of 12 de Octubre. There are no services or transport here, but another **1 hour** of road walking will bring you either to the Pan-American Highway or back to the railway station at Urbina.

Getting back: From Mechahuasca, you will reach a point on the highway 50 kilometers (31 miles) from Ambato and 44 kilometers (27 miles) from Guaranda. There is frequent bus service in both directions, but remember that travel is safest during the daytime here. To get back from Urbina or 12 de Octubre, see "Access" above.

The old railroad station at Urbina

VICUÑAS AND OTHER CAMELIDS

No picture of the Andes is complete without the graceful figures of the native camelids: llamas, alpacas, guanacos, and vicuñas. Their natural habitats are high grasslands, for which they are ideally suited with extremely warm coats of wool and a split upper lip that prevents them from destroying the roots of the fragile vegetation they graze on.

For centuries, camelids have been an integral part of life in many high Andean communities. Llamas and alpacas were domesticated and used as beasts of burden, as sources of meat and wool, and as part of religious rituals. Both guanacos (not present in Ecuador) and vicuñas have remained wild and are today found mostly in national parks and reserves. In Ecuador you are likely to see llamas—and to a lesser extent alpacas—grazing in high pastures or traditional stone corrals.

Prized for its fine fleece, the vicuña was hunted to extinction in Ecuador during the colonial era. In the 1980s small herds of vicuñas were brought from Chile, Peru, and Bolivia, and reintroduced to the high plateaus of the Reserva de Producción Faunística Chimborazo, centered around Mechahuasca. The reintroduction project has been very successful: numbers are growing steadily, and vicuñas have been sighted all around Chimborazo.

Vicuñas are the smallest of the Andean camelids, very graceful and delicate in appearance, with long, slender necks and legs. The coat on their backs is reddish-brown, and they have fluffy white bibs and undersides. Vicuña wool is extremely soft and warm; it is considered the finest animal fiber after silk, and was used by native cultures for their very best textiles. In precolonial times, vicuña garments could be worn only by the Inca emperor or his family.

Vicuñas live between 3500 and 5500 meters (11,500 and 18,000 feet) above sea level, in small herds of one male and his harem of several females and their young. Lone bachelors, which have been expelled from the family groups, are seen grazing on their own. Vicuñas are quite shy; a telephoto lens is an asset when you try to photograph them.

22 ROYAL ROAD

Rating: Moderately difficult, 33-kilometer (20.5-mile), 3- to 4-day trek.
Elevation: 2600 to 4250 meters (8500 to 14,000 feet).
Map: IGM 1:50,000: CT-ÑIV-C3 Guaranda.
Best time to visit: July and August are the driest months, but also the coldest. December is sometimes also dry. Strong winds and fog are common throughout the year.
Special gear: Cold-weather gear is essential.
Water: Available from infrequent streams along the route; start the walk with a good supply and replenish at every opportunity.
Hazards: None.
Annoyances: None.
Permits and fees: None.
Services: Basic accommodations are available at Pulingue San Pablo (Pulingue on the IGM map) along the trek. Local guides can be hired here and at neighboring La Chorrera for day trips in the area. More elaborate accommodation and meals are available at Chimborazo Base Camp, just north on the paved road. Reservations are required; phone (03)964-915.
Provisions: Riobamba is the place to shop. Only a few very basic items are available in Pulingue San Pablo.

Trekking as a form of time travel? Certainly! Of all the routes that criss-cross Ecuador, those joining the highlands with the Pacific coast are of the greatest historical importance. Among these is the Camino Real or Royal Road, perhaps already used in pre-Inca times, and particularly important during the colonial era and first decades of the Republic. Along this route endless caravans of llamas, horses, mules, and donkeys transported people and goods between the port of Guayaquil and the capital of Quito (sometimes in only 5 days). Richard Spruce traveled this road from east to west in 1860 in quest of quinine; Edward Whymper went through in the opposite direction in 1879 on route to his historical first ascent of Chimborazo.

This trek follows a particularly scenic section of the Camino Real along the southern flank of Chimborazo, joining the cities of Riobamba and Guaranda. You will have the majestic sight of Ecuador's heavily glaci-ated highest summit over your right shoulder throughout the walk. The

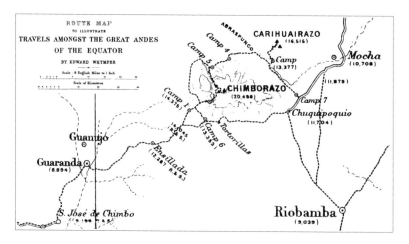

Edward Whymper's 1879 map showing the Royal Road

route is little used today: in some sections, contemporary backcountry roads following it are frequented only by local farmers and herdsmen. Other sections (especially where the road crosses the high, dry *arenal*) seem untouched since colonial times. Still other parts are completely overgrown, with bushes and trees choking the old rutted path.

Access: The trek starts in the village of Cuatro Esquinas, 15 kilometers (9.3 miles) northwest of Riobamba. Note that Cuatro Esquinas (four corners) is a very common place name, used to refer to many four-way intersections; in the vicinity of this trek there are at least two other places with the same name. The Cuatro Esquinas where this walk starts is just north of Pulinguí and reached by El Cóndor buses that leave from Parque Barriga (corner Diego Ibarra and Veloz) in Riobamba. On weekdays there are six buses between 0640 and 0815, less-frequent service later in the day. The 0640 and 1050 buses continue on school days to Sanjapamba, which is along the trek's route, saving a kilometer (0.6 mile) uphill. On Saturday there are buses every 20 minutes, but on Sunday only one at 1400. The ride takes 45 minutes and costs $.50.

Route: From Cuatro Esquinas, follow the dirt road uphill to the northwest. Cross the railway tracks, go past cultivated fields, and in **15 minutes** reach the hamlet of Sanjapamba. Continue along the same road; it climbs gradually and enters a fragrant pine forest from which you will emerge **40 minutes** later. Once out of the woods, the views of Chimborazo through the crystal-clear air are superb; it feels like you can reach out and touch the ice. At the fork to the right, continue straight. Cross the bridge over a usually dry gully, and take another fork right immediately after. Continue straight on the road that follows the deep gully on your right and climbs north. You will be in open country, surrounded by the last crops of potatoes, barley, and broad beans.

In **20 minutes** you will reach a smaller road to the left; follow this west amid tussock-covered *páramo*. In **10 minutes** a larger road comes in from the left; continue along it, still traveling west. In another **10 minutes** you will reach a four-way intersection and a waterworks tank; continue straight to the west. Soon the road starts winding and climbing; flowering bushes such as *chuquiragua* and Saint John's Wort, as well as a few cushion plants, are interspersed among the tussock grass. In **30 minutes** the road levels and then crosses the shallow valley of Quebrada Tauri Machay; in another **20 minutes** it reaches the edge of the much deeper glacial valley of Quebrada Coshne Paccha. This area is also known as Cuartel Huayco. A **15-minute** descent along the road will bring you to the valley floor, where there are camping possibilities (with more great views up to Chimborazo's glaciers) and a reliable stream for water.

The road zigzags out of the valley and in **40 minutes** climbs to a ridge. Here it widens and is lined with pines as it descends gradually to meet the paved San Juan–Chimborazo Road (access to the mountain's climbing shelters), just before a bridge over Quebrada Yuragpolvo, reached in **20 minutes**. After crossing the bridge, you can continue along the paved road for 2 kilometers (1.2 miles) to Pulingue San Pablo, or you can take the more direct route: follow one of the small trails that climbs to the right of the road and leads (in **30 minutes**) to the hamlet of La Chorrera. From there a steep path descends in **10 minutes** back to the paved road at the village of Pulingue San Pablo.

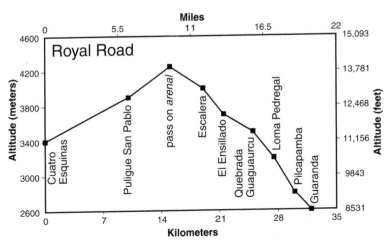

The community hall of Pulingue San Pablo (called Casa Cóndor and built in the shape of a condor) has basic accommodation for visitors, with bunk beds ($3 per person), kitchen facilities, a small shop with a very few items, and possibly meals (if given enough notice). At 3900 meters (12,800 feet), it gets very cold at night. Nearby, Chimborazo Base Camp is nicely furnished and comfortable; $25 per person including dinner and breakfast. From the village there are wonderful views of Chimborazo's five summits. The route described thus far can also be done as a day walk. If you start early, you can get to the paved road in time to catch a bus to either Riobamba or Guaranda. These buses go by around 1500. You can also take a bus to Pulingue San Pablo and start the walk here, making it a day shorter.

From Pulingue San Pablo, walk north along the path that follows the west bank of Quebrada Totorillas; it goes through barren, windswept, eroded land and in **15 minutes** turns west. **Five minutes** ahead the trail splits. The right branch crosses the streams and goes to the paved road; take the left branch, which runs alongside a barbed-wire fence. In **15 minutes** the fence ends and there are some spots by the stream suitable for camping. From here the bank of the stream gets steeper, and the trail climbs high above it. The views of the southern face of Chimborazo and the valley of Quebrada Totorillas below are beautiful. In **15 minutes** the trail ducks into a small valley with cushion plants amidst the tussock; **5 minutes** farther, an exceptionally clear spring emerges from a small tunnel. Tank up here (the area ahead is very dry). It is possible to camp nearby, but it can be very cold and windy.

From the spring continue west. There is no clear trail right here, but very shortly, on the slope of the hillside below you, the old Camino Real comes into plain sight. Follow it as it climbs steadily and in **30 minutes** reaches the flat *arenal* at 4100 meters (13,500 feet). This vast expanse of volcanic sand interrupted only by the most minute of plants and flowers, the colossus of Chimborazo looming above to your right, and the howling wind sweeping off the ice of its glaciers, combine to make you feel very small indeed. The ancient road heads across the open *arenal* and then contours along the edge of a hillside, still traveling west. The sandstone hills nearby have been sculpted into interesting shapes by the wind. In **40 minutes** the track passes through a large, dry gully. In its wind-sheltered interior, *chuquiragua* bushes and other plants thrive. It then climbs gradually for **20 minutes** to the pass at 4250 meters (13,944 feet), just north of Cerro Achu.

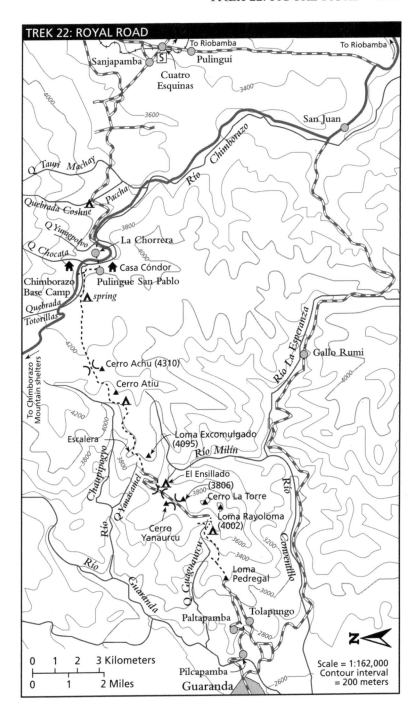

Follow the road southwest along level *arenal*. In **10 minutes** it becomes a trail again and begins to descend. Follow it down, but make sure to veer south (left) to cross above the deep gully that starts here. You will reach a clear trail heading west along the north flank of Cerro Atiu, above the south bank of the Río Chaupipogyo. The trail descends gradually, and the vegetation increases; bushes such as the *chuquiragua* reappear alongside polylepis trees. In **1.5 hours** you will reach flat ground suitable for camping near small streams—but it can be soggy underfoot, and also windy. There are magnificent views to the west, as a series of ridges descend toward the coastal plain and gnarled polylepis trees perch precariously on the windswept cliffs.

The trail continues to descend gradually. After **30 minutes** you will climb through a cut in a rocky outcrop and then cross a flat ridge top called Escalera. Once again the views of Chimborazo are superb, but the

Marcelo Guamán headed home across the arenal *of Chimborazo*

wind can be fierce. The trail descends from Escalera; **10 minutes** later it deteriorates noticeably on the slopes of Loma Excomulgado. Here are several crumbling branches of the old Camino Real and an unused aqueduct. The easiest walking is along a small path that gradually descends southwest and in **20 minutes** leads to a contemporary dirt road. Follow this road south for another **15 minutes** to a hairpin bend to the right. At the curve, leave the road and take a shortcut straight downhill, again bearing southwest. In **15 minutes** the road will lead to a grand saddle known as El Ensillado. There is plenty of flat ground for camping in this area; for water, descend to a tributary of the Río Milín to the southeast. At El Ensillado you will again meet the dirt road; follow it for **30 minutes** as it climbs steadily southwest to a small pass between the pine-covered Cerro Yanaurcu to the north and an unnamed rocky summit to the south. This summit is labeled 3806 meters (12,487 feet) on the IGM map. The road now descends gently to the southwest, and **20 minutes** farther you will have fine views down to Guaranda in the distance. Although your destination is well in sight, the most difficult part of the trek is about to begin.

Continue along the road that turns south and contours along the slopes of Cerro La Torre. In **20 minutes** it deteriorates to a very poor track that gets lost between the tussock grass and planted pines. After crossing the top of Quebrada Guaguaurcu (the drainage between Cerro La Torre and Loma Rayoloma), descend west cross-country amidst the pines for **30 minutes** to the point where a trail you will see below crosses the same drainage. This trail is once again a remnant of the Camino Real; the section between the pass by Cerro Yanaurcu and Quebrada Guaguaurcu is today totally impassable. There is a small clearing suitable for camping near the stream. The valley is very pretty, there are many flowering bushes, and pines permeate the air with a fine scent. Take water at Quebrada Guaguaurcu, as it is scarce ahead.

It is slow and difficult going from here (you must fight the dense vegetation that has overgrown the abandoned road), but you will be rewarded by fine views down to the Guaranda Valley on your right. In **2.5 hours** you will reach a grassy clearing by a large pine, and **20 minutes** farther, on a gentle ridge crest, you will meet a larger trail going downhill to the right. Cross the gate that lies ahead and continue southwest along the old worn gully, still the Camino Real. In **20 minutes**, at Loma Pedregal, you will reach an open grassy clearing; a few meters farther is a dirt road. Follow the road southwest. In **10 minutes** it will reach a fork, but "all roads lead to Rome" at this point—the Rome of Ecuador, that is. This is Guaranda's nickname, because it is surrounded by seven hills. The left branch goes via the village of Tolapungo. The right branch, described here, goes via the villages of Paltapamba and Pilcapamba.

The road to Paltapamba descends steeply over innumerable *camellones*. When it has been raining, they represent a challenge even for the most skillful trekker. In **1 hour** you will meet a much better road; another **15 minutes** will take you to Paltapamba.

Getting back: There are irregular pick-up trucks from Paltapamba to Guaranda throughout the day (20 minutes, $.50). Or you can take a shortcut straight downhill to a larger unpaved road that leads west 1 kilometer (0.6 mile) to the village of Pilcampamba (where there are also pick-ups) and then another 2 kilometers (1.2 miles) on to Guaranda.

23 HOT SPRINGS IN THE CLOUD FOREST

Rating: Difficult, 54-kilometer (33.5-mile), 5- to 7-day trek.
Elevation: 2850 to 4000 meters (9350 to 13,100 feet).
Maps: IGM 1:50,000: CT-ÑIV-F1 Volcán El Altar, CT-ÑIV-F3 Llactapamba de Alao.
Best time to visit: December through February are the driest months; April and May can be very wet.
Special gear: A machete or pruning shears may be helpful past La Magdalena; it is essential past El Placer. A fishing rod is optional.
Water: Abundant year-round throughout the route.
Hazards: None.
Annoyances: Many biting insects and ticks; take repellent. Bamboo and huge grass clog the trails at lower elevations.
Permits and fees: Foreign visitors pay a $10 fee to Sangay National Park at the ranger station outside Alao.
Services: Pack animals can be hired in Alao, but they can only go as far as La Magdalena.
Provisions: Riobamba is the place to shop. Only a few very basic items are available in Alao.

El Placer (meaning pleasure) is a most fitting name for the destination of this trek. This broad valley in the heart of Sangay National Park is not easy to reach, but the persistent trekker is richly rewarded by a comfortable shelter and soothing hot springs set in lovely, mature secondary-growth

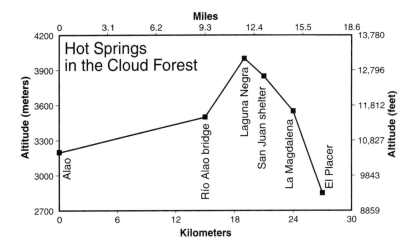

forest. Nearby is a gorgeous waterfall, as well as good fishing and chilly bathing in the headwaters of the Río Palora (one of the tributaries of the Pastaza and ultimately the Amazon).

The area teems with life, ranging from tapir and Spectacled Bear through abundant mixed-species flocks of cloud forest birds, to butterflies and all-too-common ticks, mosquitoes, and black flies. The equally impressive flora includes native trees such as the *pumamaqui*, *fical*, and alder, a variety of orchids and other colorful flowers, mosses, lichens, mushrooms, and a great many ferns.

A generation ago this area was the home of a few hardy settlers who cleared the forest to extract lumber and run cattle. Today it is protected by Sangay National Park. Trekking here, you will benefit from the efforts of the former inhabitants: some of their simple homes are now used as shelters, and the vehicle road that once ran 24 kilometers (15 miles) from Alao to La Magdalena makes for easy walking along the first part of the hike. Past La Magdalena the going is much rougher, but parts of the trail are still *empalizado* (lined with logs) or cobbled to protect against the worst of the mud. At other times you may want to curse the settlers, not only for their destruction of the primary forest, but also because two secondary-growth species—the tangled bamboo and enormous grass—frequently clog the trails at lower elevations.

For those with a taste for even more adventure, this trek can also be the start of a much longer foray into the Oriente jungle. Trails once ran from El Placer to the now-abandoned gold-mining settlement of Huamboya, as well as to the contemporary town of Palora. These routes

have long since been reclaimed by the forest. They involve several difficult and dangerous river crossings, and neither trip should be attempted
without adequate preparation and a thoroughly knowledgeable guide.
Inquiries about guides may be made in advance in Alao.

Access: The gateway for this trek is the town of Alao (see Trek 25,
High Lakes and Ridges).

Route: For route details as far as Laguna Negra, see Trek 25. It is a
7.5-hour walk from Alao to Laguna Negra, or **3.5 hours** from the quarry
turnoff (which can be reached by car) to Laguna Negra.

From Laguna Negra and the pass at 4000 meters (13,124 feet), follow the old road and descend to the east, winding back and forth along a
steep tussock-covered slope. It is tempting but not advisable to look for
shortcuts here. The descent is very abrupt, with a few small cliffs—and it
is easy to get lost in the fog. Stay on the trail. In **30 minutes** you will
reach the San Juan shelter, a rough wood and mud structure in rather
poor shape. There is room for six plus camping possibilities nearby, and a
small stream for water; if it is dry, a more reliable water source is 15
minutes down the trail (see below).

Past San Juan, the trail continues to zigzag through stands of *sigses*
and wild lupins; in **15 minutes** you will reach a series of streams tumbling over large granite slabs: the headwaters of the Río Palora. You will
cross these streams three more times down the trail. As you descend, the
vegetation increases and becomes more varied; small bushes and trees
gradually appear; bright yellow calceolarias and the first orchids are found.
The views to the east are splendid in clear weather. After **1.25 hours** you
will reach the La Magdalena camping area—a flat, sometimes soggy
meadow with a stream flowing by. Be sure to take water here.

After La Magdalena the trail deteriorates, becoming increasingly narrow and overgrown with vegetation. It heads southeast through brush at
the base of a rock face on your right. Watch your step, as the vegetation
conceals a very steep drop-off to the left. In **30 minutes** you will reach
a ridge line that the trail follows east. **Fifteen minutes** ahead, at 3400
meters (11,150 feet), is a fork; a very overgrown trail continues east along
the ridge line and soon becomes impassable, while the main trail turns
right and drops sharply to the south and west into the valley of the
Quebrada Tres Gradas. The pitch is at times very steep, and the footing
can be slippery; there are also patches of deep mud.

Here—quite suddenly—you will enter the cloud forest. Keep an eye
out for colorful gesneriads, orchids, and flowering vines. The trail also

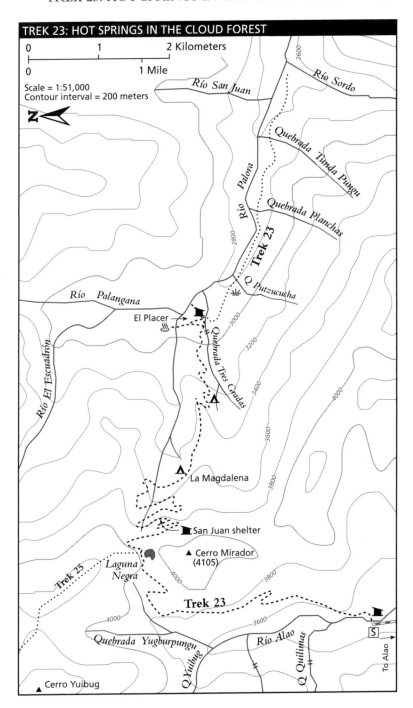

TREK 23: HOT SPRINGS IN THE CLOUD FOREST

becomes overgrown with huge *espadaña* grass, often reaching well above your head but dangling down exasperatingly to face level. Sections of old *empalizado* can be very slippery. In **1.5 hours**, at 3250 meters (10,650 feet), you will reach a small flat spot, barely big enough for one tent, next to the trail. A lovely rocky stream 50 meters (150 feet) south offers water but requires a scramble downhill through dense brush. This is the only place at all suitable for spending the night along the steep descent.

The trail continues to zigzag across the slope as it descends increasingly eastward. In addition to the tall grass there are now bamboo thickets, which inevitably get caught in backpacks and may require machete work or crawling on all fours to pass. In **30 minutes** you will reach a very small stream (a good place to take water on the way up), and **1 hour** later a clearing in the brush will allow you to see the Río Palora and surrounding valley. The trail regains the ridge line here, and there is more *empalizado*. The vegetation is also more luxuriant; note the large tree-ferns in the area. In **1 hour** you will reach a fork to the left leading to the thermal baths (signed but easy to miss); 50 meters (150 feet) ahead is a very beautiful waterfall tumbling more than 100 meters (300 feet) in three steps (hence the name of this valley: Quebrada Tres Gradas).

It is a relief to be in the flats at last. The trail continues east **10 minutes** to the shelter at El Placer. This wooden building has a good tin roof, a cooking area with a fire pit, and sleeping space on the floor for fifteen. The immediate surroundings are badly strewn with trash; please leave the area in better shape than you found it. A trail leads 5 minutes south to Quebrada Tres Gradas for water. The old pastures in the valley around the shelter are now filled with bamboo and young trees. You will have fine views to the north and west to the ridges you just descended.

The El Placer area offers several excellent day trips and shorter excursions. Although it is infrequently visited, it is best not to leave your belongings (especially valuables) unattended in the shelter.

Hot springs: There are two access trails to the baths. Both are badly overgrown and take about 30 minutes from the shelter. If nobody has been through with a machete in awhile, you will have to "bulldoze" your way through some bamboo thickets—but it is well worth the effort. The trail that starts near the Tres Gradas Waterfall is in better shape than the trail that goes directly north from the shelter. The two trails meet by a large tree; from there you continue north, cross a large stream with a collapsed bridge over it, and soon after reach the baths.

There is one large pool. The water is crystal clear but has a blue-green tinge due to algae growing on the rocks at the bottom. Be careful; the rocks are extremely slippery in and around the pool. The setting is truly idyllic; the baths are surrounded by tall trees and lush vegetation and the water is wonderfully warm. If you like it hot, head for the source of the slightly sulfurous thermal water, which tumbles into the pool through a pretty little bower of bamboo leaves (which is rather ironic, after all the grief this plant has given you along the trail). There is nowhere at all to camp near the baths, so be sure to head back to the shelter before nightfall.

Río Palora: An extremely muddy trail leads northeast from the El Placer shelter to the Río Palora, 45 minutes away. When the water level is low, lovely rocky beaches form on the banks. Down river 150 meters (500 feet) you can cross to a large rocky island. Fishermen sometimes visit this lovely area, since there are trout in the river. Trees here are thick with moss and epiphytes, butterflies flutter about, and there are many birds. From the riverbanks and island there are splendid views west, more than 1000 meters (3000 feet) back up to the pass at Laguna Negra. You can fish or take a refreshing dip in the cold water.

Exploring down river: The overgrown remains of the old trails east to Huamboya and Palora can still be followed with some difficulty near El Placer. From the water source for the shelter, cross the Quebrada Tres Gradas and head southwest, uphill through the woods, for 5 minutes,

San Juan shelter

until you reach a faint path leading south and then east. The route passes through a large bog and then heads into increasingly dense and luxuriant forest, where some great trees survive from the area's primary vegetation. This is a particularly good place to look for the prints of large animals, such as tapir and Spectacled Bear. It is a full day of hard hiking (one way) past three side streams down to the Río Sordo, which cannot be crossed safely after heavy rains. Do not proceed beyond this point without a knowledgeable guide.

Return to Alao: The walk back takes **5 to 6 hours** from El Placer to La Magdalena; **1.75 hours** to the San Juan shelter; **45 minutes** to Laguna Negra; **2 hours** to the bridge over the Río Alao; **1 hour** to the turnoff for the quarry; and **3.5 hours** to the village of Alao.

Getting back: Buses leave Alao for Riobamba between 0300 and 0500 daily. There is also a milk truck that goes sometime between 0700 and 0800. You can spend the night at the ranger station, if the rangers are in.

24 BLACK ROCK OF CUBILLINES

Rating: Difficult, 23-kilometer (14.3-mile), 4- to 5-day trek.
Elevation: 3150 to 4450 meters (10,350 to 14,600 feet).
Maps: IGM 1:50,000: CT-ÑIV-C4 Guano, CT-ÑIV-D3 Palitahua, CT-ÑIV-E2 Riobamba, CT-ÑIV-F1 Volcán El Altar; IGM 1:25,000: CT-ÑIV-F1a Laguna Pintada.
Best time to visit: December through February are the driest months.
Special gear: None.
Water: Abundant year-round throughout the route.
Hazards: Bulls.
Annoyances: None.
Permits and fees: In principle, foreign visitors pay a $10 fee to Sangay National Park, but there are no facilities for collecting the fee along this route. The beginning of the trek passes through the private properties of Haciendas Primavera, La Isabela de Sasapud, and Cubillines; ask *hacienda* staff for permission to enter.
Services: Hacienda La Isabela de Sasapud (at the beginning of the trek) has tourist cabins ($7 per person); they can also provide meals and arrange for guides and horses. Reserve in advance. Phone: (03)969-659. (Note that pack animals can only be used for the first day.)
Provisions: Riobamba has well-stocked shops with a variety of provisions.

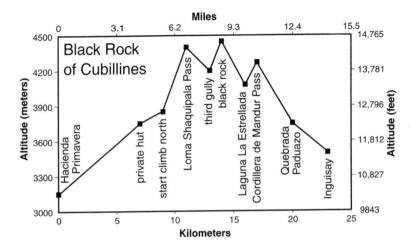

Among the mostly volcanic Ecuadorean Andes, the jet-black granite massif of Cubillines (4730 meters, 15,519 feet) is unusual in that it was formed by tectonic uplifting and folding. Subsequent glaciation has left many stark geometrical rock formations which, although they no longer have any permanent ice, become strikingly beautiful when sprinkled with a little snow. Passing alongside these impressive mountains, this trek offers access to a lovely area of lakes and waterfalls in the high *páramo*, with fine views of many of the greatest snowcapped summits of the region. The trek travels along a narrow ridge and crosses two high passes, but also includes easy walking through gentle green valleys, where a variety of hummingbirds may be seen. Cubillines is the most common local name for the massif and its surroundings, but this does not appear on the IGM maps (which refer to the large black mountain as Cerro Puerta Pailacajas).

Access: The trek begins at Hacienda Primavera. From the small bus station at Diego de Almagro and Primera Constituyente, in Riobamba, vehicles leave every 15 minutes for the town of Chambo (15 minutes, $.25). From the main plaza of Chambo you can hire a pick-up truck to take you to Hacienda Primavera (20 minutes, $5) or beyond. Or you can take one of the five buses a day from the same station in Riobamba to Guayllabamba, get off past Chambo at an area known as Barrio Sasapud, and walk 1.5 kilometers (1 mile) east along a side road to Hacienda Primavera.

Route: From Hacienda Primavera, follow the unpaved road east alongside pastures for **30 minutes** to Hacienda La Isabela de Sasapud. **Fifteen minutes** ahead is Hacienda Cubillines. Here the road becomes a trail and continues east along the north side of the valley of the Río

Ulpán (also labeled Río Guayllabamba on IGM maps), where cattle and horses roam free. **One and a quarter hours** past Hacienda Cubillines the trail passes a very large boulder covered with vegetation—a good landmark. It then climbs gently, passes to the right of a pine plantation, contours along the north side of the valley, and reaches a hut in another **30 minutes.** The hut itself is private property, but there are good sites for camping and small streams for water nearby.

The trail continues east, gradually climbing along the north side of the valley. The massive rock face of Cubillines looms ever closer as you proceed above the terminal moraine of its former glacier. Four side streams cross the trail in this area, and their respective drainages are visible some distance in advance. After the second stream there are some small stands of *fical* trees with camping possibilities. Between the second and third drainage, approximately **1 hour** past the hut, you will leave the trail to head north cross-country, climbing hard along a tussock-covered slope. Pack animals cannot continue past this point. If you follow the trail to the third stream by some woods, then you have gone too far; the flat ground ahead is very boggy and there are no good places to climb northward.

Depending on your load and stamina, the ensuing 600-meter (2000-foot) climb can take anywhere from **3 to 5 hours.** After eventually reaching the drainage of the third side stream mentioned above, the route travels northeast and then north (following the drainage) to an unnamed pass at 4400 meters (14,436 feet), just east of Loma Shaquipala. One hundred meters (300 feet) below the pass is an unusual sheet of rock, with what looks like the fossilized tracks of a giant bulldozer. Nearby is good flat ground for camping, with water and fine views of the valley below.

Try to get a very early start to cross the pass. It is **30 minutes** from the campsite to the top, where you will be greeted by superb views of the Quebrada Menestiacu far below to the north. From the pass scan the landscape to the north and east; the next part of the cross-country route presents some challenging navigation.

Descend 50 meters (150 feet) north from the pass, following a gully and small stream, and then begin to contour east below the jagged black rock to your right. This is a more difficult part of the trek, crossing several more steep ridges and gullies, all remnants of relatively recent glaciation. The moraines are still soft, and loose surface rock is barely held together by a thin layer of delicate high-altitude vegetation.

After crossing the third large gully, **2 hours** after the pass, climb eastward instead of following the gully to the north. (Note that the stream

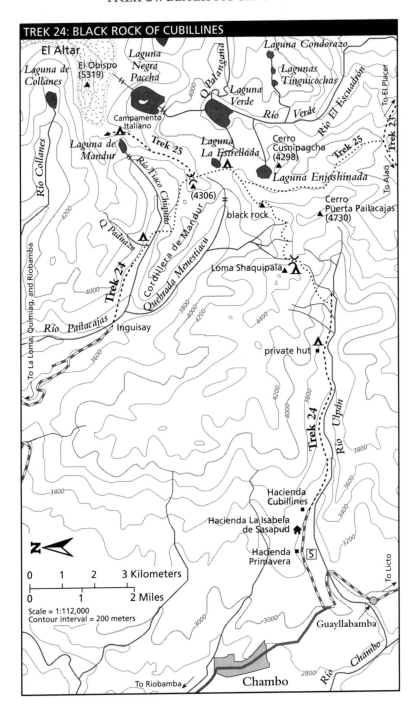

TREK 24: BLACK ROCK OF CUBILLINES

running here is not marked in the IGM maps.) You will head for the ridge line of Cordillera Pailacajas; aim for a point just south of a massive rectangular outcrop of black rock that crowns the ridge. Several tussock-covered slopes among the cliffs lead to your goal at 4450 meters (14,600 feet). The climb takes **2.5 hours** from the third gully.

Despite its mostly vertical walls, the rectangular outcrop of rock can be climbed along a grassy slope on its west side, offering stunning 360-degree views of the nearby lakes, the south face of El Altar, and several more distant peaks in good weather. The route, however, contours north-ward below the east face of the outcrop; you cannot proceed safely on the west side nor over the top. In **30 minutes** you will reach a gentler part of the Cordillera Pailacajas ridge (which may, however, be quite windy). This section also offers fine views and makes for a relaxing end to a tough day's trekking.

Follow the Cordillera Pailacajas ridge line northeast, passing above Laguna Enjoshinada at the base of Cerro Cusnipagcha to the southeast. The ridge then begins to descend steadily; in **1 hour** it will take you to the plateau around Laguna La Estrellada. As you get to the valley, go right toward the lake (the ridge straight ahead drops steeply into the canyon of Quebrada Menestiacu). There are a wide selection of spots to camp in the vicinity of Laguna La Estrellada. Since the ground can be very soggy in the wet season and it is often windy out in the open, seek slightly higher ground sheltered by the nearby hills.

This is a lovely area in which to enjoy a rest day and lazily explore your surroundings. On the east side of Laguna La Estrellada is a fine view down to the larger Laguna Verde. Walking around to the north of Laguna La Estrellada, over more boggy terrain, brings you to a view of the south face of El Altar with two high waterfalls. The first cascade tumbles 200 meters (650 feet) from the glacier to Laguna Negra Paccha (the lake itself is not visible from here). The second waterfall is just as high, from Laguna Negra Paccha to Laguna Verde—a most impressive sight overall. Looking southeast from this same area, you may be fortunate enough to see the massive silhouette of Sangay in good weather.

From the shores of Laguna La Estrellada, the route climbs north alongside the headwaters of the Quebrada Menestiacu (take water for the climb ahead) to a pass at 4270 meters (14,010 feet) in the Cordillera de Mandur. The pass is to the east (right) of the peak marked 4306 meters

(14,128 feet) on the IGM maps, **1 hour** from the lake. At the pass a trail leads right, northeast along the ridge line to Campamento Italiano (see Trek 25, High Lakes and Ridges). Our route, however, crosses the pass and descends northward along a muddy slope.

Proceed downward, north and west, to the valley of the Río Tiaco Chiquito. Along the way are lovely views of the 400-meter (1300-foot) waterfall that drops from Laguna de Mandur at the head of the valley. It is **2.5 hours** from the pass to the valley floor, where the Río Tiaco Chiquito may be forded. Follow the north side of the valley west for **30 minutes** to reach a small polylepis forest by the Quebrada Paduazo, with several good spots for camping. There may be bulls in this area.

Proceed west from the polylepis forest, contouring above the Río Tiaco Chiquito for **30 minutes**, to reach a trail that continues to descend through the valley. A **1 hour** walk along the trail will bring you to the roadhead, by a small waterworks dam (*la bocatoma*), just downstream from where the Quebrada Menestiacu joins the Río Tiaco Chiquito to form the Río Pailacajas. This area is known as Inguisay, but there is no village nor any facilities here.

Getting back: An early-morning milk truck runs daily from Inguisay to Riobamba. You can also walk from Inguisay to La Loma in 2 to 3 hours. Follow the unpaved road north along the west side of the Río Pailacajas for 1 kilometer (0.6 mile), then take the first fork left and climb west along the road to the hamlet of La Loma. From here there are irregular pick-up trucks throughout the day to Riobamba via Quimiag (1 hour to Riobamba, $1.50). There is more frequent service on Fridays.

Glacier and waterfalls on the south face of El Altar

𝟤𝟧 HIGH LAKES AND RIDGES

Rating: Difficult, 45-kilometer (28-mile), 5- to 6-day trek.
Elevation: 3100 to 4600 meters (10,200 to 15,100 feet).
Maps: IGM 1:50,000: CT-ÑIV-F3 Llactapamba de Alao, CT-ÑIV-F1 Volcán El Altar, CT-ÑIV-D3 Palitahua, CT-ÑIV-C4 Guano; IGM 1:25,000: CT-ÑIV-F1a Laguna Pintada, CT-ÑIV-D3c Cerros Negros.
Best time to visit: December through February are the driest months; April and May can be very wet. August and September are usually drier but cold.
Special gear: Be prepared for snow and below-freezing temperatures in high areas overnight.
Water: Abundant year-round throughout the route.
Hazards: Narrow ledges above the cliffs around Campamento Italiano; bulls.
Annoyances: None.
Permits and fees: Foreign visitors pay a $10 fee to Sangay National Park at the ranger stations outside Alao or Candelaria.
Services: If the rangers are in, you can spend the night at the ranger station in Alao ($1 per person). Pack animals can be hired in Alao, but these can only go as far as Laguna Negra.
Provisions: Riobamba is the place to shop. Only a few very basic items are available in Alao.

This trek crosses the heart of Sangay National Park from south to north, through beautiful *páramo* covered in plump cushion plants. Much of the hiking is along high ridges that offer magnificent views of El Altar and its surroundings, as far as the Amazon jungle to the east and Chimborazo to the west. The route also takes you by several beautiful glacial lakes, their colors changing from turquoise blue to emerald green with the mood of the sky. This is a particularly remote area, without any villages or population; you are likely to go for days without meeting other people. There are ample opportunities for observing birds that make their homes at high altitudes, including the condor, Andean Gull, snipe, *curiquingue*, and several species of ducks. Mammals are more difficult to spot, but you will see signs of the Andean Fox, White-tailed Deer, and rabbit.

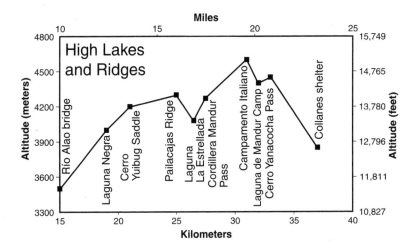

Access: The gateway for this trek is the friendly and very traditional indigenous town of Alao, about 2 hours south of Riobamba via Licto. Buses and trucks leave from Parque La Libertad (Benalcázar corner Primera Constituyente, near the San Francisco market) Monday, Wednesday, Friday, and Saturday between 1100 and 1630, Tuesday and Thursday around 1230 only, and Sunday between 0600 and 1100 (2 hours, $1). A taxi or pick-up truck from Riobamba to Alao costs $20. From Alao, on the north shore of the Río Alao, a dirt road follows the Alao Valley to the east and later north. Depending on rainfall, the first 12 kilometers (7.5 miles) of this road may be passable by vehicle. A truck can be hired in Alao for $15 to do this section.

Route: From Alao the road climbs very gradually. It parallels the river, at first traveling east for 5 kilometers (3.1 miles), then heading north for 12 kilometers (7.5 miles). It turns east again and in 2 kilometers (3.2 miles) reaches the pass at Laguna Negra and then descends steeply toward the lowlands to the east. (Note that the maps for this trek and Trek 23, Hot Springs in the Cloud Forest, begin about 5 hours from Alao, at the larger concrete bridge over the Río Alao, noted below.)

Leaving town, the road goes through green pastures that soon give way to tussock-covered *páramos*. Eleven kilometers (6.8 miles) from Alao, a fork to the left goes to La Mina, an open quarry that can be seen from the main road. This first part of the road is likely to be passable by vehicle even during rainy periods. If you are walking from Alao with a heavy load, this section will take **4 hours**. Our route continues along the right fork, following the west bank of the Alao River, through a broad valley with several flat spots appropriate for camping. **Fifteen minutes** after the fork, you will reach a small concrete bridge over Quebrada Atión, and in another **15 minutes** a landslide impassable for vehicles, but easy to cross on foot. You will then cross an area forested predominantly with small *fical* trees and bushes in the Saint John's Wort and blueberry families; **30 minutes** later you will reach a larger concrete bridge over the Río Alao; our maps begin here. Just past the bridge is a small private shelter that fits two people comfortably (up to four in a pinch), as well as some flat spots suitable for camping. (If you think you will spend the night at the shelter, ask Sr. Luis Miranda in Alao for permission.) Views of the Alao Valley and surrounding ridges are very nice. The shelter is 15 kilometers (9.3 miles) or **5 hours** of road walking from Alao, and **1 hour** past the turnoff to the quarry.

Continuing north, now along the east shore of the Río Alao, the road deteriorates and is in parts no more than a track. Small streams overflow, and water runs on the trail surrounded by moss, small bushes, and flowers. The trail climbs more steeply and offers fine views of waterfalls such as Quebrada Quilimas tumbling down to the snaking Río Alao below. The trail then turns east and zigzags up to Laguna Negra and a pass at 4000 meters (13,124 feet), **2.5 hours** from the bridge over the Río Alao.

Note that Laguna Negra does not appear on the IGM 1:50,000 map. It is a beautiful high Andean lake, nestled in the grassy *páramo* at the foot of Cerro Mirador (4105 meters, 13,469 feet)—the first of the many lakes along this route. Ducks are commonly seen here. Signs by the lake welcome you to Sangay National Park. The road continues to the east, descending to El Placer (see Trek 23). Just to the north of the road and Laguna Negra, amid the tussock, are small spots suitable for camping and a little stream for water.

From Laguna Negra, our trek leaves the road and goes cross-country. First, climb north of the lake until you reach the ridge top, then follow the ridge to the northwest. You will have splendid views, including Sangay to the southeast. In **1.5 hours** you will reach 4200 meters (13,800 feet) and a sign, "Límite Parque Nacional Sangay," which marks the boundary of the national park. Continue northwest along the ridge line for about **30 minutes**. Before an unnamed rocky summit with cliffs to the west and north, descend to the left as far as the base of the cliffs. Do not go

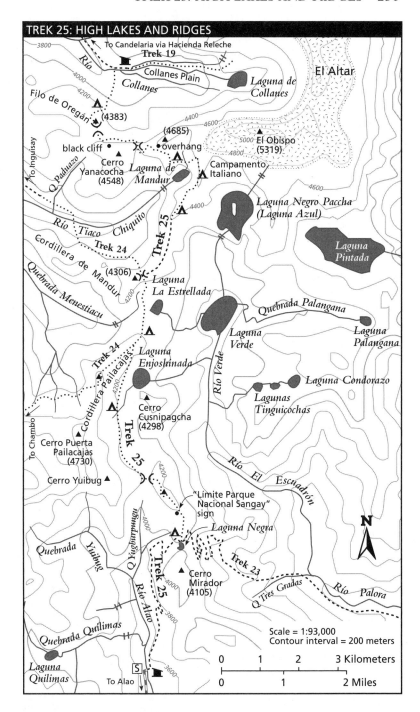

TREK 25: HIGH LAKES AND RIDGES

To Candelaria via Hacienda Releche
Trek 19

Río Collanes
3800
4000
4200
Collanes Plain
Laguna de Collanes
El Altar

Filo de Oregán
(4383)
4400
4600
El Obispo
(5319)
5000
4800

To Inguisay
black cliff
(4685)
overhang
Cerro Yanacocha
(4548)
Laguna de Mandur
Campamento Italiano
Q. Paduazo

Laguna Negro Paccha
(Laguna Azul)
4600

Río Tiaco Chiquito
Trek 24
Cordillera de Mandur
Trek 25
4400

Laguna Pintada

Quebrada Menestiacu
(4306)
4200
Laguna La Estrellada

Quebrada Palangana
Laguna Palangana

Laguna Verde
Río Verde

Trek 24
Laguna Enjoshinada
Cordillera Pailacajas
4200

Laguna Condorazo

Lagunas Tinguicochas

To Chambo
Cerro Cusnipagcha
(4298)

Río El Escuadrón

Cerro Puerta Pailacajas
(4730)
Cerro Yuibug
Trek 25
4200

"Límite Parque Nacional Sangay" sign

Quebrada Yuibug
Q. Quilimayacu
4000
Laguna Negra
Trek 23

Quebrada
Trek 25
4000
Cerro Mirador
(4105)
Q. Tres Gradas
Río Palora

N

Quebrada Quilimas
Río Alao
3800
3600

Scale = 1:93,000
Contour interval = 200 meters

Laguna Quilimas
To Alao
S
3600

0   1   2   3 Kilometers

0   1   2 Miles

down all the way to the stream of Quebrada Yugburpungu; instead, contour at the base of the cliffs and then regain the ridge. This will take about **30 minutes**. From the ridge, in clear weather you can see to the west the saddle between Cerro Yuibug and the ridge you are on. The route continues across this saddle, which you will reach in **30 minutes**. There are more special views from here: to the north is a broad green basin contrasting with the dark and imposing Cerro Cusnipagcha; behind them is your first glimpse of El Altar. To the south, you can look back at the steep valley of the upper Alao.

From the west end of the saddle, the route contours northwest and then north at about 4200 meters (13,800 feet), along the east flank of the Pailacajas range. You will cross several side valleys along the way, some with large boulders scattered about. Cattle trails can be followed on and off, several flat spots are suitable for camping, and small streams run down the hillsides. **Two hours** from the saddle, you will cross a stream with brick-red bedrock. The area north of it is particularly nice for a rest or for camping because it has excellent views. In addition to the beautiful plain below and Cerro Cusnipagcha, you will now see Laguna Enjoshinada and, to the north (towering above it all) the snowy south face of El Altar. To the east you can look through a gap in a ridge, right down to the flatlands of the Amazon basin. Directly above you, to the southwest, are the impressive black peaks of Cerro Puerta Pailacajas.

The route continues north. As before, contour through the tussock slopes at about 4200 meters (13,800 feet), crossing small side valleys along the way. Soon you will have Laguna Enjoshinada below you and to your right. In **2 hours** you will reach the main ridge of the Cordillera Pailacajas; Laguna La Estrellada will be visible to the northeast. Continue to the west side of Laguna La Estrellada, **30 minutes** ahead. There are some spots to camp along the way. (Choose high ground so it does not get too boggy, and avoid the gap of the upper Quebrada Menestiacu between the Pailacajas and Mandur ranges, which can be very windy.) At this point you have a choice of routes connecting with Trek 24, Black Rock of Cubillines.

The current trek continues to the north in quest of more high lakes and ridges. From the north end of the Pailacajas ridge, walk north following the headwaters of Quebrada Menestiacu (just a small stream at this point), where you should take water for the climb and ridge traverse ahead. Climb toward the lowest pass you see on the Cordillera de Mandur, to the right (east) of the peak marked 4306 meters (14,128 feet) on the IGM maps. From Laguna La Estrellada it is **1 hour** to the pass at 4270 meters (14,010 feet).

At the pass you will meet two trails, one descending north into the Tiaco Chiquito Valley (see Trek 24) and another climbing the ridge to the northeast, along the Cordillera de Mandur. Follow the ridge trail to the right. It is relatively easy going at first and affords wonderful views. To the left you will see the valley of the Tiaco Chiquito and, as you climb higher, the impressive waterfall formed by the outflow of Laguna de Mandur, cascading 400 meters (1300 feet) into the valley below. To the right, a gamut of sights will make you forget the weight of your pack: first Laguna La Estrellada, followed by Laguna Verde, then the beautiful waterfalls pouring directly off El Altar's glacier into Laguna Negro Paccha (also known as Laguna Azul). Later, Laguna Negro Paccha itself comes into view against the backdrop of Altar's southern peaks.

After **1 hour** on the ridge top, the terrain starts to change; there is less vegetation, and the route (now less distinct but marked by cairns) climbs more steeply on sand or scree slopes. In another **30 minutes** you will reach some large rocks where you can camp in an emergency (but there is no water, and the area is not ideal). The cairn-marked route climbs farther northeast along the ridge. In **20 minutes** the terrain becomes more level and the cairns less evident amid a boulder field. Veer a little to the left (west); in **10 minutes** you will reach a rock wall (although it is natural, it looks as if it might be manmade). Follow this wall northeast along the ridge line for **30 minutes**. (Laguna de Mandur will come into sight to your left a few minutes after you start following the wall.) Soon the route turns north and leaves the ridge line; it contours instead on the west side of its now-rocky crest, between the base of these rocks and Laguna de Mandur, 200 meters (650 feet) below to the left. Take care in this section (especially if it is icy); the ledge you are walking on is sometimes quite narrow.

In **20 minutes** you will reach Campamento Italiano, the base camp used by mountaineers for climbing El Altar's southern peaks. This is a very scenic spot by a gap in the rocky ridge you are following. A large pinnacle stands out right in the middle of the gap. There are two good tent platforms, sheltered from the wind, and less comfortable space for two more tents. Directly below and to the west is the turquoise Laguna de Mandur. To the southeast, about 1.5 kilometers (1 mile) away, is

Laguna Negro Paccha (which you can see through the gap in the ridge). The south face of El Altar is just in front of you; it feels as though you can reach out and touch the glaciers with your hand. At 4600 meters (15,100 feet), this is the highest camp along the route; temperatures are likely to fall below freezing at night, and there is a good chance of snow or sleet. Melt snow for drinking water.

From Campamento Italiano, a route marked by cairns continues to the north, maintaining an altitude of about 4600 meters (15,100 feet) and staying to the west of the rocky ridge line. (This is not the climber's route, which goes higher and heads northeast toward the glacier.) You will have impressive views down to Laguna de Mandur to your left. Be careful not to slip if the ground is icy. In **45 minutes** you will reach an area of gullies filled with loose stones. After the last cairn, take the narrow gully that descends toward Laguna de Mandur to your left. Near the bottom of the gully, the cairns reappear. Because of the gradient and loose stones, it is a difficult scramble with heavy packs. In **30 minutes** you will reach a more level area with huge boulders. Past the boulders continue descending to the west, along scree and through some grassy corridors between the rocks, to the unnamed main stream in this valley. After crossing the stream (**30 minutes** past the boulders) you will see several nice spots suitable for camping, with fine sandy patches to pitch a tent. The beautiful Laguna de Mandur, with a peninsula jutting into it, is just below you. Andean Gulls can be seen swooping over the lake and above the impressive rock cliffs to the east. You can look straight back at Campamento Italiano, 200 meters (650 feet) overhead. A notch at the outflow of the lake allows you to see many ranges to the south, including the Cordilleras de Mandur and Pailacajas. Take water here for the climb ahead.

The route continues to the northwest to an unnamed pass between Cerro Yanacocha (4548 meters, 14,922 feet) and a black rock peak marked 4685 meters (15,372 feet) on the IGM maps. Snow and sleet are common in this area. Climb west on the slope opposite the Laguna de Mandur camping area; the cairns can be difficult to distinguish because of all the stones in the surroundings. The route heads north and then west again; in **1 hour** you will reach a large rocky overhang that provides great shelter in foul weather (even a tight place to camp in case of emergency). Try not to disturb the beautiful flowers growing in this sheltered nook. From here the trail climbs steeply west for **10 minutes** and then turns north onto the west face of the 4685-meter black rock peak, mentioned above. In another **10 minutes** you will be just above and to the east of the pass, with magnificent views in all directions. Cairns continue down a small gully and in **10 minutes** reach the pass itself at 4450 meters (14,600 feet).

A very steep gully drops from the pass to the broad Collanes Plain directly below (also known as Collantes). This is a dangerous route, however; the more circuitous route described below is recommended (especially if the weather is poor). From the pass this route, marked by cairns, contours west, along the north face of Cerro Yanacocha. In **45 minutes** you will reach the base of a large black cliff. There are no cairns here, but a track contours along the base of the cliffs for **10 minutes**. The track then descends along a steep, slippery gully—but do not go this way! The recommended route continues up and around the base of the cliff to its west

Campamento Italiano (4600 meters, 15,100 feet)

side, where there are cairns again until you reach a grassy slope **10 minutes** ahead. Follow this slope, which descends north to a saddle in the Filo de Oregán. From the saddle, climb the knoll marked 4383 meters (14,381 feet) on the IGM maps. It takes **30 minutes** from the beginning of the grassy slope. There are great views from this hill. Just below, to the north and stretching eastward, is the lovely Collanes Plain and, beyond it, El Altar's complete *cirque* and crater lake. Also to the north and farther afield is Tungurahua; in the distance, to the west, are the snowcapped peaks of Chimborazo and Carihuayrazo.

The next landmark along the route is the Collanes shelter, at the west end of the Collanes Plain. The thatched-roof buildings can be seen from the hilltop. Continue along the Filo de Oregán to the northwest. Just before it starts to rise again, leave the ridge and descend to the northeast. The terrain is steep, but there is good footing because of the tussock grass and cushion plants. (Try to step above the fragile cushion plants, instead of on them.) In **15 minutes** you will reach a flat, grassy area suitable for camping. (You will have great views of the Collanes Plain and El Altar's *cirque* from here.) Continue to the north, descending toward the Río Collanes. (It is easier to travel along the low ridge tops than the valleys.) It will take you **1 hour** to reach the river. Note that the lower areas near the river are boggy. Ford the river, which may be above knee level; from here it will take **15 minutes** to reach the shelter.

From the shelter you can either first go to El Altar's crater (highly recommended) or leave the area via Hacienda Releche and Candelaria, 8 kilometers (5 miles) or **6 hours** walk down to the northwest. Details about the shelter and both these options are found in Trek 19, Crater of El Altar.

Getting back: See Trek 19.

Chapter 13
TREKS FROM CUENCA

Altitude, 2550 meters (8400 feet)
Population, 600,000

Cuenca is the smallest and most congenial of Ecuador's three major cities. It is the capital of the province of Azuay and the hub of all of El Austro, the southern region of the country. Endowed with a charming colonial center and strong traditions in the arts and academia, Cuenca offers many urban attractions as well as access to interesting trekking areas. Crime and pollution (air and noise) are unfortunately present here, but they are less severe than in Guayaquil or Quito. Several agencies can organize treks from Cuenca; the most common routes are all in nearby Cajas National Park.

The Inca Empire left more of a mark on El Austro than on other parts of Ecuador. Easy Trek 26 explores part of this legacy. Trek 27 delves into a different southern Ecuadorean tradition: gold mining. This long, difficult, and very scenic Gold-Rush Trail follows the miners' footsteps through deep canyons and over high *páramos*.

26 INCA TRAILS

Rating: Easy, 15-kilometer (9.3-mile), full-day hike.
Elevation: 2700 to 3100 meters (8800 to 10,200 feet).
Maps: IGM 1:50,000: CT-ÑVI-A1 Sígsig, CT-NVI-B2 Girón. The latter is optional.
Best time to visit: June through September are the driest months; March to May, and October, are the wettest.
Special gear: None.
Water: There is none along this ridge route, so take plenty from the start.
Hazards: None.
Annoyances: Soft clay mud.
Permits and fees: None.
Services: The trailhead is at Hacienda San Pedro de Yunga, a convenient place to spend the night before the trek (especially since an early start is recommended). Accommodation at this working farm costs $12 per person,

including dinner and breakfast. If you wish to do the route on horseback, it is $50 per person, including a guide and food (less if there is a group). Longer equestrian tours are also offered. Advance reservations are required for all services. Phone Montaruna Tours (see Appendix A, "Companies Offering Treks in Ecuador"). There are no accommodations in Cumbe. **Provisions:** Cuenca has well-stocked shops and supermarkets.

Aided by its well-developed road system, the Inca Empire expanded gradually north into Ecuador from what is today Peru. Inca occupation in Ecuador was relatively short, and vestiges of its presence are most evident in the south of the country. Based on sixteenth-century Spanish chronicles and on the remains of *tambos* (shelters) found along the ancient roads, the route followed by the Capac Ñan can be traced (see "The Capac Ñan" at the end of this trek description). In the Cuenca area, the main north-south road took the top of a lower intermediate range, between the Cordilleras Occidental and Oriental. It came north from Nabón; a spur descended west to Tomebamba (the Inca city at Cuenca) and continued north to Ingapirca and Achupallas. The latter section, from Ingapirca to Achupallas, is the Inca Trail visited by most trekkers.

   This pleasant day walk follows a small piece of what was the great Inca road, from Yunga to Cumbe, south of Cuenca. The route goes through several patches of forest with beautiful flowers and many birds. This section of the Inca road is not cobbled, nor are there remains of fortifications along the way. Rather, it offers magnificent vistas of the surrounding valleys as well as both the eastern and western *cordilleras*—and even a view down to the Pacific Ocean. Traveling the overgrown remains of so great a

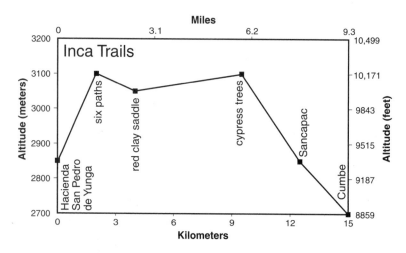

highway makes one reflect on the ephemeral nature of man's achievements.

Although the road does not have cobblestones, it does have an abundance of red clay (as the weight of your boots will testify). Red clay is a key ingredient in the manufacture of ceramics. Since pre-Inca times, and until today, Cuenca has produced many beautiful ceramic wares. Toward the end of the walk is Loma Caullín, a hill with Inca terracing, where ancient artifacts have been found.

Access: Hacienda San Pedro de Yunga is located southeast of Cuenca, 17 kilometers (11 miles) by road through Turi or 26 kilometers (16 miles) via Tarqui. Take a bus for Guillanshapa (sometimes written Huillanzhapa) from the Feria Libre, at Avenida de las Américas in Cuenca. There is service at 0530, 0730, 1115, and 1415 (1 hour, $.30). Get off at the turnoff for Yunga, just south of Guillanshapa; from there it is 6 kilometers (4 miles) to the *hacienda*. Follow the dirt road southeast. Stay right at the intersections, and keep left of Quebrada Yunga. The road ends at Hacienda San Pedro de Yunga, 1.5 hours ahead.

Route: From the *hacienda*, take a trail that climbs southeast above the valley of Quebrada Yunga. There are two forks near the beginning; go left at the first and right at the second. The trail climbs gradually above the valley; in **15 minutes** it reaches a small, flat clearing. Continue through it; in **5 minutes** the trail ducks into a nice patch of forest. Look for *gañal* bushes with rounded leaves and lovely large white flowers. There are also orchids, including the mauve *flor de Cristo* and another with small yellow bell-shaped flowers, dwarf *chuquiraguas*, and calceolarias. Try to catch a glimpse of the flocks of birds passing by (you are sure to hear their songs). The area has hummingbirds, tanagers, and woodpeckers. The route (with a couple of parallel branches here) continues to climb, now to the northeast. In **30 minutes** it emerges from the forest at the edge of Quebrada Ashcujambi, with nice views to the ridges farther north. Continue climbing along the edge of the *quebrada* through some brushy vegetation for **10 minutes** to reach the ridge top where six paths meet.

Our route, the Inca road south, contours the east flank of the peak labeled 3170 meters (10,400 feet) on the IGM map, neither climbing to the scrubby summit nor dropping east toward Quingeo. Follow the trail south along the eroded hillside; it turns southwest, then drops a bit to cross a patch of forest. In **1 hour** the trail descends a little more to a windy saddle of eroded red clay, north of Loma Bayón (3168 meters, 10,394 feet). You can now look back at the Yunga Valley to the northwest. If it is clear to the southwest, you can also see right down to the Pacific Ocean.

The trail, here muddy and slippery, climbs up from the saddle and in **15**

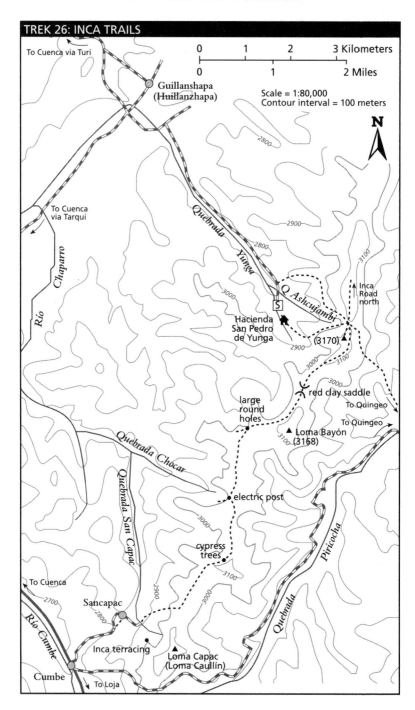

minutes reaches a pasture where it becomes faint. On the far side of the pasture, it again enters the woods and travels southwest through nice forest, rich in mosses and bromeliads. In **20 minutes**, you will go by a pasture to your right with more nice views. The trail now travels west; several paths branch off here, so always stay on the ridge top. In **35 minutes** you will reach some large round holes in the ground (a curious sight in the forest) and a fork. Take the left branch; it climbs southwest, wide and muddy through the forest. The trail then turns south along the ridge top and in **30 minutes** emerges at a clearing with good views east to the Cordillera Oriental. As the route continues south through more forest, a few small paths again branch off along the way. Stay on the main trail; in **30 minutes** it emerges at another clearing, above Quebrada Chocar to the west (right).

Continue toward the electric post ahead on the ridge top. Here a clear trail descends to the right. Do not take it; instead, look for the trail that heads south and passes left of the eroded rocky ground beyond the post. This trail goes along the east flank of the ridge and in **15 minutes** returns to the ridge line, where there are wonderful views west. Follow the ridge line south. In **15 minutes** you will reach a pasture with a few large cypress trees. Continue south along the ridge top, with more fine views in all directions. In **25 minutes** the trail leaves the ridge top and starts descending to the southwest (right). Head toward a hillside with impressive Inca terracing, locally called Loma Caullín but labeled Loma Capac on the IGM map. After **30 minutes** of steady descent you will cross Quebrada San Capac and meet a dirt road. **Ten minutes** along the

Hacienda San Pedro de Yunga

road is the village of Sancapac. The road continues to wind its way down to Cumbe, but you can take a shortcut south past the church. In **1 hour** you will reach Cumbe and the paved Cuenca–Loja Highway.

Getting back: Buses run frequently from Cumbe to Cuenca (27 kilometers, 17 miles) between 0500 and 1700 (45 minutes, $.50). If you get out after 1700, walk to the highway and wait for a Loja–Cuenca bus or try to find a taxi ($10). It is best not to be on the road after dark.

THE CAPAC ÑAN

The Inca Empire, the most powerful nation of pre-Columbian South America, achieved its grandeur thanks in part to an incredibly well-organized system of communications. This was based on an extensive road network, which totaled some 23,000 kilometers (14,000 miles). There were two main roads. The Capac Ñan (chief or great road) was for the exclusive use of the ruling class. It ran through the highlands and joined Cusco and Quito, the empire's two capitals. A coastal road went from Tumbes, in what is today northern Peru, south to the Río Maule in Chile. These two north-south highways were interconnected by numerous perpendicular roads that also continued east toward the Amazon basin.

The conquering Spanish were so impressed by the Inca roads that they waxed eloquent about them in their chronicles. In 1553 Pedro Cieza de León wrote:

> .... [A]nd they built a road, the most haughty seen in the world, the longest, because it left Cusco and arrived in Quito and it joined the one going to Chile. Its greatness is unmatched in all human history, carved along deep valleys and high sierras, over snow-capped mountains and quagmires, alongside raging torrents, hewn out of the living rock. Through these places it went, level and cobbled, with foundations along the slopes, well cut into the mountains, carved into the cliffs, with retaining walls along the rivers, with steps and landings in the snow; everywhere clean and swept. Along the way it was full of lodges, storehouses laden with treasure, temples of the sun, post-houses. Oh! What grandeur can we ascribe to Alexander the Great, or any of the mighty kings that ruled the world, that they should build such a road? Neither the great Roman road that passed through Spain, nor others we read about, can compare to this road. El Señorío de los Incas, Segunda parte de la Crónica del Perú (Lima: Instituto de Estudios Peruanos, 1967), pp. 213–214, translated by Robert Kunstaetter

27 GOLD-RUSH TRAIL

Rating: Difficult, 65-kilometer (40-mile), 5- to 7-day trek.

Elevation: 1100 to 3700 meters (3600 to 12,150 feet).

Maps: IGM 1:50,000: CT-NVI-C4 Paccha, CT-NVI-D1 Manú, CT-NVI-D2 Nabón, CT-NVI-D3 Selva Alegre. Note that there are many discrepancies between local usage and the names given in the IGM maps; these differences are indicated in the route description below. The map in this book includes only local names.

Best time to visit: The Río León Valley receives very little precipitation at any time of the year. Farther west, the rainy period is January to May. The Cerro de Arcos area can have mist and wind at any time; it is driest, coldest, and windiest here from June to September.

Special gear: Hiking boots.

Water: Plenty on route but spread out, so stock up at every opportunity.

Hazards: Poisonous snakes at lower elevations.

Annoyances: None.

Permits and fees: None.

Services: Oña is a good place to stay before you start this trek. It has a couple of basic hotels: Buenos Aires is best ($5 per person), located near the main highway, a 15-minute walk from the center of town. The Alvarado sisters run a very good traditional place to eat on the same street. Pick-up trucks can be hired at the hotel or in town. Alfonso Vallejo, at the hardware store on the street behind the church, is knowledgeable about the area and can help arrange a local guide. Phone: (07)434-173. Zaruma, at the end of the trek, is a city with all services.

Provisions: Cuenca and Loja are best for major shopping. Basic supplies are available in Oña, Lluzhapa, La Curva, and Tauarcocha along the route. You can therefore travel light and buy food as needed.

All that glitters is not gold—but where there is the slightest shimmer, man is sure to go after it. The aboriginal peoples of Ecuador were skilled goldsmiths who created the most diverse ornaments (a tradition carried on today). The conquest of America was largely driven by the search for "El Dorado," the ultimate mother lode—and native mines were quickly taken over by the Spanish. The coastal province of El Oro owes its name to ancient gold mines near Zaruma. Mines were worked by the Spanish starting in 1539, and by French, British, and U.S. companies since the

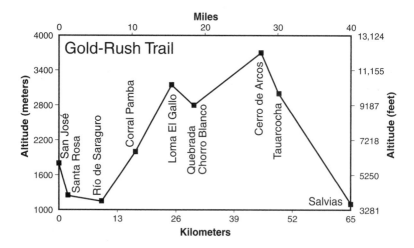

1800s. Countless people have been lured to Zaruma by the golden dream—and many never emerged from the mines.

This trek follows the route west taken by miners from their homes in the highlands of southern Azuay and northern Loja. Starting near the town of Oña, halfway between Cuenca and Loja, the route at first follows Ecuador's "Grand Canyon": the spectacular valley of the Río León. The trek then climbs a mountain range called Cordillera de Huandú, and drops to another deep valley before crossing the Cordillera Occidental. For a finale, it climbs to the unusual rock formations atop Cerro de Arcos, from which it descends 2600 meters (8500 feet) toward Zaruma in the western foothills of the Andes. Colonial Zaruma is indeed a gem worth taking extra time to explore. Some of the mines are still operating and (sadly) still dumping cyanide and mercury into the rivers.

This route is far off the tourist track. Although old-timers in Oña claim to have walked to Zaruma in 3 days, it is nonetheless a long and demanding hike. You will cross a few roads along the way, however, that will allow you to finish sooner if you wish. The trek includes an impressive diversity of climatic zones; mangoes grow in the hot, dry valley of the Río León, but it can be very cold and wet on the *páramo* of Cerro de Arcos.

Access: There are ten daily buses in each direction on the route Cuenca–Oña–Loja. From Cuenca or Loja to Oña takes 2.5 hours and costs $3. The turnoff for the trailhead is 5 kilometers (3 miles) south of Oña. From here a dirt road heads west another 7 kilometers (4.4 miles) to the village of San José, then 1 kilometer (0.6 mile) farther to the start of the trek. A pick-up truck from Oña to the trailhead costs $5.

Route: This trek starts on a ridge northeast of Quebrada del Alumbre. The trail zigzags down through irrigated fields and past a few houses. In **15 minutes** it crosses a small irrigation canal (not shown on our map). Take the right fork just after the crossing; soon you will cross the canal again. The trail continues descending; in **15 minutes** it turns west and goes through a patch of trees. The predominant species here are the spiny *faique*, with very narrow leaves, and *molle*, with larger leaves and seeds like black pepper.

Shortly the trail turns north and descends steeply to the small and silty Quebrada del Alumbre, just before this joins the Río León. Cross the *quebrada*; its water contains large amounts of alum and is not safe to drink (even when purified). This area is known as Santa Rosa. A few houses have mango and palm trees, whose shade is most welcome at any time of the year. From April to June, the aroma of ripe mangoes is a real delight. You can buy fruit here, and also ask for some water; it is piped in from San José, but you should purify it as always.

The trail continues west along the south shore of the Río León. In **15 minutes** it crosses a dry gully; **30 minutes** ahead it crosses a second, larger, dry gully; and in another **15 minutes** it reaches a third gully with just a trickle of water. The little stream, a welcome sight in the hot dry climate, is surrounded by shady vegetation. It is labeled Quebrada Manzano on the IGM map, but locals call it Quebrada Jurupe. A small white cross marks a grave here, dating to 1920—perhaps one of the gold miners.

From Quebrada Jurupe, a trail continues west close to the edge of the high bank above the Río León. It is narrow and can be dangerous if you have a large backpack. An alternative trail that goes west up on the hillside is a safer choice. In **20 minutes** you will reach the hamlet of Zapotepamba, named after the *zapote* that grows in the area. The sticky resin of these broad-leaved trees is collected to make glue.

The route continues west along the south shore of the Río León. There are several parallel trails here; aim for the powerline in the distance. You will cross an irrigation ditch twice (not shown on our map), then a small gully; in **20 minutes** you will reach an electric post. The trail splits here. Continue along the right branch, which travels west, contouring at about 1200 meters (3950 feet), still parallel to the river. You will pass south of and above some fields and houses. The pastures are velvety green below the irrigation canal, in stark contrast to the extremely dry surroundings.

In **30 minutes** the river below turns north, getting farther away from the trail, which drops to cross the deep Quebrada Chayazapa

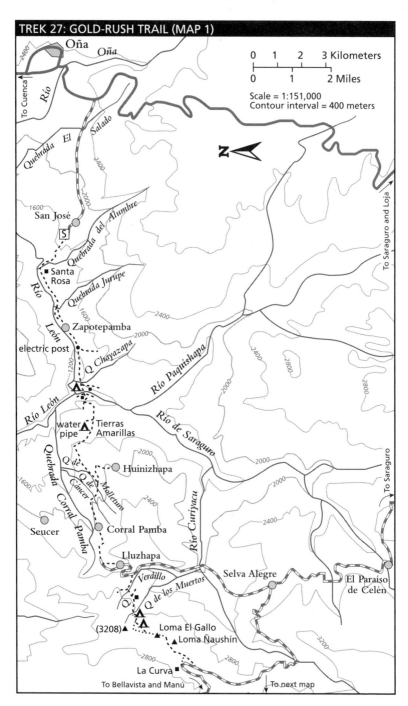

TREK 27: GOLD-RUSH TRAIL (MAP 1)

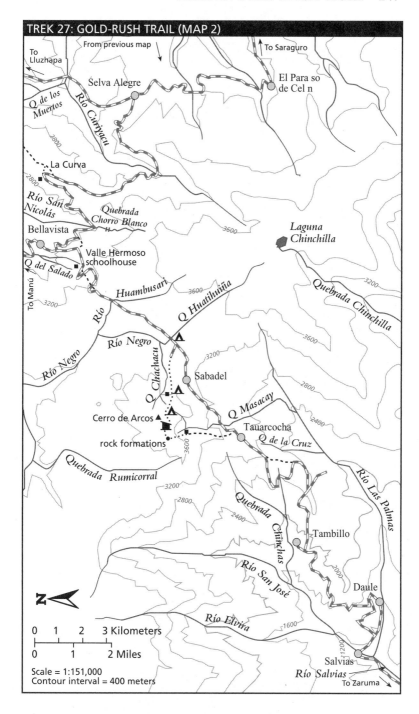

(Quebrada Jurupe on the IGM map). From here it climbs steeply, in **15 minutes** reaching a small notch between the hills and a fork. Take the right branch; it descends west, passes a house (ask here for permission to camp and use the *tarabita* ahead), and in **20 minutes** continues to the Río de Saraguro (Río Naranjo on the IGM map). There is ample flat ground here for comfortable camping.

If the Río de Saraguro is low (knee to waist deep), it can be forded. Otherwise you must use the *tarabita*, a primitive cable car that is difficult to use if you are not familiar with it. When in doubt, ask for assistance. Take water for the hot, dry climb ahead. On the west shore of the river is another shady mango grove. A path climbs from it, crosses an irrigation ditch (not shown on our map), and immediately reaches a house. Several trails branch out from here. Follow the one that zigzags steeply west over a parched clay slope, passing above the house and in **20 minutes** reaching a broad, dry plateau deeply incised by a convoluted tangle of canyons. There are splendid views in all directions: north to the great canyon of the Río León, east back the way you came, south up the valley of the Río de Saraguro, and west to what seems like an impenetrable wall of mountains (which is also the way forward). The trail again forks here. The right branch goes west, down into the canyons ahead; follow the left branch, which goes south, to contour around the canyons.

After **30 minutes** of climbing you will reach a second plateau with more great views. Nearby are a few widely scattered houses. The trail now swings northwest and in **15 minutes** crosses a large, dry, unnamed *quebrada*. Immediately after emerging from this gully, take the left fork; it climbs northwest along the northern rim of the *quebrada* you just crossed. In **10 minutes** you will reach a small water pipe, another valuable opportunity to fill up since it is still hot and dry ahead. This area, known as Tierras Amarillas, has flat ground for camping. Ask for permission at one of the houses.

The trail continues to climb steeply northwest along the northern rim of the *quebrada*. In **30 minutes** it turns north and ascends more gradually. If you look carefully among the bushes here, you might see some nice birds: doves, hummingbirds, and the bright-red Vermilion Flycatcher. After **20 minutes** the trail turns 90 degrees southwest into the spectacular canyon of Quebrada Corral Pamba (also called Quebrada Zurín on the IGM map), which offers outstanding views down into the great abyss and up toward the green slopes ahead. The trail climbs steadily along the south edge of this huge *quebrada*. In **30 minutes** the vegetation becomes more lush; there are flowers along the path, and bird songs are heard in the small Quebrada de Molleturo on your right (a welcome change from the arid landscape below).

Another **30 minutes** ahead you will reach a fork. The left branch climbs back east and south, towards Huinizhapa (Huiñazhapa on the IGM map). Take the right branch, which continues west, crosses Quebrada Molleturo and Quebrada de Cáncer, and in **45 minutes** reaches the village of Corral Pamba. This is a friendly little place where you can ask permission to camp in the school-yard or someone's field. From Corral Pamba the trail climbs southwest for **45 minutes**, past the cemetery, pastures, and cultivated fields. It then descends and in **10 minutes** reaches a dirt road. Follow the road south and take a shortcut **15 minutes** to Lluzhapa (Lluzhpa on the IGM map). This village has some shops. At 0400 there is a daily bus to Selva Alegre, Saraguro, and Loja (5 hours, $3). You can ask to stay at the *casa comunal*.

The trek continues over the Cordillera de Huandú, an intermediate range between the Cordilleras Oriental and Occidental. Follow the road to Selva Alegre, south out of Lluzhapa. You will head for the top of a hill high above and southwest of town. Either continue along the road for **30 minutes** to a wide trail that goes west on the north shore of Quebrada Verdillo, or take a couple of steep shortcuts (not shown on our map). The trail climbs gently west at first, past some houses, and then more steeply. In **45 minutes** it reaches a fork; take the left branch southwest. There are planted pines and eucalyptus in this area and views east, all the way back to the mountains around Oña. In **10 minutes** the trail drops to cross Quebrada Verdillo, then climbs again in **15 minutes** to reach the ridge line on the south side of this *quebrada*. Just as you reach the top, another trail comes in from below, to your left. Do not take it; instead, continue west, contouring along a barbed-wire fence and then climbing by a house with tall eucalyptus trees. The trail continues to a large, level pasture; when you reach it, turn left briefly and then right to cross it. **Thirty minutes** from the last fork, you will cross Quebrada de los Muertos. Shortly after is a second, smaller stream. This is a suitable spot to camp and take water for the thirsty climb ahead.

From the stream the route contours briefly before striking steeply uphill to the west, through a deep path worn into the red clay soil. In **1 hour** you will reach a plateau suitable for camping (but no water is available). The area ahead, going over the top of Cordillera de Huandú, is less traveled and trails are indistinct, but the topography is easy to follow.

There is a choice of routes. One faint trail crosses the pasture and climbs up the slope to the southwest; a second trail continues west along the northern edge of the pasture and then climbs to the ridge top south of the point marked 3208 meters (10,526 feet) on the IGM map. The first trail is a more direct route, while the second offers spectacular views and is recommended in good weather. From the top of the ridge along the second route, reached in **20 minutes**, you can see east back to the Cordillera Oriental and the entire route you have traveled so far. To the west you can see down to the deep valley of the Río San Nicolás, beyond to the village of Bellavista, and all the way to the *páramo* in the Cordillera Occidental (your route ahead).

Follow the ridge line south. In **20 minutes** you will meet the first route mentioned above, coming up from the plateau. Continue along the top of the ridge due south, through some bushes, to the summit of Loma El Gallo, reached in **30 minutes**. There are more wonderful 360-degree views. An old rutted trail begins to descend east; do not take it. Rather, continue south cross-country along the crest of the ridge, which in **15 minutes** drops steeply to the saddle between Loma El Gallo and Loma Ñaushín. Here you will join a large trail again. Follow it southwest as it contours along the western slopes of Loma Ñaushín, going through some forest fragments along the way. In **40 minutes** you will reach a fork; the main trail continues south, while a small trail turns right, to the west. Cross under a barbed-wire fence to take the right fork. Shortly it will cross an irrigation canal and (in **10 minutes**) reach the Saraguro–Manú Road. If you missed the turnoff, the main trail also leads to the same road but is quite a detour. In either case, turn right on the road; you will be at a hairpin bend aptly called La Curva (the curve), where there are two small shops. Five daily buses travel this road to Saraguro (2.5 hours, $1.50) and Loja (4 hours, $3).

From La Curva on a clear day you can see southwest to the *páramo* for which you are headed. A 500-meter (1600-feet) abyss—the valley of the Río San Nicolás—lies between you and this goal, however. Follow the road southwest to get around it. **One hour** down the road you will pass the lovely 100-meter (300-foot) waterfall of Quebrada Chorro Blanco. Continue **20 minutes** along the road past another small stream, a church on the right, and a third stream—where the road makes a sharp turn right. Beyond this turn, take a rutted path on your left; it climbs steeply

Colonial Zaruma is a gem worth taking time to explore.

toward an area called Valle Hermoso. After climbing west for **30 minutes**, the trail turns sharply north and levels off. In **10 minutes** it meets a dirt road coming up from Bellavista. This road is very poor, and suitable for vehicles only in the dry season. (Even then, it sees almost no traffic.) Follow the road uphill, crossing the broad scenic valley of Quebrada del Salado. In **30 minutes** you will reach the schoolhouse of Valle Hermoso, on your right. Take a rutted trail south here; it starts on your left, directly opposite the school. The trail climbs steeply, soon crosses the road again, and continues uphill to emerge once more at the road in **30 minutes**.

The trail continues through a planted pine forest; it shortcuts the winding road a few more times, but becomes increasingly overgrown. When you have had enough of shortcuts, continue uphill along the road. In **30 minutes** you will emerge from the forest onto open *páramo*; the road climbs gently and then begins to descend to the Río Huambusari, a small meandering stream (reached in **10 minutes**). The road continues to the southwest over the *páramo*. (It can be very muddy.) In **1 hour** you will reach the Río Negro (called Quebrada Huatihuiña upstream). There is a pedestrian bridge to the right of the road, and across the river are good camping spots amidst small bushes. Take water here.

Five minutes along the road past the Río Negro is a fork. The left branch goes southwest to the broad and beautiful valley around Sabadel and on to Tauarcocha (Taurococha on the IGM map). This is the direct route for those in a hurry. Weather permitting, there is a truck that picks up cheese from the farms at Tauarcocha on Fridays, so you might be able to get a ride. A more interesting alternative, however, is along the right branch west to Cerro de Arcos. Along this route, the road ends abruptly in **20 minutes** and a series of poorly defined trails continue west over the straw-covered *páramo*, on the south side of Quebrada Chachacu. Gradually move away from the *quebrada* and climb to the ridge running east-west between it and the Sabadel Valley to the south (on your left). In **1 hour**, you will reach a flat area with huge boulders that provide some wind shelter for camping. There is no water here, but there are superb views south to Sabadel. Below you to the north (right) is a lone homestead with some trails leading to it. Do not follow them; instead, head northwest to cross the southernmost source of Quebrada Chachacu. Continue up this valley and climb amid the straw to your right, to reach a small windy northwest-southeast ridge that separates Quebrada Chachacu from the easternmost sources of Quebrada Masacay. There is wind shelter by some bushes and usually a trickle of water in

Quebrada Masacay. You can camp here, **30 minutes** from the boulders.

The elliptical straw-covered summit of Cerro de Arcos lies to the northwest. It is easy to climb if you wish, but more interesting are the rock formations southwest of the summit, at point 3719 meters (12,202 feet) on the IGM map. A trail climbs west from the suggested camping spot by Quebrada Masacay to reach a shelter in **30 minutes**. It is an unfinished adobe house with a roof but no windows or floors. The area is windy; there are few sheltered spots to camp nearby, and only a small pond for water. A trail continues west from the shelter and in **30 minutes** reaches the *arcos* (arches), eroded rock formations with interesting shapes. The *arcos* are worth exploring; note the flat rock platform with a shallow pond near the top.

Descend from the *arcos* and travel south cross-country over the open *páramo*. Below to the east, near another source of Quebrada Masacay, is a house with a straw roof; stay west and well above it. Look for a clear trail ahead to the south, reached in **45 minutes**. The trail descends steadily south along the ridge west of Quebrada Masacay; views down to the valleys and back up to the arches are lovely. Along the way are several forks to pastures or houses; always continue south. In **1.25 hours** you will see the village of Tauarcocha well below you to the southeast; here a wide rutted trail branches left and in **15 minutes** descends steeply east to the dirt road just before Tauarcocha. You will be back at the road you left after crossing the Río Negro. In the village is a shop, and you can ask permission to camp in a field. (The area ahead is too steep for camping.)

The road winds its long way down to Zaruma, but more splendid views make you forget the distance. **Thirty minutes** from Tauarcocha there is a rutted shortcut to the left, from which you will emerge in **35 minutes**. The road then goes through some pretty forest fragments. In **30 minutes** you will reach a fork. Take the right branch northwest, mostly through pastures. In **2 hours** you will reach another fork near Tambillo. Go left (south). **Three hours** farther, past turnoffs to Daule (a detour), you will reach the village of Salvias. Here are some shops but no accommodations; you can ask to stay in the *casa comunal*.

Getting back: Hourly *rancheras* run from Salvias to Zaruma between 0600 and 1700 (1 hour, $.50). The scenic ride on the open-sided vehicle makes a lovely finale to the trek. Along the way you can see several *chancadoras*, rock-crushing equipment still used for mining. There are several daily buses from Zaruma to Loja (5 hours, $4) and Cuenca (6 hours, $5.50).

Chapter 14
TREKS FROM VILCABAMBA

Altitude, 1600 meters (5200 feet)
Population, 5000

Vilcabamba is the rainbow at the end of Ecuador's "*gringo* trail." This once-isolated village in the far south of the country attracts many expatriate residents as well as travelers. They are drawn by an ideal climate and idyllic surroundings, which combine to create a special air of tranquility. Vilcabamba first came to the country's attention as a fabled fountain of youth; many people there lived more than a hundred years, at a time when the average life expectancy in Ecuador was barely sixty. Today it is a small, prosperous resort with very good facilities and access to wonderful trekking.

Tour agencies in Vilcabamba are small and informal. Horseback riding is very popular; trips generally venture east into the foothills of Podocarpus National Park. At the close of this edition, llama trekking was just being introduced to the area. A popular day walk is to the top of Mandango, a spectacular rock formation near town. (Alas, there have been a few hold-ups on this trail.)

Trek 28, Natural High, climbs east from Vilcabamba, amid beautiful orchid-clad cloud forest, to the crest of the Cordillera Oriental. It returns along a different set of ridges to make a moderately difficult 4- to 5-day loop. Starting south of Vilcabamba, Trek 29 is a difficult and rewarding westward traverse of the Cordillera Oriental. This route crosses the Pass of the Winds to reach a unique and seldom-visited corner of Ecuador.

28 NATURAL HIGH

Rating: Moderately difficult, 30-kilometer (18.6-mile), 4- to 5-day trek.
Elevation: 1600 to 3600 meters (5200 to 11,800 feet).
Map: IGM 1:50,000: CT-NVII-B4 Vilcabamba.
Best time to visit: November is the driest month in the high *páramo*, but there may be fog, mist, and rain here at any time. At lower elevations to the west, the weather is milder and suitable for walking year-round,

but there is some rain from December to February. July and August can be very windy everywhere.

Special gear: None.

Water: Available year-round in streams; tank up before the ridge climbs.

Hazards: Hypothermia is a risk in the wet and windy conditions along the Continental Divide.

Annoyances: A few biting insects, ticks, and chiggers in the forest.

Permits and fees: This trek goes through Podocarpus National Park and two private reserves abutting on the park. The national park entry fee is $10 but there are no facilities for collecting it. You must obtain permission to walk through the private reserves. For Las Palmas Reserve, contact Charlie or Sarah Nodine, Cabañas Río Yambala, at the trailhead. For the reserve around Refugio El Gavilán, contact Gavin Moore at Caballos Gavilán in Vilcabamba. (See Río Yambala and Caballos Gavilán, respectively, under "Companies Offering Treks in Ecuador" in Appendix A.)

Services: There is a comfortable shelter at Las Palmas with running water, hot shower, and cooking facilities ($7 per person). Get the key at Cabañas Río Yambala, a convenient place to stay before or after the trek ($10–$12 per person, including breakfast and dinner). You can also arrange for pack animals or a fully organized tour here. On the descent is Refugio El Gavilán, another very nice shelter. To stay here, you must make prior arrangements with Gavin Moore, as indicated above. He also offers a full range of services. There is plenty of space to camp outside both shelters.

Provisions: Vilcabamba has a reasonable variety of provisions and Loja a wider selection.

There are many different ways to experience Vilcabamba. Foremost among the town's attractions are its magnificent natural surroundings, but some foreigners come to experience *San Pedrillo* (a hallucinogenic cactus juice) and other recreational drugs. They seem especially superfluous here— where the sky is often filled with real rainbows, and a couple of hours' walk brings you to enchanting forests overflowing with the most amazing orchids. The Cordillera Oriental towers 2000 meters (6500 feet) above Vilcabamba— a natural high that puts all the others in the shade.

East of Vilcabamba lies Podocarpus National Park, named for the only conifers native to Ecuador. Crystal-clear streams and waterfalls abound, and (farther afield) shining lakes nestle in the *páramo*. The rich

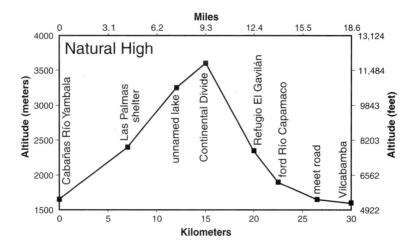

topography, flora, and fauna of the park are shared with several private reserves. Trees include alder, *cascarilla*, *higuerón*, *pumamaqui*, and of course podocarpus. Mosses and epiphytes are particularly abundant; in some areas there are so many bromeliads that it seems they were planted along the trail. Orchids of all colors, shapes, and sizes abound. Birds are also numerous; one study at Las Palmas identified 150 different species. The keen observer can see toucans, guans, parrots, and many hummingbirds. Mammals are more difficult to spot, but you may run across signs of deer, puma, Mountain Tapir, and Spectacled Bear.

This trek makes a loop east from Vilcabamba to the Continental Divide on the Cordillera Oriental and returns along a different set of ridges. It starts in the Río Yambala Valley, goes up to Las Palmas Reserve, and continues to an unnamed lake in the *páramo*. It then traverses south to return along the watershed of the Río Capamaco.

Access: The trailhead is at Cabañas Río Yambala, 4 kilometers (2.5 miles) southeast of Vilcabamba. From Vilcabamba's main plaza, follow the street Diego Vaca de Vega east. An unpaved road continues to the villages of Yamburara Bajo and Yamburara Alto, and on to the Río Yambala. A pick-up truck can be hired at the plaza in Vilcabamba. The trip to the cabañas costs $3.

Route: Cabañas Río Yambala has a small system of marked trails. Follow the red trail, which has some signs at the beginning and later red paint on rocks and trees. It climbs steeply south, zigzagging up the north flank of the ridge between the Río Yambala and the Río Capamaco. In

15 minutes you will reach the ridge line, and the trail climbs more gradually to the east. You will be surrounded by open pastures and have fine views back to Vilcabamba. In **30 minutes** you will reach a fork. The right branch continues to climb along the ridge toward Cerro Los Helechos. Take the left fork through a metal gate, dropping slightly and then undulating northeast along the northwest flank of the ridge. You will cross several small streams, pass a couple of farm houses, and in **40 minutes** reach Quebrada Palto.

Cross the stream and go through a wooden gate. The trail climbs steeply at first, east along the nose of the ridge that separates Río Yambala and Quebrada Palto. In **30 minutes** it levels off and then contours along the northwest flank of the ridge. It then drops steeply north to the Río Yambala, reached in **20 minutes**. A log bridge here was washed away in June 2001. The water level is about knee deep, but beware: it rises quickly after rain upstream.

The trail crosses the river and enters forest. It follows the north shore of the Río Yambala, which soon divides into the Quebrada de Solomaco and the Quebrada las Palmas. In **15 minutes**, just above the confluence of the rivers, the trail drops slightly to Quebrada de Solomaco, which is crossed on a one-log bridge or at an adjacent ford. On the east shore is a small clearing suitable for camping, with room for one or two tents.

From the river the trail climbs east, zigzagging steeply along the nose of the ridge between Quebrada de Solomaco and Quebrada Las Palmas. It then climbs more gradually along the ridge line, through secondary forest alternating with open country. In **30 minutes**, the ridge line dips slightly and there are views of a pretty waterfall upriver in Quebrada de Solomaco.

Shelter at Las Palmas Reserve

TREK 28: NATURAL HIGH

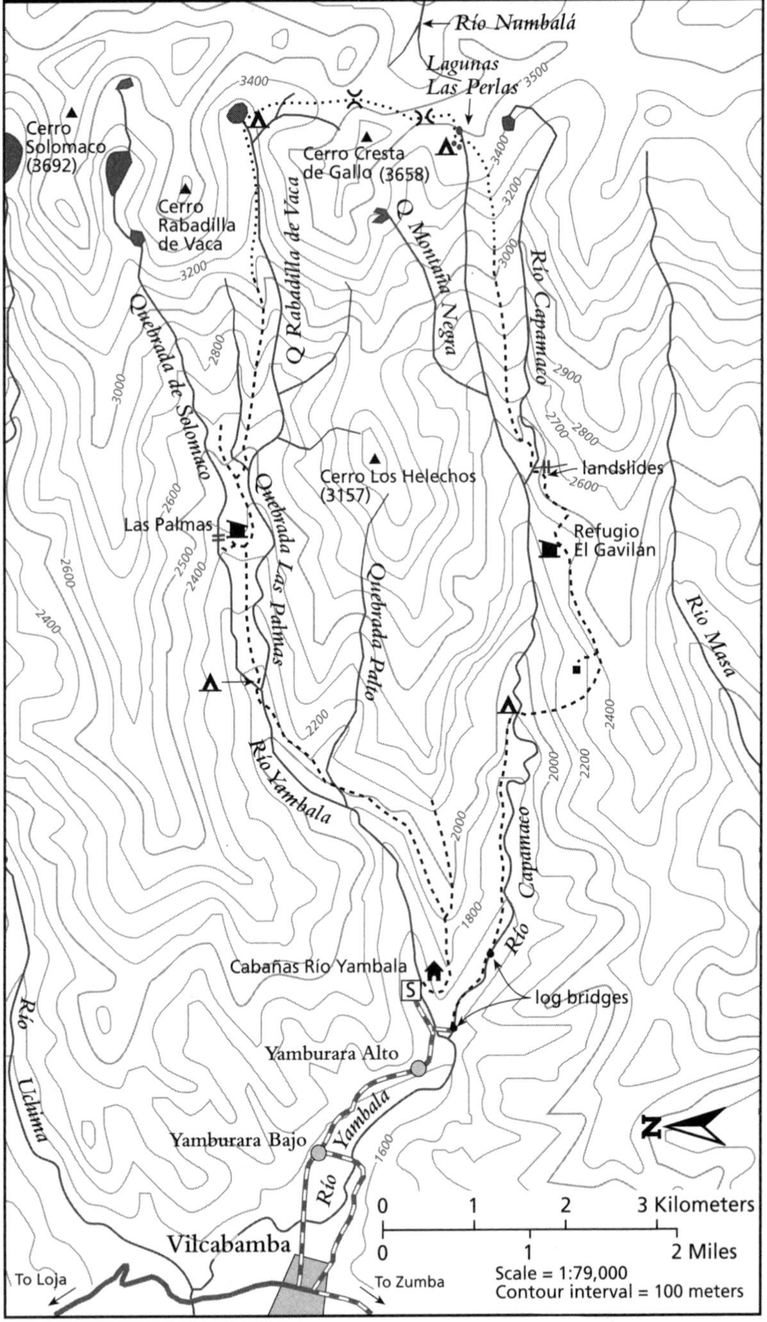

Río Numbalá

Lagunas
Las Perlas

Cerro Solomaco (3692)

Cerro Rabadilla de Vaca

Q. Rabadilla de Vaca

Cerro Cresta de Gallo (3658)

Q. Montaña Negra

Río Capamaco

Quebrada de Solomaco

Cerro Los Helechos (3157)

landslides

Las Palmas

Refugio El Gavilán

Quebrada Las Palmas

Quebrada Palto

Río Masa

Río Yambala

Río Capamaco

Cabañas Río Yambala

log bridges

Yamburara Alto

Río Uchima

Yamburara Bajo

Río Yambala

Vilcabamba

To Loja

To Zumba

| 0 | 1 | 2 | 3 Kilometers |
| 0 | | 1 | 2 Miles |

Scale = 1:79,000
Contour interval = 100 meters

The path continues to climb along the ridge line. In **20 minutes** you will reach a metal gate, the entrance to Las Palmas Reserve. Continuing **15 minutes** farther east, just north of the ridge line, you will reach the shelter at Las Palmas, surrounded by a large flat area suitable for camping.

Nearby in Quebrada de Solomaco are two magnificent waterfalls more than 50 meters (160 feet) high—well worth a visit. A side trail goes north from the shelter. When it splits in a few meters, take the left fork, which drops steeply 150 meters (500 feet) into the Solomaco canyon, winding its way through pretty forest. The trail is not safe during heavy rains; always be careful by the falls, since the rocks are slippery. The walk to the falls takes 30 minutes each way.

Our trail continues along the top of the ridge, just south of the shelter. Follow it east, climbing gradually through scrub with ferns, *achupallas*, and *gañales* (bushes with round waxy leaves and large white flowers). In **20 minutes** it starts to descend and enters nice forest with many epiphytes and birds. **Ten minutes** ahead you will reach a fork. The left branch goes northeast toward Cerro Rabadilla de Vaca. Follow the right branch, which heads southeast, contouring at first and then dropping to cross an unnamed stream in another **10 minutes**. This is a very pretty spot; it is surrounded by vegetation and has a small pool for a refreshing dip. Take water here for the ridge climb ahead.

After the ford, the trail climbs steadily east through more lovely forest along the nose of the ridge, north of Quebrada Rabadilla de Vaca. In **15 minutes** you will emerge again on a relatively clear ridge top with ferns, bamboo, bushes, and some small trees. The views looking back west are great. Continue climbing east on the ridge line. After **1.25 hours** the trail descends slightly, before reentering the woods and resuming its climb east along the ridge. You will be surrounded by lush cloud forest, the trees laden with mosses and orchids. The many terrestrial *huicundos* make the area look like a bromeliad garden. The path is narrower here and the going slower if you have a large backpack. You will duck under, over, and around the tree trunks. At about 3100 meters (10,200 feet), the forest begins to thin out; **2 hours** after the start of the woods, you will emerge at a clearing on the ridge top. The views in all directions are gorgeous; back west over Vilcabamba there is a wide panorama of dry mountains stretching to the north and south. To the east is Cerro Rabadilla de Vaca and, on its south flank, the *cirque* above the lake for which you are headed.

The trail now deteriorates and leaves the ridge line. It descends steadily to the east, through scrub forest and into the valley of Quebrada Rabadilla de Vaca. In **15 minutes** it emerges from the low scrub into open *páramo*. From here it climbs gradually east above the north shore of the stream. The ground is boggy, and you will often walk into a brisk wind, making the going slow. In **1.25 hours** you will reach the pretty, unnamed lake at the head of Quebrada Rabadilla de Vaca. There are nice views over the water to the *cirque*. You may see ducks in this and other lakes in the area, and snipes in the *páramo*. A number of spots are suitable for camping near the lake, but the area is wet and windy. If you intend to make it from here to Refugio El Gavilán in one day, you must start very early the next morning and set a good pace.

Our route continues south from the lake. Cross the outflow, just where it leaves the lake, and proceed south over the undulating *páramo*. Some small animal trails appear and disappear in this area; there is no one distinct path. Identify your goal: the pass east of the point marked 3658 meters (12,002 feet) on the IGM map, not a higher pass to the northwest of that point. Shortly you will cross a small stream. If you have not taken water from the lake, be sure to tank up here. (Water is scarce ahead.) After **45 minutes** of gentle climbing south across the boggy *páramo*, you will reach the base of the pass. Look for more animal tracks here; it is **20 minutes** of steep climbing to the top of the pass at 3550 meters (11,648 feet).

Your next goal is the south end of the very broad pass stretching south from point 3658. From the first pass, descend a little southwest (again using animal tracks) to cross above the headwaters of the Río Numbalá, a large drainage to the east. Then climb southwest toward the second pass. This is the Continental Divide, which offers superb views both east and west. It can, however, be extremely windy. In good weather, follow the ridge line south. Beware of the steep drop-off west (to your right). If it is very windy, stay just east of the ridge line. **One and a half hours** from the first pass, you will reach a point where the ridge begins to rise sharply and, looking down to the west, you will see a small lake and an adjacent cluster of ponds. These are unnamed on the IGM map, but known by locals as Lagunas las Perlas. Look for a tall slab of rock standing vertically just east of the ridge line at 3600 meters (11,800 feet); west of it is a narrow route that in **15 minutes** descends very steeply to the lake. You can camp in this area, although the ground is soggy. Be sure to take water from here for the long ridge-line descent ahead. After this point there are no areas suitable for camping until you reach Refugio El Gavilán, about 6 hours of walking ahead.

Make your way southwest between the ponds; then climb to a knob that is the eastern end of the long east-west ridge running along the north side of Río Capamaco. From the top of the knob, **30 minutes** away, are more outstanding 360-degree views: east to the *cordillera* from which you have just descended; north to the heavily eroded Cerro Cresta de Gallo (Cocks Comb Hill); west to the great panorama of dry mountains and valleys behind Vilcabamba; and south to the deep canyon of the Río Capamaco. Note, however, that neither the lake at the source of Quebrada Montaña Negra nor the one at the source of the Río Capamaco are visible anywhere along this route.

The route descends west along the top of the ridge. At about 3300 meters (10,800 feet), the *páramo* blends into a low, scrubby forest. A poorly defined trail weaves its way through the scrub, but it is often overgrown and difficult to follow. Stick to the ridge line in the more open areas and look for the trail in the bush. Around 3100 meters (10,200 feet), larger trees appear and you will gradually enter magnificent cloud forest, **1 hour** from the top of the knob. The trail becomes clearer here, although you will once again have to make your way around the crossed tree trunks. **Three hours** after the start of the cloud forest, the trail leaves the east-west ridge line and begins to descend steeply to the southeast, toward the Río Capamaco. It reaches the river in **30 minutes**, at a point upstream from its confluence with Quebrada Montaña Negra. On the south shore of the river are a lovely 75-meter (250-foot) waterfall and several large landslides dating to 1998. If it has been dry, it is easy to cross the river on some large rocks. (You won't even have to get your boots wet.) If there has been heavy rain upstream, however, it might be impossible to cross. Should you need to take shelter while you wait for the level to drop, there is a rocky overhang 20 meters (65 feet) back up the trail you came on.

On the south side of the river, the trail climbs very steeply at first, zigzagging over the bare landslide and then through dense forest, parallel to the waterfall. After **20 minutes** of steep ascent, the trail turns southwest and continues to climb more gently through the woods. (Be careful not to take a small fork right, back down to the river.) In **15 minutes**, the trail emerges into a patch of low, scrubby forest with good views. Continuing through alternating woods and scrub to skirt an old overgrown pasture, the trail reaches Refugio El Gavilán in another **15 minutes**.

From Refugio El Gavilán a big horse trail contours southwest around the 2400-meter (7900-foot) level through pastures and open scrub. In **1 hour** it reaches a fork above two houses. The right branch descends to the first house, while the left trail continues west above the houses. Take the left branch, which in **1 hour** winds steeply down to the Río Capamaco. There are good camping possibilities along the river's edge, especially on the south shore. When the river is low, the ford is knee deep and there are lovely swimming holes.

Our trail proceeds west, gradually down river, well above the north shore of the Río Capamaco. A few paths branch off to farms along the way. In **1.5 hours** you will descend back to the level of the river, where a one-log bridge crosses it. Do not cross the river; rather, continue along the north shore. The preferred route hugs the shore when water is low (and at times you will walk right in the river). In **30 minutes** you will reach another log bridge across the river and a dirt road coming in from the north. Follow the road north; it connects the Río Capamaco with the Río Yambala, which you will reach in **5 minutes**. Here is a ford for vehicles and a pedestrian bridge.

Getting back: If you wish to return to Cabañas Río Yambala, turn right and walk 0.6 kilometer (0.4 mile) east. Vilcabamba is 3.5 kilometers (2.2 miles) west.

29 PASS OF THE WINDS

Rating: Difficult, 52-kilometer (32-mile), 4- to 6-day trek.
Elevation: 1200 to 3600 meters (3950 to 11,800 feet).
Maps: IGM 1:50,000: CT-NVII-D3 Amaluza, CT-NVII-D4 Valladolid; both are *reservado* (see "Maps and Navigation" in Chapter 3).
Best time to visit: Rain on the eastern slopes is likely at all times of the year. November is considered the best month to cross the *cordillera*. West of the pass, dry conditions prevail from May to December. June through August can be very windy everywhere.
Special gear: None.
Water: Abundant on the eastern side; stock up for the ridge climb and descent on the western side.
Hazards: Hypothermia at higher elevations, snakes in the lowlands.
Annoyances: None.
Permits and fees: None.
Services: Palanda has two very basic hotels ($1.50 per person), and a

few equally basic places to eat. Pick-up trucks can be hired here for the ride to Valle Hermoso (see "Access" below). Pack animals can be arranged in Fátima; ask for Luís Girón or for his brothers Angel or Isauro. They will not go all the way to Amaluza, but they can help haul your gear for part of the climb.

At the western end of the trek, Amaluza has a couple of simple hotels (El Rocío is best at $2 per person), and a few restaurants. If you are coming from or going to Peru, there are border crossings at Zumba, south of Palanda, and Jimbura, southwest of Amaluza.

Provisions: Loja has a wide range of supplies, and Vilcabamba is reasonably well stocked. Only basic items are available in Palanda, but there is slightly more variety in Amaluza.

Southern Ecuador is a land of striking contrasts. Extremely wet conditions in the Oriente and on the eastern slopes of the Andes exist alongside semidesert in the inter-Andean valleys and ranges to the west. As humidity from the east rises along the outer slopes of the Cordillera Oriental, it quickly condenses to form great banks of cumulus cloud. From the west, it looks like a cloud-making machine has gone out of control: cloud after cloud is expelled over the mountains, only to dissipate in the bright blue sky. Right at the height of the *cordillera*, the wind that accompanies this phenomenon can be incredibly strong.

Just like the clouds that are blown from one side of the Andes to another, the people of this region have also been buffeted by the winds of

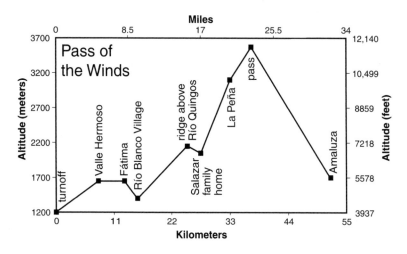

fate. According to historians, many settlers here during the late 1500s were Marrano Jews fleeing the Inquisition in Lima. In the more recent past, when severe drought struck the already dry valleys of southern Loja in the 1960s and 1970s, *lojanos* dispersed all over the country. Many went to colonize the Oriente. Some chose to defy the wind-swept *cordillera* by crossing due east, clearing the forest to make their new homes (and trading arid soil for mud). Colonization brought the destruction of great expanses of tropical forest in Oriente, but the cleared land soon proved poor for agriculture. Today, *lojanos* from both sides of the *cordillera* are migrating again, alongside other Ecuadoreans looking for a better life in North America and Europe.

This trek goes from Palanda, in the province of Zamora Chinchipe, west across the Continental Divide to Amaluza, in the dry Espíndola region of Loja near the border with Peru. Although a great deal of forest has been cleared along the way, enough remains to keep the route varied and interesting. Good visibility to the west makes for outstanding vistas and unforgettable sunsets.

Access: The first buses headed south to Zumba leave Loja at 0500 and 0530 daily, passing Vilcabamba between 0600 and 0700. There are more buses later in the day. Vilcabamba to Palanda takes 3 to 4 hours for the 53-kilometer (33-mile) ride ($3). This trek starts along a dirt road (not shown in the IGM map) going west off the Loja–Zumba Road. This turnoff to the villages of Valle Hermoso and Fátima is 13 kilometers (8 miles) south of Valladolid and 6.5 kilometers (4 miles) north of Palanda. If it is relatively dry, a pick-up truck hired in Palanda can take you as far as Valle Hermoso ($12)—or perhaps beyond to the Río Nanguira. If it has been raining, trucks can go only a few kilometers up the road before it becomes impassable.

Route: From the turnoff described above, walk **2.5 hours** west along the dirt road to the hamlet of Valle Hermoso. Continue west along the road; you will cross a couple of streams and in **45 minutes** reach a pedestrian bridge over the Río Nanguira. **Five minutes** beyond the bridge is another stream with pretty waterfalls. Along the watercourses are some lovely patches of rainforest; look for the bright heliconias. Continue west along the muddy road; after **1 hour** you will reach the village of Fátima, also known as Nanguira, perched high above the rushing Río Palanda.

From Fátima a muddy trail drops west, gradually at first and then very steeply to a pedestrian suspension bridge over the Río Blanco, reached in **1 hour**. Cross the bridge and follow the trail **10 minutes** south to the hamlet of Río Blanco, where the Río Blanco and the Río Jíbaro join to form the Río Palanda. You can ask for permission to pitch your tent here, or to stay in the schoolhouse.

From Río Blanco, a trail climbs northwest through pastures. In **20 minutes** you will reach a fork. The left branch goes straight up the ridge that separates the valleys of the Río Blanco and the Río Jíbaro. This is an old route over the *cordillera* to Amaluza, the trail shown on the IGM map. Locals discourage use of this route because of its long traverse in exposed, windy *páramo*. Instead, take the right branch at the fork. The muddy trail continues to climb steadily to the northwest, along the pastures above and south of the Río Blanco. In **45 minutes** it reaches the home of the Abad family. (Señor Abad is interested in showing visitors some ruins found on his property.) The trail continues climbing northwest, but now more gradually; it occasionally dips to cross several small streams. At one of these streams, **2 hours** from the Abad house, there is some flat ground and room for two tents. The forest fragments along the streams are alive with bird songs and fluttering butterflies, and the open pastures provide fine views of the Río Blanco Valley.

After crossing several more side streams, the trail climbs to a patch of flat ground with some boulders, situated between two streams (**1 hour**). This is another good spot to camp. From here, drop to the next stream, which runs through a small boggy area. Instead of following the main trail northeast here, look for a smaller path that climbs steeply north from the boggy area to a notch between the hills. You will reach the notch in **20 minutes** and emerge on a ridge high above a house and surrounding pastures on your right.

A good trail (smaller than the one you have been following) continues to climb steadily northwest, still above the south shore of the Río Blanco. Small patches of cloud forest alternate with pastures and recently cut or burnt trees—a sad sight. The trail contours and again undulates to cross several small streams. In **2 hours**, it reaches the top of a bare north-south ridge, from which you will have grand views down to the Río Quingos (a tributary of the Río Blanco) coming in from the west. Descend steeply along the ridge. There are a few zigzags to ease the 200-meter (650-foot) drop to a wooden bridge over the Río Quingos (**30 minutes**). A rock overhang on your left just before the bridge is too small to pitch a tent, but makes a good dry bivouac in poor weather.

Immediately after crossing the bridge, the trail divides. Take the left

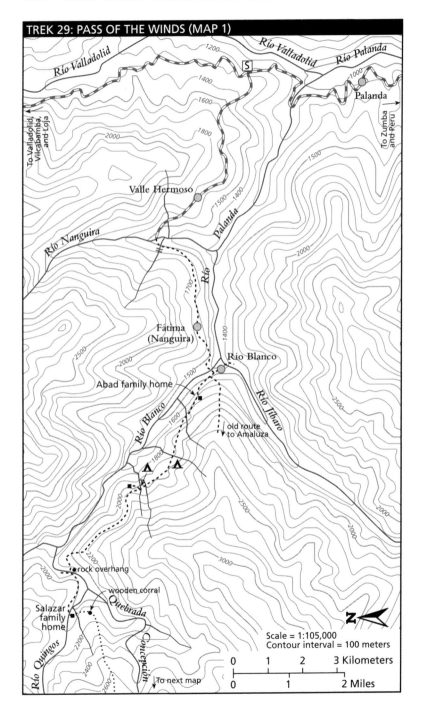

TREK 29: PASS OF THE WINDS (MAP 1)

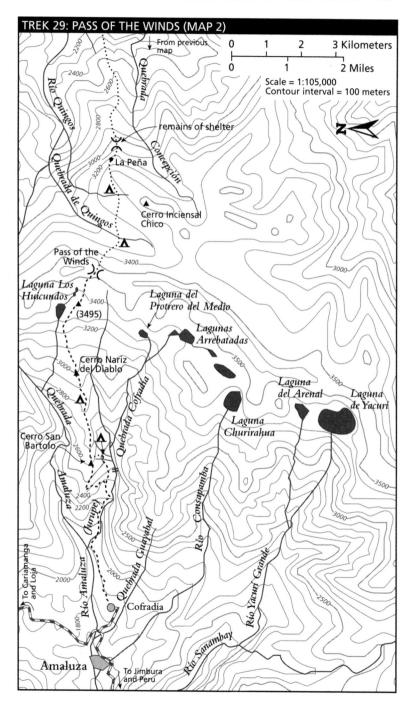

TREK 29: PASS OF THE WINDS (MAP 2)

branch, which follows the Río Quingos upstream. It climbs steeply at first, then drops to a pasture from which it climbs more gradually west above the north shore of the Río Quingos, through patches of lovely forest interspersed with pastures and landslides. In **2 hours** you will begin to drop back down toward the Río Quingos, amid a large pasture. On the far side of the pasture is a sort of doorway made of logs on the hillside. From here you can see a couple of small houses on the south side of the river.

Locals usually call out from this spot to let people know they are arriving; it is a good idea to do likewise, so you can be guided to the best place to cross the river. The trail drops steeply from the doorway to fields by the river's edge. Look for a rough log bridge over the Río Quingos; after crossing, find the path that climbs up to the houses (home of the Salazar family), which you will reach in **10 minutes**. You can ask permission to camp here (they are very friendly people). Be sure to get Señor Salazar's advice about the weather before continuing up to the *cordillera*.

The route continues up a grassy ridge south of the Salazar home. Take water for the long climb ahead. Cross the small *quebrada* south of the house and climb steeply south along the nose of the ridge. In **1 hour** you will reach a flat patch at the top, with a wooden corral. Turn west and follow a small trail that climbs more gently along the ridge separating the Río Quingos from Quebrada Concepción (unnamed on the IGM map). The trail continues to travel west along the ridge line, rising more steeply at times for 360-degree views of the deeply incised valleys and several lovely cascades. When you are **1.5 hours** from the corral, you will begin a hard climb up a forested slope; look for *incienso* trees, with large round leaves and yellow resin used as incense. Another local summit is reached in **45 minutes**; there are fine views west to a rugged unnamed ridge and the headwaters of Quebrada Concepción.

Continue west along the ridge line through alternating cleared areas and cloud forest rich in epiphytes and mosses. (There are many orchids here.) After a small dip, the trail climbs along a forested slope with smaller trees, more moss, and bambusoid grass. In **45 minutes**, you will reach the nose of a cleared ridge. The trail then cuts briefly north across this pasture before continuing to climb west at the edge of a patch of forest. There are views back to the Río Blanco Valley to the east, the Río Quingos to the north, and the Río Concepción to the south—a real top-of-the-world feeling. Continue climbing gradually west along the ridge. In **15 minutes**, it drops steeply to a saddle that divides the watersheds of the Río Quingos and Quebrada Concepción. At the saddle are remains of a shelter, a few boards but no roof, and sometimes a trickle of water. The spot is small and unattractive, but it is sheltered from the wind.

The trail now begins a very steep climb to the northwest. It zigzags along the almost-vertical nose of a 250-meter-high (800-foot-high) ridge known by locals as La Peña (the cliff). This stretch is not for those with a fear of heights, but there are grand views in clear weather. Be sure to watch your step. **One hour** from the saddle, the terrain levels off briefly before continuing a less vertical (but nonetheless steep) climb to the northwest.

After **45 minutes**, the trail leaves the ridge line and begins to climb more gently west through open *páramo*, along the north flank of Cerro Inciensal Chico. In **20 minutes**, it reaches 3400 meters (11,150 feet) and starts to descend gently, still traveling west. As it levels off, there are several sites suitable for camping near small, meandering streams. The ground is boggy, however, and you must look for wind shelter behind bushes or large boulders (of which there are several strewn about). In another **20 minutes** you will pass a nice rocky area with stunted shrubs, which looks like a bonsai garden. Continue west across a series of low ridges and valleys, with the rocky cliffs of Cerro Inciensal Chico to your left (south). In **30 minutes** you will reach the rim of a broad glacial valley, the Quebrada de Quingos. Drop steeply west, pass a small waterfall, and reach the river in **20 minutes**. The ford is ankle deep but subject to flooding after heavy rain. Here too are some picturesque but soggy spots to camp. Take as much water as you can here for the climb to the pass and subsequent descent.

The route continues northwest, climbing steadily along straw-covered slopes. Enjoy the great views back to the craggy summits towering over Quebrada de Quingos. As you climb, the wind begins to sweep over the *páramo*, driving the clouds west. At the pass (3570 meters, 11,713 feet), reached in **1.5 hours**, there is often a roaring gale, with winds strong enough to topple you over. The descent is equally windswept, and gusts will seem to come at you from all directions at once. When the clouds begin to dissipate in the now-dry air, however, the views make it all worthwhile. Below you to the northwest are Laguna Los Huicundos (with frothy whitecaps whipped by the wind) and two small ponds farther east. To the southwest lies a large bowl—probably once the site of lakes as well.

After the pass, the trail widens and drops west along the narrow ridge separating the lakes and the bowl. It reaches a small saddle and then climbs the hill marked 3495 meters (11,467 feet) on the IGM map (**30 minutes** from the pass). There are more splendid views here, down to Amaluza's deep valley and beyond to the endless dry mountains of Peru. The trail continues to descend, zigzagging northwest and then west along the ridge that separates Laguna Los Huicundos and its forested outflow from the headwaters of Quebrada Cofradía. The wind remains ferocious at first, but very gradually diminishes as you descend. In **1 hour** you will pass the large black boulder of Cerro Nariz del Diablo (the Devils Nose) and the first spots sufficiently flat and wind-sheltered for camping. (It is still quite exposed here, however, and there is no water.) Overhead, the juggernaut of clouds continues to sweep by and evaporate into an incredibly blue sky.

The trail continues to descend west for **1.5 hours** along the ridge that joins Cerro Nariz del Diablo with Cerro San Bartolo (San Bertolo on the IGM map). Along the way are several more spots with flat ground for camping. They are sheltered by forest, but there is no water here. Despite the lack of rainfall, the area is misted by the constantly passing clouds—creating beautiful cloud forests with many orchids and bromeliads. As you approach Cerro San Bartolo, the trail begins to climb gently. Just before it becomes steep, you can take a shortcut used by locals on foot. Otherwise, continue west along the main route (a more circuitous but easier mule trail).

To take the shortcut, when you reach a barbed-wire fence with pines planted behind it, keep left to follow the fence. Then cross a rough wooden gate (just a pile of logs) to turn south along a ridge coming off Cerro San Bartolo. The trail is less distinct here, but the topography is easy to follow and you can see where you are headed. Follow the ridge down—at first along a fence and then more steeply on the ridge line, zigzagging through alternating forest and steep open slopes, to reach a larger trail traveling east-west (**30 minutes** after the wooden gate).

The route to Amaluza continues west, but there is a lovely little stream in a shady patch of forest 5 minutes east of this junction, the first water since Quebrada Quingos. Five minutes farther east, on the trail above the stream, is a pasture suitable for camping.

The route continues west along the trail. It descends gradually through open country alternating with planted pine forest and crosses a few more small streams. Looking down the valley of Quebrada Cofradía, you can see Amaluza in the distance, with its backdrop of high, dry mountains. In **45 minutes**, you will meet the mule trail that wound its way around Cerro San Bartolo. From this point there is a lovely view back to waterfalls on Quebrada Cofradía. The trail continues to descend steadily west; in **1.5 hours** it reaches a concrete bridge over Quebrada Cofradía. (Note that locals call both this river and the Río Amaluza lower down "Río Jurupe.")

Cross the concrete bridge and continue west along the south shore— at first alongside the river, then climbing gradually southwest away from it. In **45 minutes** you will reach the hamlet of Cofradía. An unpaved road descends west from here and meets the main Loja–Amaluza Road in **30 minutes**. Take the Loja–Amaluza Road left. Amaluza is **10 minutes** ahead.

Getting back: There are several daily buses from Amaluza to Loja (6.5 hours, $4). Buses, vans, and shared taxis (Taxi Rutas) run from Loja to Vilcabamba (1 hour, $1).

Daisy bracing against the wind above Laguna Los Huicundos

Section III
APPENDIXES

CAMINANTE NO HAY CAMINO
SE HACE CAMINO AL ANDAR

APPENDIX A: RESOURCES

Additional updated information, Internet links, resources, references, and an expanded trekker's vocabulary are all found on the website *www. trekkinginecuador.com*.

Note: Changes were made to the Ecuadorean telephone numbering system in late 2001. All cellular phones (area code 09) and phones in the provinces of Pichincha (02) and Guayas (04) currently have seven digit numbers, as shown below. All other phone numbers have only six digits. There are plans to change the remaining numbers to seven digits by 2003. Please consult the website *www.trekkinginecuador.com* for updated telephone information.

EMERGENCY CONTACTS
Emergency Phone Numbers. 911 in Quito, 101 in the rest of Ecuador (although the latter may not always work).

Your Embassy. _____
Phone numbers for embassies and consulates are listed in the Quito telephone directory, or you can obtain them from the foreign affairs department of your government before you leave home.

Hospitals and Clinics
Quito
Clínica Pichincha
Veintimilla E3-30 y Páez
Phone: (02)256-2296

Hospital Metropolitano
Mariana de Jesús y Av Occidental
Phone: (02)226-1520

Hospital Voz Andes
Villalengua Oe2-37 y 10 de Agosto
Phone: (02)226-2142

Med Center Travel Clinic
Foch 476 y Almagro
Phone: (02)252-1104

Guayaquil
Clínica Alcívar
Coronel 2301 y Azuay
Phone: (04)258-0030

Clínica Kennedy
Av San Jorge y la Novena
Phone: (04)228-9666

Cuenca
Clínica Santa Inés
Daniel Córdova Toral 2-113 y Agustín Cueva
Phone: (07)817-888

Hospital Monte Sinaí
Miguel Cordero 6-111 y Av Solano
Phone: (07)885-595

Snakebite Treatment Centers
Coast
Hospital Augusto Egas
Santo Domingo de los Colorados
Phone: (02)275-0336

Oriente
Hospital Voz Andes
Shell (near Puyo)
Phone: (03)795-172

Search and Rescue
ASEGUIM
Quito
Phone: (02)223-4109

ASEGUIM'S office is seldom staffed. Try to contact through Safari Tours, Quito. Phone: (02)255-2505 or (02)250-8316. Or contact Compañía de Guías de Montaña, Quito. Phone: (02)250-4773.

Air Ambulance

Icaro
Palora Oe3-20 y Amazonas (south of airport terminal)
Quito
Phone: (02)245-0928 or (09)980-2513

TOPOGRAPHIC MAPS
Ecuador
Instituto Geográfico Militar (IGM)
Telmo Paz y Miño (up from Avenida Colombia)
Quito
Phone: (02)254-5090

Europe
Cordee
3a De Montfort Street
Leicester LE1 7HD, U.K.
Phone: 0116-2543579; fax: 0116-2471176
e-mail: *info@cordee.co.uk*
website: *www.cordee.co.uk*

GeoCenter
Schockenriedstrasse 44
70565 Stuttgart, Germany
Phone/fax: 0711-781946-54
website: *www.geocenter.de*

Stanford's
12-14 Long Acre, Covent Garden
London WC2E 9LP, U.K.
Phone: 020-7836-1321; fax: 020-7836-0189
e-mail: *customer.services@stanfords.co.uk*
website: *www.stanfords.co.uk*

North America
Omni Resources
1004 South Mebane Street
Burlington, NC 27216-2096, U.S.A.
Phone: (336)227-8300; fax (336)227-3748
e-mail: *custserv@omnimap.com*
website: *www.omnimap.com*

Treaty Oak
P.O. Box 50295
Austin, TX 78763, U.S.A.
Phone: (512)326-4141; fax: (512)443-0973
e-mail: *maps@treatyoak.com*
website: *www.treatyoak.com*

CONSERVATION ORGANIZATIONS
Andean Tapir Fund
P.O. Box 456
Minden, NV 89423, U.S.A.
Phone: (775)267-3484; fax: (775)747-1642
e-mail: *ccdowner@yahoo.com*
website: *www.dexlen.com/Tapir/andean_tapir.htm*

Corporación Ornitológica del Ecuador (CECIA)
La Tierra 203 y Los Shyris
Quito
Phone/fax: (02)227-1800 or (02)246-4359
e-mail: *cecia@uio.satnet.net*
website: *www.geocities.com/avesecuador/*

Fundación Arcoiris
Segundo Cueva Celi 03-15 y Clodoveo Carrión
P.O. Box 11-01-860
Loja
Phone/fax: (07)577-449
e-mail: *arcoiris@utpl.net*
website: *www.arcoiris.org.ec*

Fundación Ecológica Rumicocha
Antonio Ante 343 y Vargas, office 209
P.O. Box 17-15-13B
Quito
Phone/fax: (02)258-4619
e-mail: *ferumico@pi.pro.ec*

Fundación Jatun Sacha
Pasaje Eugenio de Santillán N34-248 y Maurián
Urbanización Rumipamba
P.O. Box 17-12-867
Quito
Phone: (02)243-2246; fax: (02)245-3583
e-mail: *jatunsacha@jatunsacha.org*
website: *www.jatunsacha.org*

Fundación Jocotoco
Shyris N39-281 y Gaspar de Villarroel
Centro Comercial La Galería, local 47
P.O. Box 17-16-337
Quito
Phone: (02)226-9260, ext 147
e-mail: *fjocotoco@andinanet.net*
website: *www.jocotoco.org*

Fundación Maquipucuna
Baquerizo Moreno E9-153 y Tamayo
P.O. Box 17-12-167
Quito
Phone: (02)250-7200; fax: (02)250-7201
e-mail: *maqui@ecua.net.ec*
website: *www.maqui.org*

Fundación Natura
Av República 481 y Almagro
P.O. Box 17-01-253
Quito
Phone/fax: (02)250-3391
e-mail: *natura@fnatura.org.ec*
website: *www.ecua.net.ec/fnatura/*

INTERNET SITES

Ecuadorean daily newspapers (all in Spanish)
El Comercio (www.elcomercio.com)
El Hoy (www.hoy.com.ec)
El Universo (www.eluniverso.com)

Ecuadorean Embassy in Washington (English and Spanish)
www.ecuador.org

Ecuadorean Ministry of Tourism (English and Spanish)
www.vivecuador.com

EcuadorExplorer (English)
www.ecuadorexplorer.com

Explored (Spanish)
www.explored.com.ec

The Latin American Travel Advisor (English)
www.amerispan.com/lata/

National Geophysics Institute (volcano advisories in Spanish)
www.epn.edu.ec

South American Explorers (English)
www.samexplo.org

Trekking in Ecuador (English)
www.trekkinginecuador.com

Health Information for International Travelers

Centers for Disease Control, U.S.A.
www.cdc.gov

Scottish Center for Infection and Environmental Health
www.fitfortravel.scot.nhs.uk

World Health Organization
www.who.int/ith/

COMPANIES OFFERING TREKS IN ECUADOR
Australia
Contours Travel
Level 6, 310 King Street
Melbourne.Victoria 3000, Australia
Phone: 3-96706900; fax: 3-96707558
e-mail: *contours@contourstravel.com.au*
website: *www.contourstravel.com.au*

Europe
Andísimo
Merrillweg 9a
50996 Köln, Germany
Phone: 2236-96-70-50; fax: 2236-96-70-49
e-mail: *admin@andisimo.com*
website: *www.andisimo.com*

Avventure Nel Mondo
Circonv. Gianicolense, 41
00152 Roma, Italy
Phone: (06)5880661; fax: (06)5809540
e-mail: *info@viaggiavventurenelmondo.it*
website: *www.viaggiavventurenelmondo.it*

Journey Latin America
12 and 13 Heathfield Terrace
Chiswick, London W4 4JE, U.K.
Phone: 0208-7478315; fax: 0208-7421312
e-mail: *adventure@journeylatinamerica.co.uk*
website: *www.journeylatinamerica.co.uk*

Nouvelles Frontières
France
website: *www.nouvelles-frontieres.fr*

SNP Natuurreizen
Bijleveldsingel 26
6512 AT Nijmegen, The Netherlands

Phone: 024-327-7000; fax: 024-327-7099
e-mail: *sales@snp.nl*
website: *www.snp.nl*

North America
G.A.P.
19 Duncan Street, Suite 401
Toronto, ON, Canada M5H 3H1
Phone: (800)465-5600 or (416)260-0999; fax: (416)260-1888
e-mail: *adventure@gap.ca*
website: *www.gapadventures.com*

Mountain Travel Sobek
6420 Fairmount Avenue
El Cerrito, CA 94530, U.S.A.
Phone: (888)687-6235 or (510)527-8100; fax: (510)525-7710
e-mail: *info@mtsobek.com*
website: *www.mtsobek.com*

Wilderness Travel
1102 Ninth Street
Berkeley, CA 94710, U.S.A.
Phone: (800)368-2794 or (510)558-2488; fax: (510)558-2489
e-mail: *info@wildernesstravel.com*
website: *www.wildernesstravel.com*

Ecuador
Otavalo
Ernesto Cevillano
El Mirador Cabins, Cuicocha
Phone: (06)648-039 or (09)990-8757

Suni Tours
Morales y Sucre
Phone: (06)923-383 or (09)993-3148
e-mail: *ivansuarez@hotmail.com*

Yuratours
Morales 505 y Sucre
Phone/fax: (06)921-861
e-mail: *info@yuratours.com*
website: *www.yuratours.com*

Quito
Angermeyer's Enchanted Expeditions
Foch 726 y Amazonas
Phone: (02)256-9960; fax: (02)256-9956
e-mail: *angerme1@angermeyer.com.ec*
website: *www.angermeyer.com*

Compañía de Guías de Montaña
Jorge Washington 425 y 6 de Diciembre
Phone/fax: (02)250-4773
e-mail: *guiasmontania@accessinter.net*
website: *www.companiadeguias.com*

Exploratur
Shyris 760 y República de El Salvador
Phone: (02)276-0791; fax: (02)246-0801
e-mail: *exploratur@andinanet.net*
website: *www.exploratur.com*

Pamir
Juan León Mera 721 y Veintimilla
Phone: (02)254-2605; fax: (02)254-7576
e-mail: *info@pamirtravels.com.ec*
website: *www.pamirtravels.com.ec*

Safari
Calama 380 y Juan León Mera
Phone: (02)255-2505 or (02)250-8316; fax: (02)222-3381
U.S.A./Canada toll free: (800)434-8182;
e-mail: *admin@safari.com.ec*
website: *www.safari.com.ec*

Sierra Nevada
Pinto 4E-150 y Cordero
Phone: (02)255-3658; fax: (02)255-4936
e-mail: *snevada@accessinter.net*
website: *www.hotelsierranevada.com*

Surtrek
Amazonas 897 y Wilson
Phone: (02)256-1129; fax: (02)256-1132
e-mail: *surtrek@surtrek.com*
website: *www.surtrek.com*

Vasco Tours
Calama E7-49 y Reina Victoria
Phone: (02)254-0227
e-mail: *vascotours@andinanet.net*

Latacunga
Estambul Tours
Hotel Estambul
Belisario Quevedo 6-46 y Padre Salcedo
Phone: (03)800-354

Neiges
Guayaquil 5-19 y Quito
Phone/fax: (03)811-199
e-mail: *neigestours@hotmail.com*

Panzaleo Tour
Quito 16-32 y Padre Salcedo
Phone: (03)800-302
e-mail: *panzaleo_tour@hotmail.com*

Ruta de los Volcanes
Padre Salcedo 4-55 y Quito
Phone: (03)812-452

Selvanieve
Guayaquil y Quevedo
Phone: (09)990-6045

Tovar Expeditions
Guayaquil 5-38 y Quito
Phone: (03)813-080 or (09)971-8262
e-mail: *tovarexpeditions@hotmail.com*

Baños
Deep Forest Adventure
Rocafuerte y Halflants
Phone/fax: (03)741-815
e-mail: *deepforestadventure@hotmail.com*

Expediciones Amazónicas
Oriente 11-68 y Halflants
Phone/fax: (03)740-506
e-mail: *expoamazon@hotmail.com*

Geotours
Ambato y Halflants
Phone/fax: (03)741-344
e-mail: *geotours_@hotmail.com*
website: *www.ecuadorexplorer.com/geotours*

Rainforestur
Ambato 800 y Maldonado
Phone/fax: (03)740-743
e-mail: *rainfor@interactive.net.ec*
website: *www.rainforestur.8k.com*

Guaranda
Cashcaventura
Convención de 1884 #1112 y García Moreno (no sign)
Phone/fax: (03)980-725

Riobamba
Alta Montaña
Daniel León Borja 3517 y Uruguay
Phone/fax: (03)942-215
e-mail: *aventurag@laserinter.net*

Expediciones Andinas
Las Abras, Km 3 via a Guano
Phone: (03)964-915; fax: (03)969-604
e-mail: *sales@expediciones-andinas.com*
website: *www.expediciones-andinas.com*

Julio Verne
5 de Junio 21-46 y 10 de Agosto
Phone/fax: (03)963-436
e-mail: *julioverne@andinanet.net*
website: *www.julioverne-travel.com*

Cuenca
Ecotrek
Calle Larga 7-108 y Luis Cordero
Phone: (07)842-531; fax: (07)835-387
e-mail: *ecotrek@az.pro.ec*

Montaruna Tours
Hermano Miguel 4-46 y Calle Larga
Phone/fax: (07)846-395
e-mail: *montarun@az.pro.ec*
website: *www.montaruna.ch*

Río Arriba
Hermano Miguel 7-14 y Presidente Córdova
Phone: (07)840-031; fax: (07)830-116
e-mail: *negro@az.pro.ec*

Vilcabamba
Biotours
José Antonio Eguiguren y Olmedo
Loja
Phone: (07)578-398; fax: (07)574-696
e-mail: *biotours@loja.telconet.net*

Caballos Gavilán
Sucre y Diego Vaca de Vega
Phone: (07)580-281
e-mail: *gavilanhorse@yahoo.com*

Llamandina
Vilcabamba (no storefront, contact in advance)
Phone/fax: (07)580-061
e-mail: *anneli@llamandina.com*
website: *www.llamandina.com*

Río Yambala
Past Yamburara Alto
Phone: (07)580-299 (messages only)
e-mail: *rio_yambala@yahoo.com*
website: *www.vilcabamba.cwc.net*

CAMPING STORES IN ECUADOR
Quito
Los Alpes
Reina Victoria N23-45 y Baquedano
Phone: (02)223-2362

Altamontaña
Jorge Washington 425 y 6 de Diciembre
Phone: (02)252-4422

The Altar
Juan León Mera 615 y Carrión
Phone: (02)252-3671

AltuSport
Juan León Mera N23-15 y Veintimilla
Phone: (02)290-3654

Andísimo
9 de Octubre 479 y Roca
Phone: (02)250-8347

Antisana
Centro Comercial El Bosque, ground floor
Phone: (02)245-1605

Camping
Colón 942 y Reina Victoria
Phone: (02)252-1626

Equipos Cotopaxi
6 de Diciembre 927 y Patria
Phone: (02)250-0038

The Explorer
Reina Victoria E6-32 y Pinto
Phone: (02)255-0911

Tatoo
Wilson y Juan León Mera
Phone: (02)290-4533

Baños
Varoxi
Maldonado 651 y Oriente
Phone: (03)740-051

APPENDIX B: FURTHER READING

TRAVEL GUIDEBOOKS

Box, Ben. *South American Handbook 2002*. 78th ed. Bath, U.K.: Footprint Handbooks, 2002.

Gómez, Nelson. *Pocket Guide to Ecuador*. Quito: Ediguías, 2001.

Kunstaetter, Robert, and Daisy Kunstaetter. *Ecuador and Galápagos Handbook*. 3rd ed. Bath, U.K.: Footprint Handbooks, 2001.

Pearson, David, and David Middleton. *New Key to Ecuador and the Galápagos*. 3rd ed. Berkeley, CA: Ulysses Press, 1999.

Rachowiecki, Rob. *Ecuador and the Galápagos Islands*. 5th ed. Melbourne: Lonely Planet, 2001.

Smith, Julian. *Moon Handbooks Ecuador*. 2nd ed. Emeryville, CA: Avalon Travel, 2001.

TREKKING AND MOUNTAINEERING

Brain, Yossi. *Ecuador: A Climbing Guide*. Seattle: The Mountaineers, 2000.

Rachowiecki, Rob, Mark Thurber, and Betsy Wagenhauser. *Climbing and Hiking in Ecuador*. 4th ed. Chalfont St Peter, UK: Bradt Publications, 1997.

Serrano, Marcos, Ivan Rojas, and Freddy Landázuri. *Montañas del Sol*. Quito: Campo Abierto, 1994.

TRAVEL AND TREKKING MEDICINE

Bezruchka, Stephen. *The Pocket Doctor*. 3rd ed. Seattle: The Mountaineers, 1999.

Van Tilburg, Christopher. *First Aid, A Pocket Guide*. 4th ed. Seattle: The Mountaineers, 2001.

Wilkerson, James, ed. *Medicine for Mountaineering and Other Wilderness Activities*. 5th ed. Seattle: The Mountaineers, 2001.

GEOGRAPHY AND GEOLOGY

Gómez, Nelson. *Manual de Elementos de Geografía del Ecuador*. 3rd ed. Quito: Ediguías, 2001.

Hall, Minard, et al. "Tungurahua Volcano, Ecuador: Structure, Eruptive History and Hazards." In *Journal of Volcanology and Geothermal Research*, 91(1999), 1-21. Elsevier Science, 1999.

Mothes, Patricia, ed. *El Paisaje Volcánico de la Sierra Ecuatoriana.* Quito: Corporación Editora Nacional, 1991.

RESERVES AND NATURAL AREAS

Gómez, Desider, Laurence Lebrun, and Luís Germán Flores. *Un Paseo Cultural y Botánico en el Parque Omaere.* Quito: Fudación Omaere, 1998.

Jiggings, Chris, et al. *Ecuador Nature Guide: Southwest Forests.* Edmonton: Lone Pine Publishing, 2000.

Rodríguez, Luis. *Guía de Parques Nacionales y Reservas del Ecuador.* Quito: INEFAN-GEF, 1998.

FLORA

Jorgensen, P., and S. León-Yánez. *Catalog of the Vascular Plants of Ecuador.* Saint Louis: Monographs in Systematic Botany from the Missouri Botanical Garden 75, 1999.

Patzelt, Erwin. *Flora del Ecuador.* Quito: Banco Central del Ecuador, 1996.

Valencia, R., N. Pitman, S. León-Yánez, and P. Jorgensen, eds. *Libro Rojo de las Plantas Endémicas del Ecuador.* Quito: Herbario QCA, Pontificia Universidad Católica del Ecuador, 2000.

FAUNA

Canaday, C., and L. Jost. *Common Birds of Amazonian Ecuador: A Guide for the Wide-Eyed Ecotourist.* Quito: Ediciones Libri-Mundi, 1997.

Guarderas, Lidia, and Iván Jácome. *Fauna Nativa Amazónica.* Quito: Abya-Yala, 1999.

Moreno, Miguel, Xavier Silvia, Germania Estévez, Inés Marggraff, and Paul Marggraff. *Mariposas del Ecuador.* Quito: Colección el Ecuador Secreto, Imprenta Mariscal, 1997.

Patzelt, Erwin. *Fauna del Ecuador.* Quito: Imprefepp reprint, 2000.

Ridgely, R., and P. Greenfield. *Birds of Ecuador.* Ithaca: Cornell University Press, 2001.

Tirira, Diego. *Mamíferos del Ecuador.* Quito: Editores CBA, 1999.

HISTORY

Gómez, Nelson, ed. *Charles Marie de la Condamine: Diario del Viaje al Ecuador, 1745.* Quito: Ediguías, 1994.

Honigsbaum, Mark. *The Fever Trail: The Hunt for the Cure for Malaria.* London: Macmillan, 2001.

Lourie, Peter. *Sweat of the Sun, Tears of the Moon.* Lincoln: Bison Books, University of Nebraska Press, 1998.

Wallace, Alfred Russell, ed. *Notes of a Botanist on the Amazon and Andes.* London: Macmillan, 1908.

Whymper, Edward. *Travels Amongst the Great Andes of the Equator.* London: Murray, 1891. Reprint, Salt Lake City: Gibbs M. Smith, 1987.

COFFEE-TABLE BOOKS

Acosta-Solis, M., et al. *Ecuador a la Sombra de los Volcanes.* Quito: Ediciones Libri Mundi, 1991.

Anhalzer, Jorge Juan. *Andes.* Quito: Imprenta Mariscal, 1997.

———. *Ecuador from Above.* Quito: Guías de Montañas/Andes Editores, 1993.

Cruz, Marco. *Mountains of Ecuador.* Quito: Dinediciones, 1993.

APPENDIX C: TREKKER'S VOCABULARY

Local Spanish/ Quichua*	English
abajo	down
acampar	to camp
acequia	irrigation ditch
agua	water
ahí no más	nearby
aldea	village, hamlet
arenal	sandy slope or plain
arriba	up
arriero	muleteer
arroyo	stream
asfaltado	paved
auxilio	help, rescue
bestia	beast, pack animal
bosque	woods, forest
brújula	compass
burro	donkey
caballo	horse
camellones	transverse ridges on a muddy trail
caminata	trek, walk
camino	road, trail, path
camino de herradura	horse/mule trail
camión	truck
camioneta	pick-up truck
campamento	camp
campesino	rural dweller
canal de riego	irrigation canal
cargador	porter
carpa	tent
carro	vehicle, car, bus
carta topográfica	topographic map
casa comunal	community hall
cascada	waterfall
cerco(a)	fence

cerro	hill, mountain
chaquiñán*	small trail, foot path
chorrera	waterfall
choza	primitive hut
cocha*	pond, lake
conocedor	local expert, guide
cordillera	mountain range
cortar camino	to take a shortcut
cruce	crossing
cuchilla	ridge
cueva	cave
cultivo	crop, worked field
cumbre	summit
derecha	right (direction)
derrumbe(o)	landslide
deshecho	path
Dios le pague	may God repay you, thank you
empalizado(a)	trail lined with logs
empedrado	cobbled, lined with stones
empinado	steep
enderezo	shortcut (used in the south)
enfermo(a)	sick
escuela	school
este	east
filo	ridge
fuente	fountain, spring
ganado	cattle
ganado bravo	fighting bulls
ganado de lidia	fighting bulls
ganado manso	tame cattle
garúa	mist
glacial	glacier
granizo	hail
guagua*	child, baby
guía	guide, guide book
hacienda	farm, ranch
helada	frost

herido(a)	injured
hospedaje	accommodations
hospedería	simple accommodations
hostal	hotel, inn
hotel	hotel
izquierda	left (direction)
lago	lake
laguna	pond, lake
lastrado	graveled
loma	hill
*machay**	cave, overhang
macho	male, male mule
mapa	map
médico	doctor
*minga**	community work project
mirador	lookout
monte	woods, forest
motel	accommodation for short-stay couples
mula	female mule
neblina	fog
nevado	snow-capped mountain
niebla	fog
nieve	snow
norte	north
oeste	west
ojo de agua	spring
paja	straw, tussock grass
pajonal	straw-covered *páramo*
*pampa**, *pamba**	plain, plateau
Panamericana, Pana	Pan-American or any major highway
pantano	swamp
parada de bus	bus stop
páramo	high Andean moorland or grassland
paso	step, pass
pendiente	slope, steep
peña	cliff
perro	dog

plano	flat
pogyo★	spring
portón	gate
potrero	pasture
precipicio	cliff
pueblo	town, village
puente	bridge
puente colgante	suspension bridge
puente peatonal	foot bridge
pungu★, *punku*★	door, gate, gateway
quebrada	ravine, gully, valley, canyon
ranchera	open-sided bus (used in the south)
rancho	primitive hut
refugio	shelter
riachuelo	stream
río	river
rumi★	stone
sacha★	jungle, forest, wild
seguir filo filo	to follow the ridge line
selva	jungle
sendero	trail
siga	continue, go ahead
siga no más	go ahead (imperative)
soroche	altitude sickness
subtrópico	subtropics, warm lowlands
sur	south
tambo★	inn, rest stop along trail
tarabita	primitive cable car
tembladera	quaking bog (used in the Llanganates)
tempestad	storm
temporal	storm
terminal terrestre	bus station
tienda	shop, general store
toro	bull
toro bravo	fighting bull
urcu★, *ucu*★	mountain
vaca	cow

vado	ford
valle	valley
venenoso(a)	poisonous
vertiente	spring
vía carrosable	vehicle road
viento	wind
yacu★	water, river
yegua	mare

INDEX

Trekking centers are in **boldface type**. Page references to sidebars are printed in *italic type*.

ABOUT THE AUTHORS

Caminante, no hay camino, se hace camino al andar. Robert and Daisy first heard these words in southern Mexico in 1990, and immediately adopted them as their mantra. Daisy had begun trekking long before, in her native Ecuador at age five, where she promptly fell into a *quebrada*. Little did she imagine how many more *quebradas* lay ahead.

Daisy's trail eventually led her to Montreal, Canada, for university, where she met Robert and his idea of traveling for "a year or so." Since their training in medicine and occupational therapy had prepared them for a rather different set of challenges, they continued their education at the National Outdoor Leadership School (NOLS) in Wyoming, U.S.A., before hitting the road. The year became two, and then four, and then more, as they traveled and trekked throughout Latin America—and acquired the new profession of travel writing along the way.

Having tasted the forbidden fruit of freedom, there was no turning back. Instead they broke trail on projects as varied as tourism programs in Antarctica and a radio program called *Travel Latin America*. Since 1993, Robert and Daisy have again made their home in Ecuador, from where they continue to travel, trek, and write. They are founders of the *Latin American Travel Advisor,* authors of the *Ecuador and Galápagos Handbook,* and contributors to various other publications. Notoriously leisurely on the trail, you might find them enjoying an after-lunch siesta in the *páramo*, or pondering the foggy way forward while mumbling their mantra: *caminante, no hay camino . . .*

(Photo: Carmen Sánchez)

THE MOUNTAINEERS, founded in 1906, is a nonprofit outdoor activity and conservation club, whose mission is "to explore, study, preserve, and enjoy the natural beauty of the outdoors...." Based in Seattle, Washington, the club is now the third-largest such organization in the United States, with 15,000 members and five branches throughout Washington State.

The Mountaineers sponsors both classes and year-round outdoor activities in the Pacific Northwest, which include hiking, mountain climbing, ski-touring, snowshoeing, bicycling, camping, kayaking and canoeing, nature study, sailing, and adventure travel. The club's conservation division supports environmental causes through educational activities, sponsoring legislation, and presenting informational programs. All club activities are led by skilled, experienced volunteers, who are dedicated to promoting safe and responsible enjoyment and preservation of the outdoors.

If you would like to participate in these organized outdoor activities or the club's programs, consider a membership in The Mountaineers. For information and an application, write or call The Mountaineers, Club Headquarters, 300 Third Avenue West, Seattle, WA 98119; 206-284-6310.

The Mountaineers Books, an active, nonprofit publishing program of the club, produces guidebooks, instructional texts, historical works, natural history guides, and works on environmental conservation. All books produced by The Mountaineers Books fulfill the club's mission.

Send or call for our catalog of more than 500 outdoor titles:

 The Mountaineers Books
1001 SW Klickitat Way, Suite 201
Seattle, WA 98134
800-553-4453

mbooks@mountaineersbooks.org
www.mountaineersbooks.org

 The Mountaineers Books is proud to be a corporate sponsor of Leave No Trace, whose mission is to promote and inspire responsible outdoor recreation through education, research, and partnerships. The Leave No Trace program is focused specifically on human-powered (nonmotorized) recreation.

Leave No Trace strives to educate visitors about the nature of their recreational impacts, as well as offer techniques to prevent and minimize such impacts. Leave No Trace is best understood as an educational and ethical program, not as a set of rules and regulations.

For more information, visit *www.LNT.org*, or call 800-332-4100.

Available at fine bookstores and outdoor stores, by phone at (800) 553-4453, or on the Web at www.mountaineersbooks.org

Trekking in Bolivia: A Traveler's Guide by Yossi Brain. $16.95 paperback. 0-89886-501-8.

Trekking in Nepal: A Traveler's Guide, 7th Edition by Stephen Bezruchka, M.D. $16.95 paperback. 0-89886-535-2.

Trekking in Tibet: A Visitor's Guide, 2nd Edition by Gary McCue. $18.95 paperback. 0-89886-662-6.

Trekking in Russia and Central Asia: A Traveler's Guide by Frith Maier. $16.95 paperback. 0-89886-355-4.

Ecuador: A Climbing Guide by Yossi Brain. $16.95 paperback. 0-89886-729-0.

Wilderness Navigation: Finding Your Way Using Map, Compass, Altimeter, & GPS by Mike Burns and Bob Burns. $9.95 paperback. 0-89886-629-4.

GPS Made Easy: Using Global Positioning Systems in the Outdoors, 3rd Edition by Lawrence Letham. $14.95 paperback. 0-89886-802-5.

The Pocket Doctor: A Passport to Healthy Travel, 3rd Edition by Stephen Bezruchka, M.D. $6.95 paperback. 0-89886-614-6.

Wilderness 911: A Step-By-Step Guide for Medical Emergencies and Improvised Care in the Backcountry by Eric A. Weiss, M.D. $16.95 paperback. 0-89886-597-2.

First Aid: A Pocket Guide, 4th Edition by Christopher Van Tilburg, M.D. $3.50 paperback. 0-89886-719-3.

Emergency Survival: A Pocket Guide by Christopher Van Tilburg, M.D. $3.50 paperback. 0-89886-768-1.

Everyday Wisdom: 1001 Expert Tips for Hikers by Karen Berger. $16.95 paperback. 0-89886-523-9.

Backcountry Cooking: From Pack to Plate in 10 Minutes by Dorcas Miller. $16.95 paperback. 0-89886-551-4.

Staying Alive in Avalanche Terrain by Bruce Tremper. $17.95 paperback. 0-89886-834-3.

Outdoor Leadership: Technique, Common Sense, & Self-Confidence by John Graham. $16.95 paperback. 0-89886-502-6.